MW01709794

Thanx for your interest - art speaks! ~ Darrie

Uncommon Clay

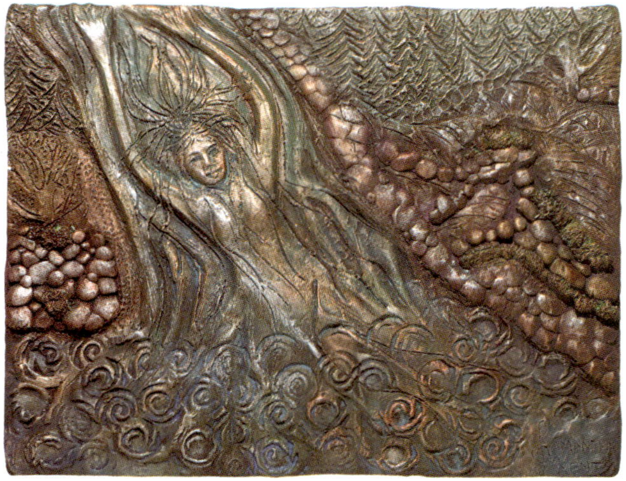

Canada Council for the Arts   Conseil des Arts du Canada   Canada   Newfoundland Labrador

We gratefully acknowledge the financial support of the Canada Council for the Arts, the Government of Canada through the Book Publishing Industry Development Program (BPIDP), and the Government of Newfoundland and Labrador through the Department of Tourism, Culture and Recreation for our publishing program.

Cover Design and Tile Photography by Eric Walsh
Layout by Joanne Snook-Hann and Todd Manning
Printed on acid-free paper

Published by
CREATIVE PUBLISHERS
an imprint of CREATIVE BOOK PUBLISHING
a Transcontinental Inc. associated company
P.O. Box 8660, Stn. A
St. John's, Newfoundland and Labrador A1B 3T7

Printed in Canada by:
TRANSCONTINENTAL INC.

Uncommon clay : the Labrador
mural / edited by Dorrie Brown.

ISBN 978-1-897174-57-9

1. Tiles--Newfoundland and Labrador--Labrador.
2. Mural painting and decoration--Newfoundland and
Labrador--Labrador. 3. Native art--Newfoundland and
Labrador--Labrador. I. Brown, Dorrie, 1950-

NK4670.7.C3L32 2010   738.6'097182   C2010-900507-4

FSC Mixed Sources
Product group from well-managed forests, controlled sources and recycled wood or fiber
www.fsc.org Cert no. [illegible]V-COC-0009[illegible]2
© 1996 Forest Stewardship Council

Uncommon Clay

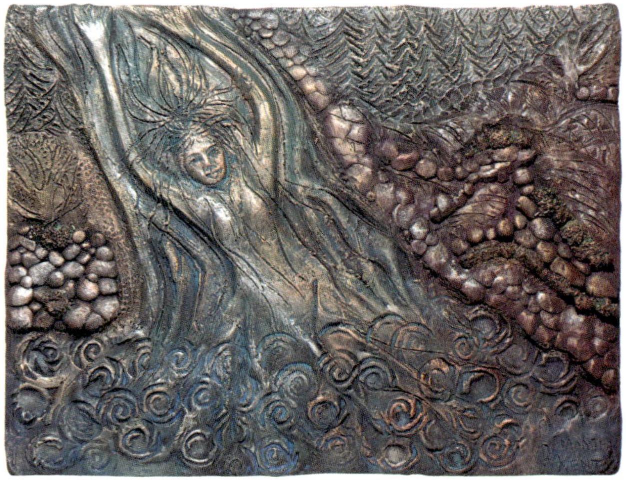

The Labradoria Mural
Dorrie Brown

CREATIVE PUBLISHERS
St. John's, Newfoundland and Labrador
2010

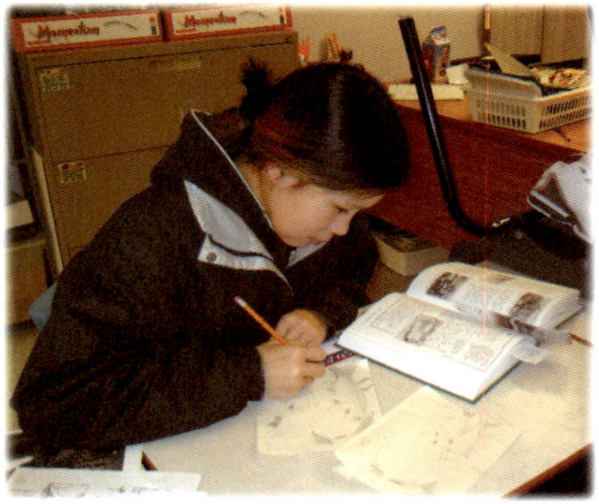

Dedicated to the memory of
Kitora Boase

Preface

As a long time member of the Canadian Society for Education through Art, (CSEA) and as an art educator for more than thirty-five years, I was delighted to attend a National CSEA conference in Goose Bay, Labrador, in November, 2005. This conference dovetailed with the local Labrador Creative Arts Festival, orchestrated by Dr. Tim Borlase who also directed the Labrador Institute of Memorial University. In the context of this vibrant event, I was proud to receive a CSEA National Affiliate Award for British Columbia and I also had the pleasure of delivering the keynote address about the community based art program that I had taught for many years at Cowichan Secondary School in Duncan, BC. As a result of this presentation, (which particularly highlighted more than 270 painted, mosaic and ceramic murals my students had created for hospitals, community centres, nursing homes, schools, universities, and even three for the Royal BC Museum in Victoria), I was asked by Martha MacDonald to return the following November of 2006 for the Festival. I would work with nineteen middle and high school students who would come to Goose Bay for the Arts Festival and who had agreed to be part of an intense four-day mural workshop I would be teaching. In the context of this event, I met Dorrie Brown, a recently retired art teacher from Goose Bay who chaired the Festival Committee and helped coordinate many of its events. She had arranged for the delivery of clay from Alberta to Labrador and took care of all the behind-the-scenes details so that the days I spent making mural panels with the students would be a success. Dorrie popped in whenever she could to see how the students were proceeding and, in spite of her demanding schedule, managed to create a clay panel herself so she would learn the process along with the students.

The theme of *Labradoria* was chosen and an intense day was spent doing research, drawing and learning compositional skills to develop each student's chosen topic. The next four days were used to transfer the designs and develop them in a *bas relief* style on the 15" x 19" clay slabs that my great friend and retired art teacher, Victorinne Dionne from Maine, had rolled for the students. Each day, we assembled the clay panels to analyze their development, so that by the end of the process, the standard of excellence, to my mind, had been achieved by all students. I have always believed "there is an artist in everyone" and if you give students a great project, in a short period of time and get them to "go public" amazing things can happen!

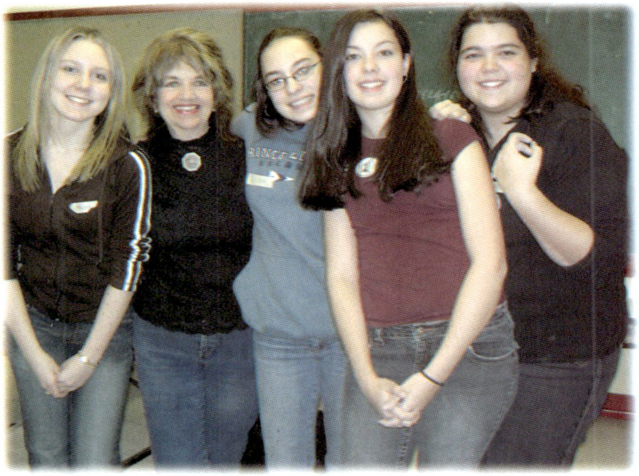

"The Girls From Churchill" with artist Lynda Faulks: from left, Krista Collins, Lynda Faulks, Laura Bonnell, Heidi Kent, Samantha Kent. (And they thought they couldn't do it!)
November 2006, Labrador Creative Arts Festival workshop

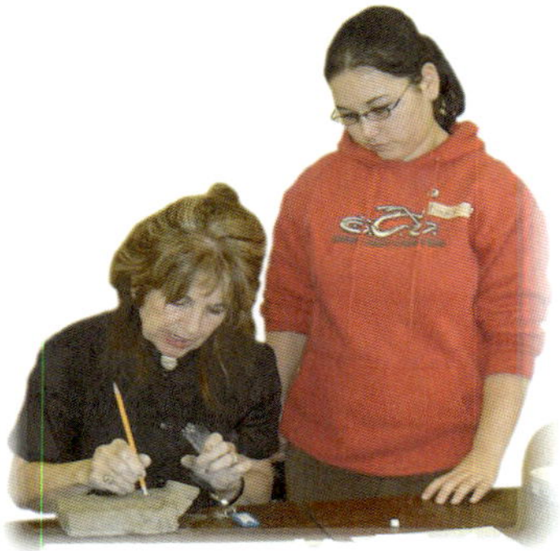

Lynda Faulks demonstrates clay techniques as Dinah Wolfrey of Rigolet looks on.

November 2006, Labrador Creative Arts Festival workshop

I left Dorrie with firing instructions for the clay and with the help of Viola Hodder, who owned a small kiln, the pieces were successfully fired. In January of 2007, Dorrie flew out to British Columbia to stay with my husband and I for five days to learn antiquing techniques for finishing the mural panels and installing skills needed to assemble the Labrador mural in the future.

In the meantime, Dorrie had seen an amazing opportunity to extend this mural project and to develop it with another thirty-four panels by flying into other communities of Labrador and working with interested students so that a larger more-inclusive *Labradoria* mural might be created for the new, soon to be opened, community arts centre in Goose Bay. As they say, "the rest is history!"

Dorrie is to be congratulated for her vision, hard work and her tenacity in the face of so many obstacles to develop this mural project which serves as a permanent repository of history for Labrador. It is a daily reminder of the amazing potential of young people, who if they are challenged, inspired and loved are capable of amazing things.

I am proud that my background as an art educator and mural artist, and my week spent developing the first part of this mural project with students became a catalyst for something truly wonderful. All of the student artists, and especially Dorrie Brown, are to be congratulated for amazing work.

Lynda Faulks, M. Ed.

Uncommon Clay: The *Labradoria* Mural

Introduction

Clay. Of the earth. Earth itself. What could be more common?

And by *common* we might infer that something is simple, basic, ordinary, as in, 'a common rowboat'. Or, perhaps that something is familiar, frequent and expected, as in, 'it was common to see ice on the ponds by October'. Or, we might refer to something shared; we speak of having something 'in common' with one another.

All of these apply to clay. Clay is simple and basic. It is familiar and found frequently in our environment. And if, as we are told, we are all 'made of clay', then we share 'in common' our origins; our humanity.

These definitions equally apply to the *Labradoria* Mural. This mural is made of simple, ordinary clay. Mud. What can be more basic than that? It is made up of familiar, frequent, and in some cases, expected images. And it was created by fifty-four people from all over Labrador who hold this wild and varied region in common with one another.

And yet, this is *uncommon* clay, for, held in its forever-grip are stories unique to the cultures, landscapes and histories of this enigmatic land "God Gave to Cain".

In November of 2006, the Labrador Creative Arts Festival invited artist Lynda Faulks to teach students how to create *bas relief* images in clay. Mrs. Faulks, a national award winner in arts education, had already helped many students in her home province of British Columbia create numerous extraordinary clay murals prestigiously displayed in colleges, community centres, the University of Victoria, and the Royal British Columbia Museum. It seemed a fitting thing that a mural created by Labrador students should grace the anticipated new regional arts centre in Goose Bay.

Clay for the workshop had to come from Alberta, and by October, when we ordered it for the Festival, a heated trailer was required to prevent the clay from freezing en route. It was less expensive to bring an entire palette of clay (enough to make eighty tiles) than to bring only twenty blocks for Lynda's workshop, so that's what we did. But next, the task of getting it to Labrador proved daunting to the shipper, who had no idea where we were, and offered to ship it at cost if we could get it past Quebec City, where he apparently 'lost our scent'.

The clay arrived with about one day to spare. Lynda arrived and set to work. It would be an understatement to describe Lynda as a powerhouse. She worked with nineteen students from Nain, Churchill Falls, Happy Valley-Goose Bay, Black Tickle and Rigolet, packing into four days what usually takes a month to accomplish.

The process began with an introduction to *bas relief,* used by ancient peoples to record their histories in stone. The making of these tiles would similarly record, in a permanent installation, images of Labrador created by these young people: what the students were making would be seen by their grandchildren — an idea that was at first novel to most, but resonated powerfully with some.

Mrs. Faulks showed photos of other tiles done by students, to give an idea of what would work, and what wouldn't. Then came the question: "If I were to say 'Labrador' to you, what would you think of?" And then came the images — lists and lists of ideas. Books, magazines and online searches followed, and more ideas were added.

Each student then made thumbnail sketches of four possible subjects. The one eventually selected either showed the most promise, or held the most interest for the artist. A short course in composition came next; the sketches were revisited and redrawn, applying principles of composition just learned.

Finally, the developed sketch was drawn once more on a large piece of newsprint the same size as the slab, and 'poked' onto the clay using a large needle. And then, the real work began. Now everyone was playing with mud, finding clever ways to form it into necessary shapes; creating textures with sculpting tools and everyday objects; discovering 'accidents' that worked!

There were reports of some students wanting to bail after the first day, believing that they couldn't possibly do this work, or that others had far more art training or that 'clay project' meant making a simple scene from playdough. This was a much bigger project than they had bargained for! There was one report of a wise and unrelenting teacher sending her charges back in for Day Two, telling them this was "the chance of a lifetime" — a prediction later verified by those same young artists.

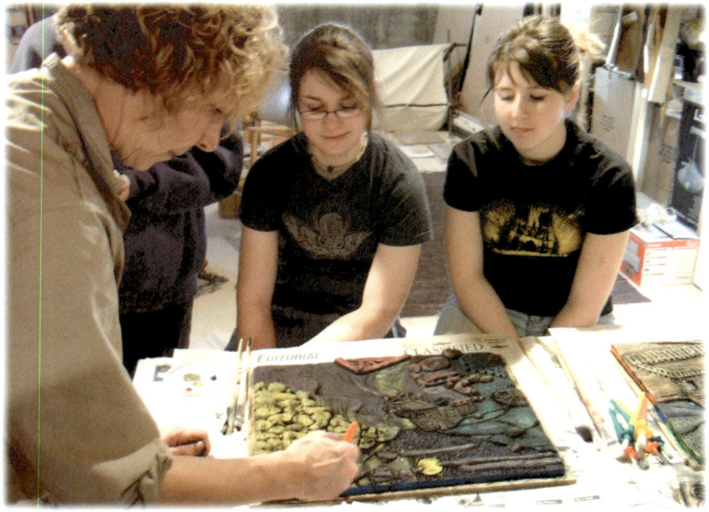

Dorrie Brown works with Leanna Kippenhuck (left) who brought her friend, Chantelle Aylward along to cheer her on during the painting process.

Occasionally, someone in the workshop would ask, "What's going to happen to our tiles? How will they be fired? How will we paint them? And what's going to happen to the rest of the clay?" And I, at this point in the role of Lynda's Novice Apprentice, would blithely say, "Oh, don't worry. This is only the beginning of the project. I'll see that they are fired… and I will set up painting sessions with you…and I'll take the clay to other communities…" and my voice would trail off.

A noble idea, coming from one who wasn't sure we had a working kiln in the community; who had *never worked with clay*; who was learning *with the students in the workshop* (albeit, one day behind, and only because I'd been coaxed into working on the extra slab); and who had no idea where the money would come from to enable such a grand plan!

A 'grand plan' indeed, in that Labrador is an immense territory embracing 294,300 square kilometres (larger than the rest of the combined Atlantic provinces), whose harsh climate and rugged landscape have limited where people can live and what they can do. Five regions (northern/Torngat, Labrador West, central/Lake Melville, south coast, and The Straits) are home to people of Innu, Inuit, Metis, and European heritage. Even so, only 29,231 residents are spread among thirty-two communities, most of which are scattered along 7,886 kilometres of coastline. There are two major roads, each stretching 500 kilometres either north-south, or east-west, but neither of which is paved, and neither of which would serve the destinations of this project. All of the travel necessary to continue with the mural would be by air, and it would be "weather-permitting".

But, from January to June 2007, this grand plan took shape. At 6:00 a.m. each Monday morning, my husband Herb drove me to the airport, with one hundred pounds of clay rolled flat in four slabs, forty pounds of tools and materials, and a small bag of personal items.

On each trip, the airline personnel would greet me with, "We may not be able to get all of your stuff on the plane. If we can't, which do you want to leave behind?" The clay was of no use without the tools; the tools were of no use without the clay. It always came down to my personal items. OK, keep the toothbrush! Yet, nothing was ever left behind. Consider also that the clay could not freeze, and it was travelling *in cargo, in winter, in Labrador*. What were we thinking? Yet, it never froze.

With the help of cooperating principals and teachers, I spent a week in eight additional communities, working with three to five students after school and long into the evening to make tiles. Students from Hopedale, Natuashish, Makkovik, Postville, Northwest River, Sheshatshiu, Mud Lake, and Cartwright all added contributions to the mural.

Each weekend, I brought the tiles back to Goose Bay, where they cured for four to six weeks, and were then fired, six at a time, by Mrs. Viola Hodder in her small kiln that dates from the days of the U.S. Air Base in Goose Bay.

After being fired, the tiles were returned to their creators to undergo three painting processes. This required a second week in each community. The results? Harmonious metallic hues of copper, bronze, gold and silver, with undertones of color.

By July 2007, all but one tile had been painted. The last tile was painted in May, 2009. In the meantime, all of the tiles lay on my basement floor, awaiting their intended and permanent home in the lobby of the new Lawrence O'Brien Auditorium in Goose Bay. But they did not lay idle: they were viewed and admired by people from all over the world. Finally, the mural was installed in June 2009 and was unveiled in September of that year.

This work, costing approximately $33,000, was enabled by funding and in-kind support from the Labrador Creative Arts Festival, Voisey's Bay Nickel (now Vale Inco), NL Hydro, Labrador Airways, Provincial Airlines, Labrador School Board, *Makkovimiut* Trust, Happy Valley-Goose Bay Rotary, the Zippie Ikkiatsiak Award and the Government of Newfoundland & Labrador Department of Labrador Affairs.

Fifty-four tiles have now been completed by young Labrador artists of Inuit, Innu, Metis and non-aboriginal heritage. The mural represents natural and cultural history of the region. Concepts and images were chosen, developed and researched by youth ranging in age from twelve to eighteen years, and rendered by their hands. Many of the images were based on archival photographs from the *Them Days Magazine* collection; others were original compositions based on visual research.

Among the tiles, one sees the image of Kitora Boase, an outstanding elder from Hopedale, created from a photograph by her great-granddaughter Marea Mitsuk. Mrs. Boase's namesake, great-granddaughter Kitora, molded magnificent images of codfish, no longer plentiful in Labrador waters. Maria Lidd from Nain created *The Ghosts of Hebron,* based on a photograph from the Hebron reunion in 1999. A ghost story from Spotted Island takes shape under the creative hands of Krista Williams of Cartwright. From Postville, Herbie Jacque's hunter's eye translates clay into an exquisite Labrador Black Duck. Roxi Wolfrey from Rigolet recalls the days of dogteams. Cheryl Rich, from Natuashish, honors her grandparents' way of life framed in an Innu drum.

Common clay makes building blocks. Building blocks make walls.

Uncommon clay gives life to images, which give life to stories, which whisper and breathe from walls that remember and celebrate.

These images, these stories, now in common clay, are forever. And these images, these stories, will be admired, considered, treasured, *and heard,* by all who understand their uncommon nature.

Dorrie Brown
September, 2009

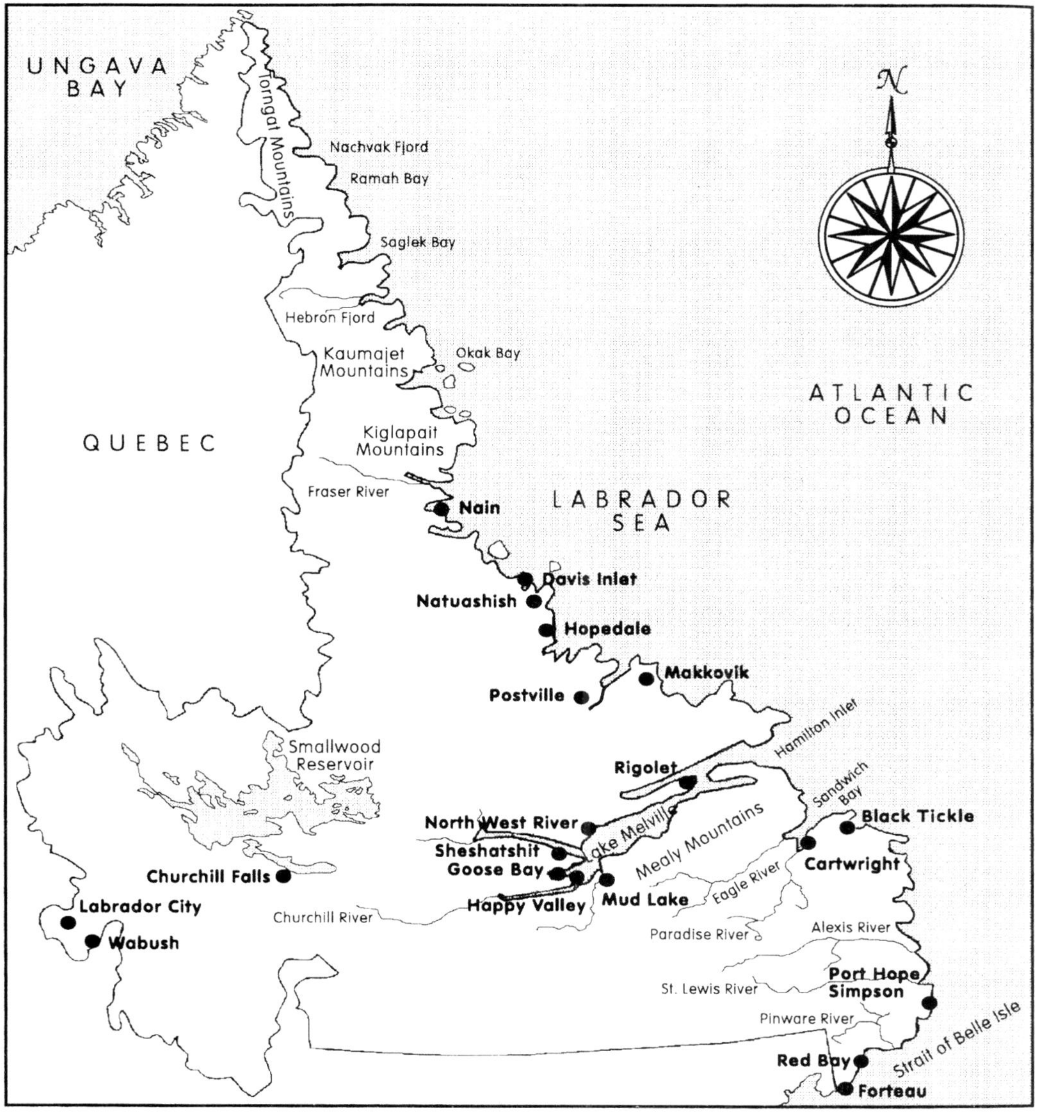

UNGAVA BAY
Torngat Mountains
Nachvak Fjord
Ramah Bay
Saglek Bay
Hebron Fjord
Kaumajet Mountains
Okak Bay
Kiglapait Mountains
QUEBEC
ATLANTIC OCEAN
Fraser River
Nain
LABRADOR SEA
Davis Inlet
Natuashish
Hopedale
Makkovik
Postville
Hamilton Inlet
Smallwood Reservoir
Rigolet
Sandwich Bay
North West River
Lake Melville
Black Tickle
Sheshatshit
Mealy Mountains
Cartwright
Goose Bay
Churchill Falls
Mud Lake
Eagle River
Labrador City
Happy Valley
Churchill River
Paradise River
Alexis River
Wabush
Port Hope Simpson
St. Lewis River
Pinware River
Strait of Belle Isle
Red Bay
Forteau
N

Clay. Of the earth. Earth itself.

The Tiles

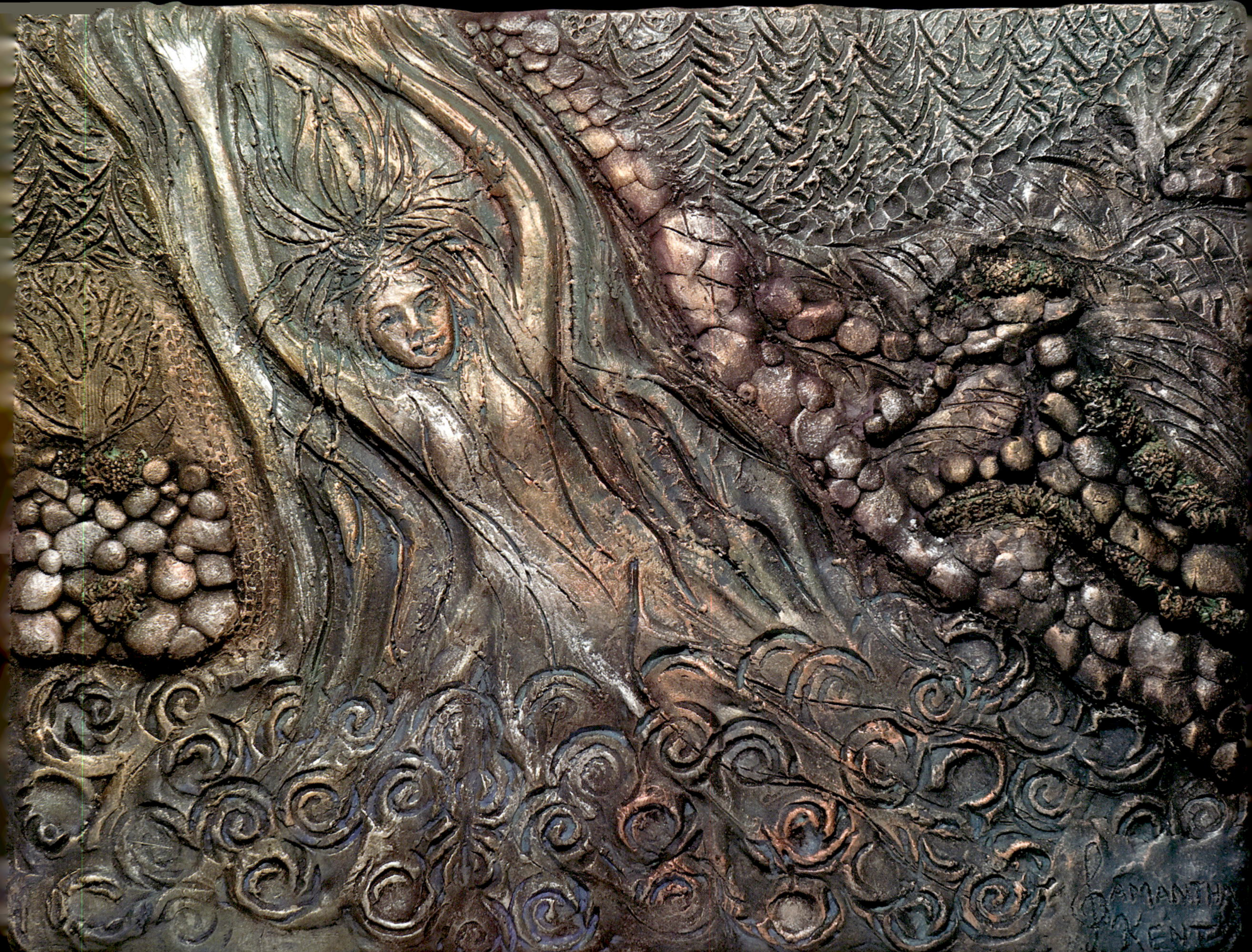
SAMANTHA
KENT

Pichitawno

Samantha Kent, Churchill Falls

Pichitawno, The Legend of the Falls, tells the story of an Innu woman who fell into Churchill River's famous falls as she washed her clothing. Her spirit still lives there and her face can still be seen in the falls.

This story, and my tile which is based upon it, shows how deep and rich the culture of Labrador is, even in a community as relatively new as Churchill Falls. Ours is a community that has grown up to harness the falls for energy; yet our very 'reason for being' is steeped in culture and tradition. Wealth comes in many forms.

The first day we worked on the tiles with Mrs. Faulks, I felt pride, excitement and not just a little apprehension. We were going to complete in four days what others do in a month? Overwhelming! But by the end of the first day we had our designs and our clay slabs began taking shape. Mrs. Faulks' guidance was incredible – especially for a self-proclaimed 'artistically challenged' person!

I am so proud that our mural will be displayed permanently in the new regional arts centre.

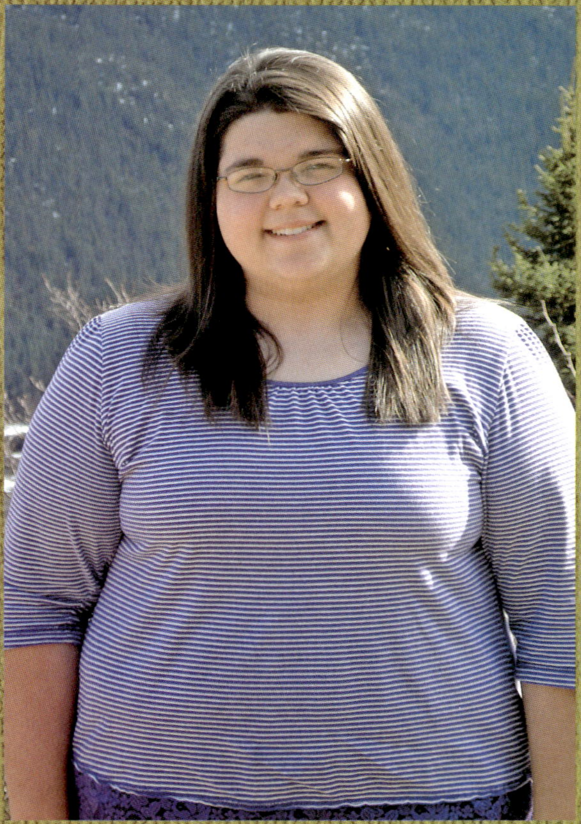

This story, and my tile which is based upon it, shows how deep and rich the culture of Labrador is, even in a community as relatively new as Churchill Falls.

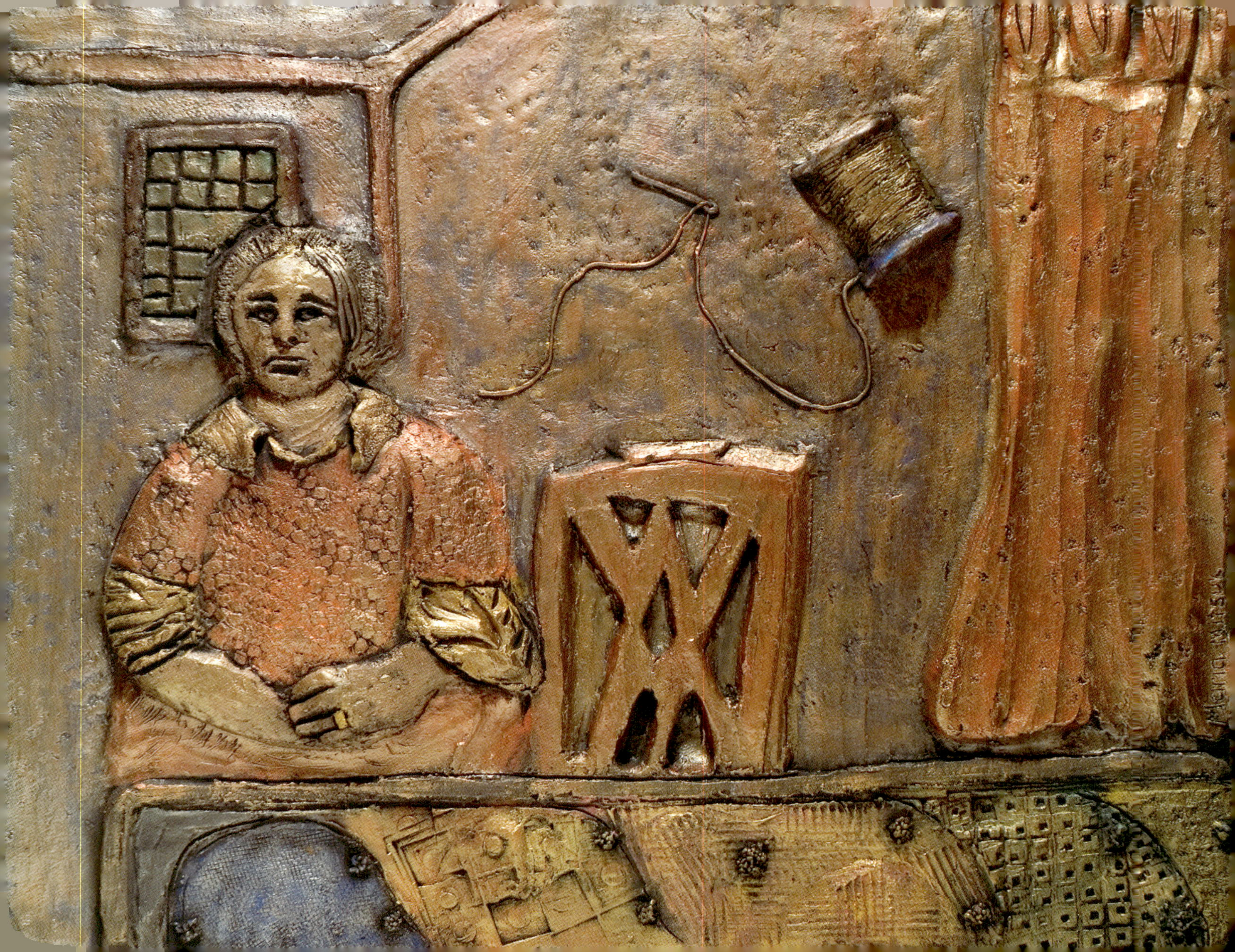

Great-great grandmother Kitora Boase

Marea Mitsuk, Hopedale

I chose to make an image of my great-great-grandmother, Kitora Boase. My family members tell me that she was a beautiful woman; a kind, nice person. She was an important elder in Hopedale. She made things with her hands, like the quilt you can see in front of her. I added the spool of thread and needle to add to that idea of her sewing and making things; to show that she was resourceful.

When I was invited to make a clay tile for the mural, I was excited. A few days into the work, I was getting confused and stressed, because it was harder than I thought! Some things were difficult to do, but I wanted to see how it would turn out, so I kept going. And I love it! Doing this clay work was awesome.

My uncle, who was raised by Grandmother Boase, tells me he recognized her right away in the clay, so it must have worked!

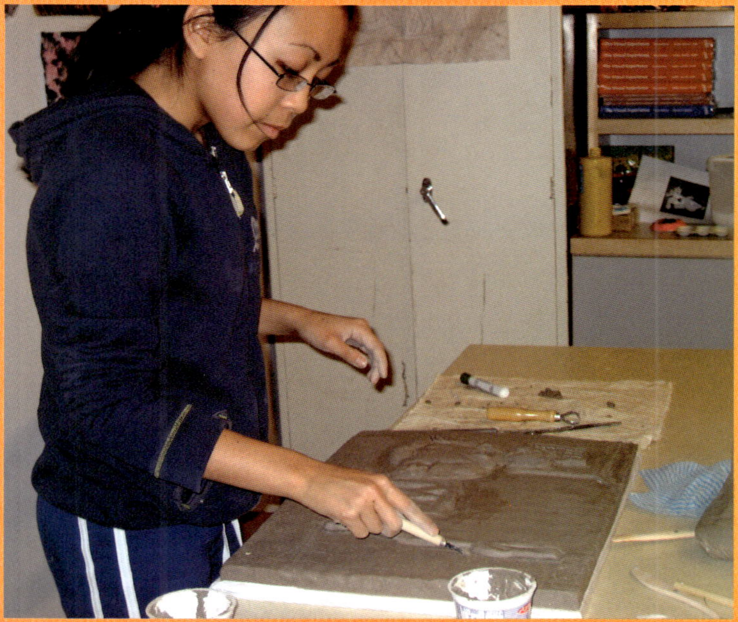

I chose to make an image of my great-great-grandmother, Kitora Boase. My family members tell me that she was a beautiful woman; a kind, nice person.

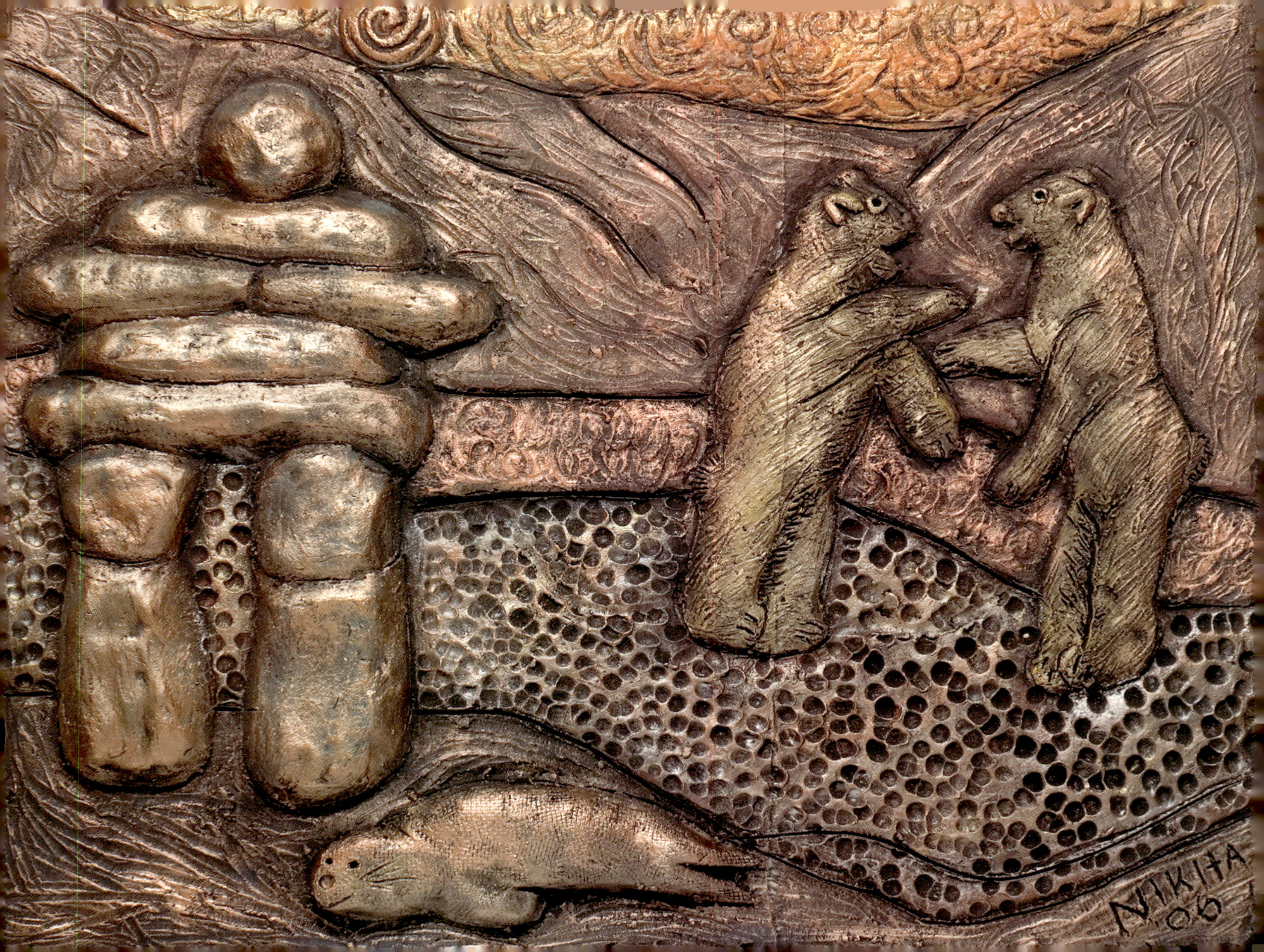
NIKITA
06

Inukshuk

Nikita Keefe, Black Tickle

If you go up to the gulch near Black Tickle, you'll see an **Inukshuk**. In the spring of the year, a polar bear sighting might happen once a week, or even once a day. Seal-hunting is something I've done with my Pop for as long as I remember.

I grew up around all three of these images. It's just the way of life. These are the things one misses most about not being home; they have great value. And so, I put all three of them together in my tile image.

During the tile-making process I thought, "Man, I'm not artistic. Mine is going to look lame." But then I got farther along and became more at ease and comfortable with the clay. It took a lot of time and effort, but in the end I could say, "Wow! I made that!"

And no matter that it wasn't Picasso material, it was still mine, and something to be proud of. Having it displayed is like winning the lottery. People will remember me for my piece. It will always be there. I have earned my own private place in a little corner of Labrador's history.

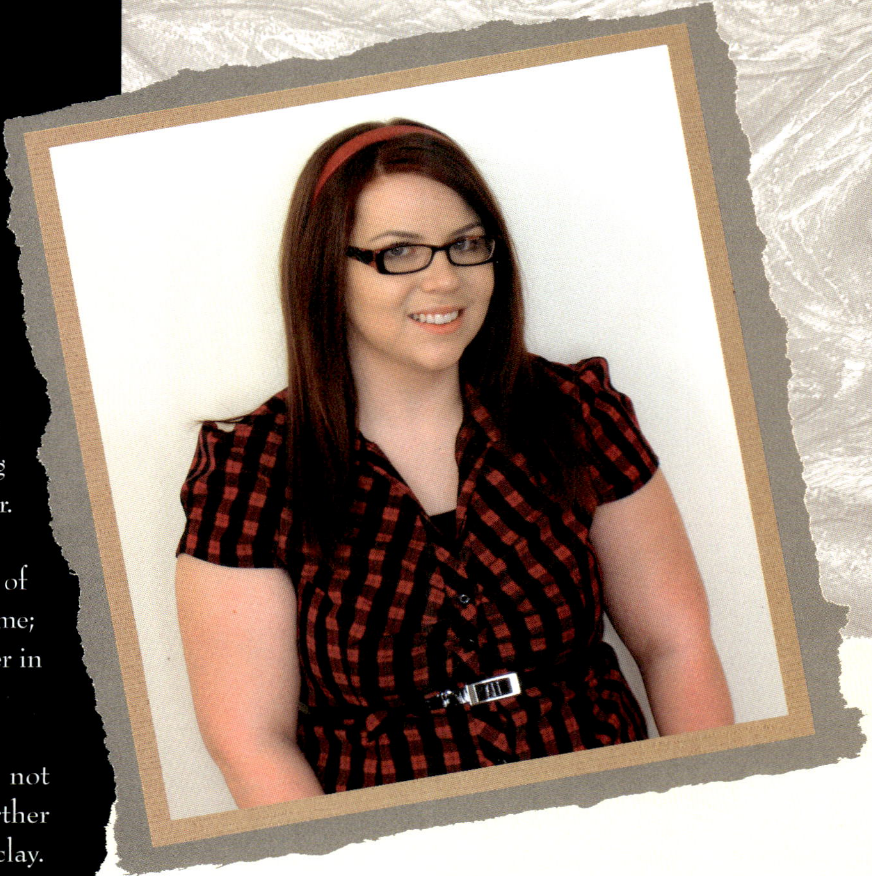

I grew up around all three of these images. It's just the way of life. These are the things one misses most about not being home; they have great value. And so, I put all three of them together in my tile image.

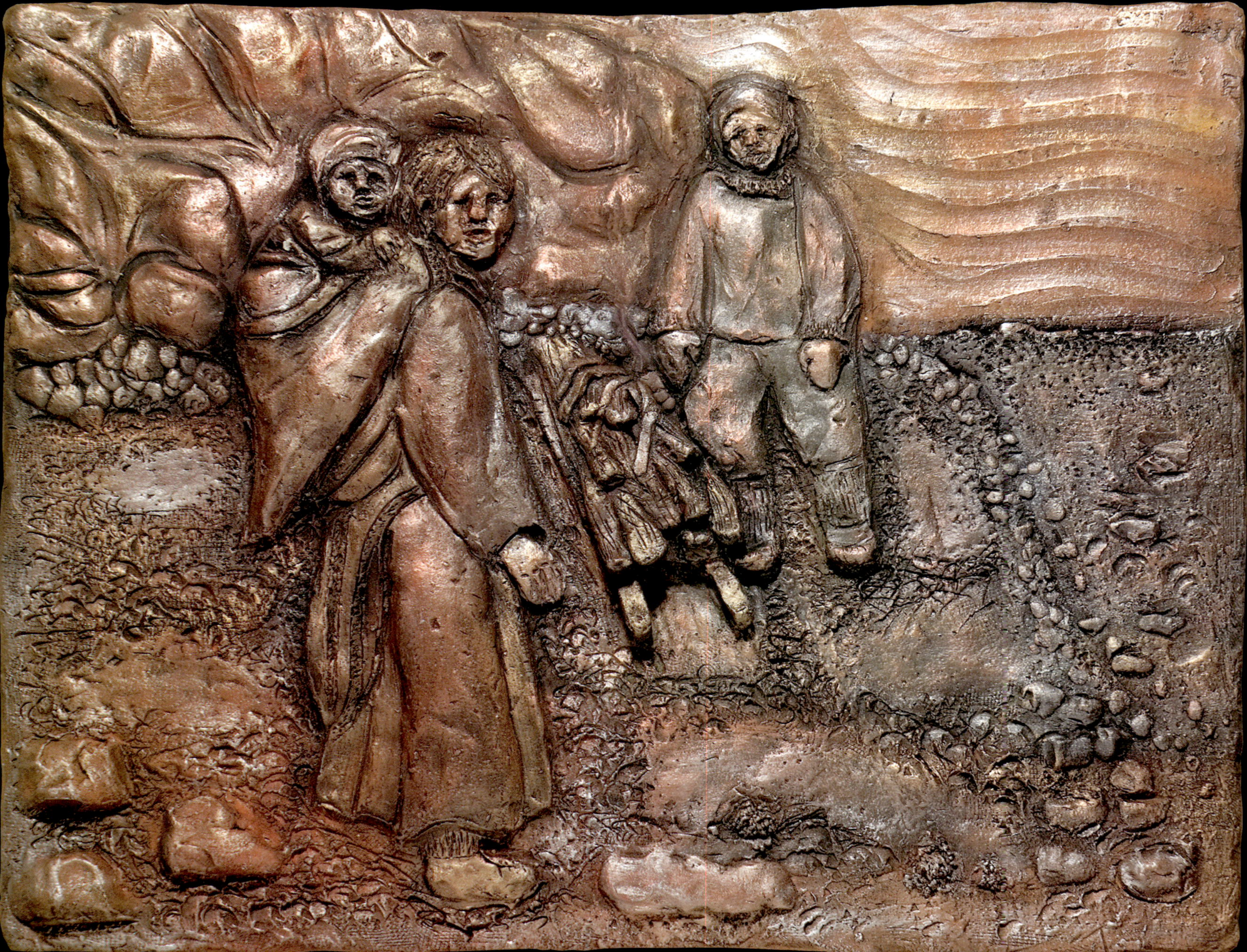

Amautik & Komatik: Carrying Precious Things

Dorrie Brown, Happy Valley - Goose Bay

One of the categories we discussed when first talking about image ideas was clothing. I immediately thought of the *amautik*, the outer garment traditionally worn by Inuit women. It has long 'tails' in front and back that reach to the knees, and a very large hood where a baby can ride, warm and snug, nestled on mother's back.

I found a photograph that showed a young family – mother and babe in an amautik, father standing beside a loaded Komatik, or sled – taking firewood back to their community. They had obviously travelled some distance to collect it. It is spring and snow is in spotty short supply. The Komatik is grounded on the beach. Clearly, arduous work is ahead, to either drag the heavy load across the mud and stones, or to unload and re-load the sled, once snow has been regained. Nonetheless, everyone is still smiling in the picture, undaunted. It seems to be just part of the package, living in the north.

It struck me that both the Komatik and the amautik carry necessary precious things. The first carries things that are precious to life. The second carries life itself.

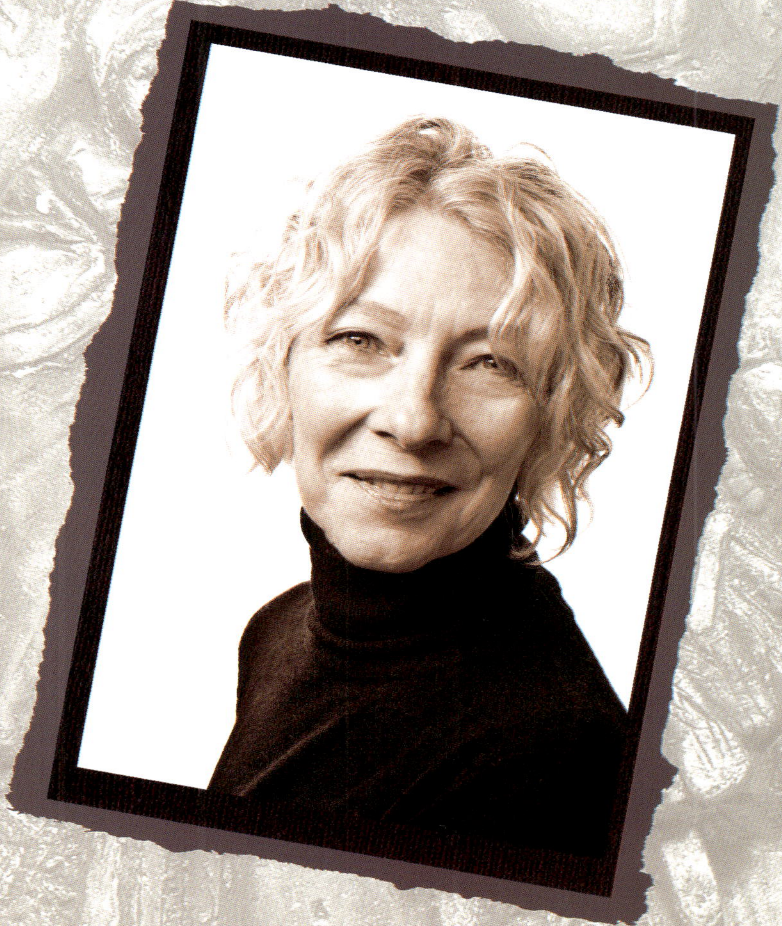

It struck me that both the Komatik and the amautik carry necessary precious things. The first carries things that are precious to life. The second carries life itself.

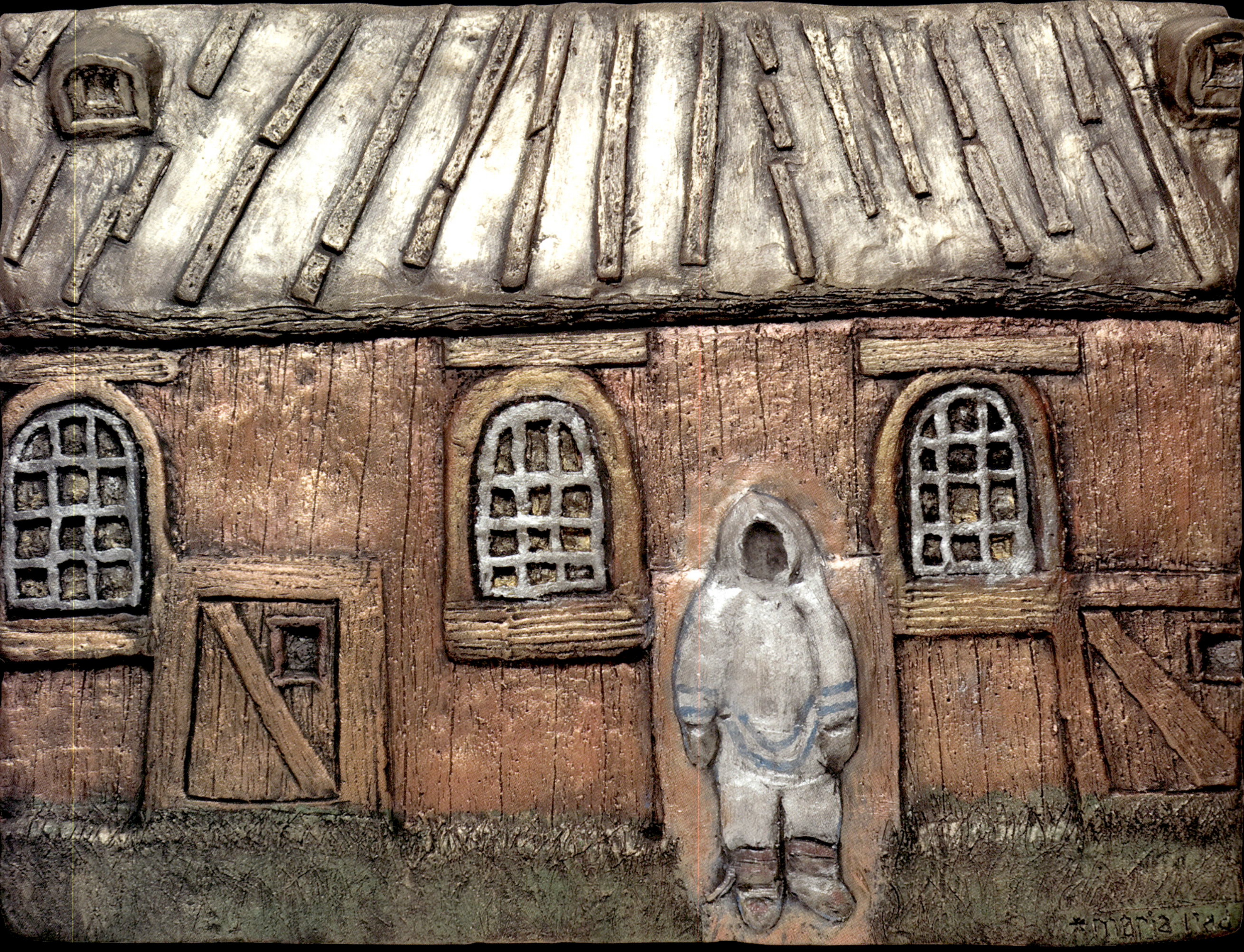
*maria

The Ghosts of Hebron

Maria Lidd, Nain

I took my inspiration for this piece from my mother, who is from Hebron. I wanted to show something of her life there; to show others what life was like back then in the north.

Hebron was re-settled in 1958. Many people go back there for trips, just to see their home again and to remember. My tile image was taken from a photograph of a grand reunion of Hebron residents held in 1999.

If you stay over-night in Hebron, some people say you will see ghosts of those who passed away there. Sometimes they appear if you do something bad, like steal something from the old buildings. They may appear just because they want to.

If you look closely at the windows and shutters on my tile, you will see smiley faces. I put them there because you don't need to be scared to go there – it's not all about ghosts in Hebron. It's a beautiful place to visit.

Hebronip IjuguKutingit

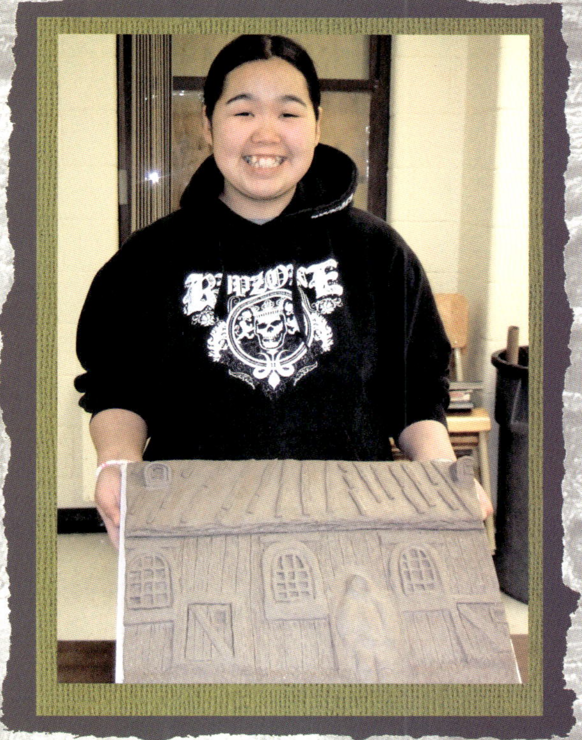

Isumatsasiutlunga tânna sanalauttaga Anânaga pijugiutigitlugu Hebronimiungummat. Takutitsigumatlunga Kanuk inosiKaKattalaummangâta taggâni.

Hebronimiut nottitaulaukKut 1958-timi. Unuttuit suli utiKattavut Hebronimut ikKaumamut amma takugumaummigamik nunavinimminik.

Tânna sanalauttaga atjinguamit tigutlugu Inuit utittitaugalâniammata Hebronimut 1999-nami.

Sinittaguvit Hebronimi unikkautauKattavuk ijugugajattutit ajuliKattasimajuvininnik taikani, piungitosimaguvit uffalu tilliKattasimaguvillonet illuvininginnit. Ilangani affitagumatuinnatlutik sakKisonguvut ijugungit Hebroniup.

Sanasimajagani KimikKuguvit Hebronip katimmavingita igalânginni takugajakKutit kenanik Kungajunik. Tamaunga ililauttaka itsinalungimat, nunatsiangummat Hebroni aiviugami.

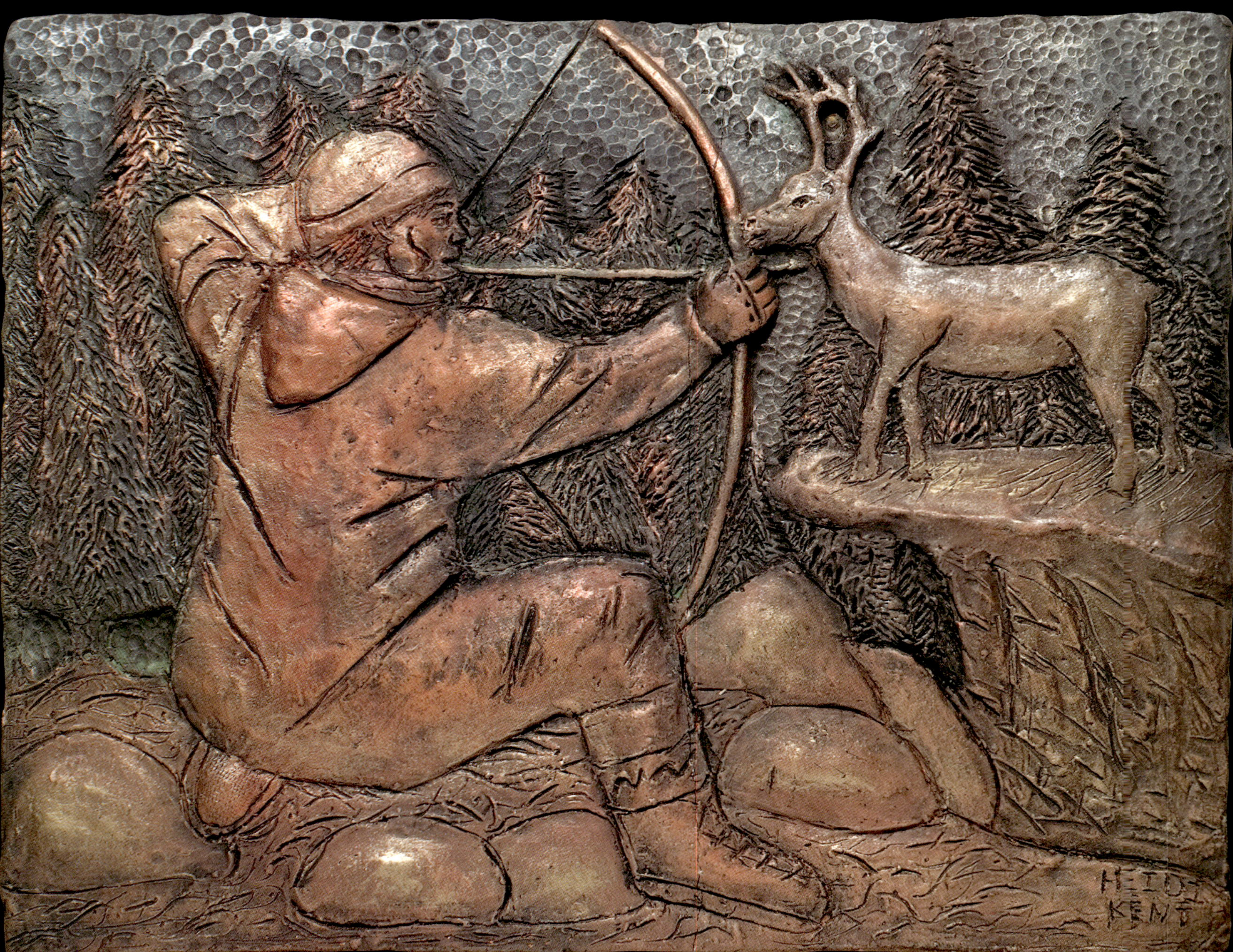
HEID
KENT

Innu Hunter

Heidi Kent, Churchill Falls

Caribou has always been a source of food, of shelter, of clothing – of life! – for the people of Labrador. Every year hundreds of thousands of caribou migrate in herds from the north, flooding the forests and barrengrounds. Traditionally, the Innu followed the deer through the interior, leading a nomadic life and becoming known as the People of the Deer. The caribou is crucial to Innu culture in Labrador.

Caribou are still hunted today, carefully monitored in three principal groups. The George River herd is enormous, the Mealy Mountain one is much smaller, and the Red Wine herd is endangered. They are prized for their meat, and admired for their unrivalled majestic beauty.

To be honest, as I headed into this mural work I felt a good deal of stress. I didn't know that I was getting into such a large-scale project. Through the experience, I have gained a great deal of pride in both my art and in Labrador.

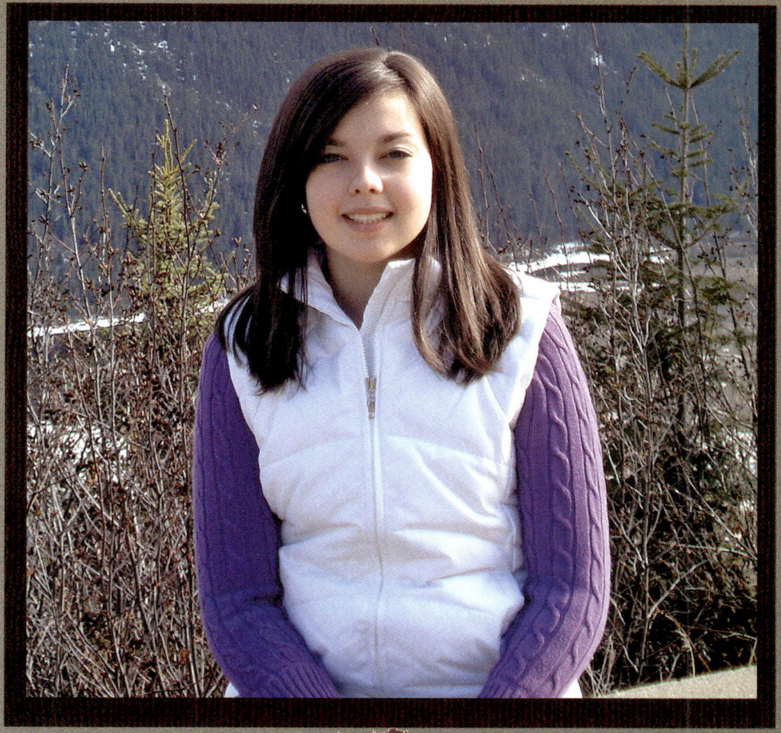

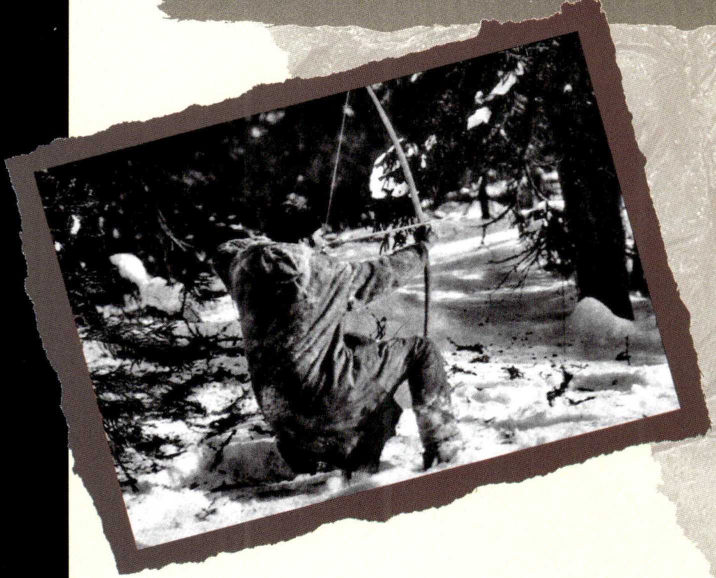

Through the experience, I have gained a great deal of pride in both my art and in Labrador.

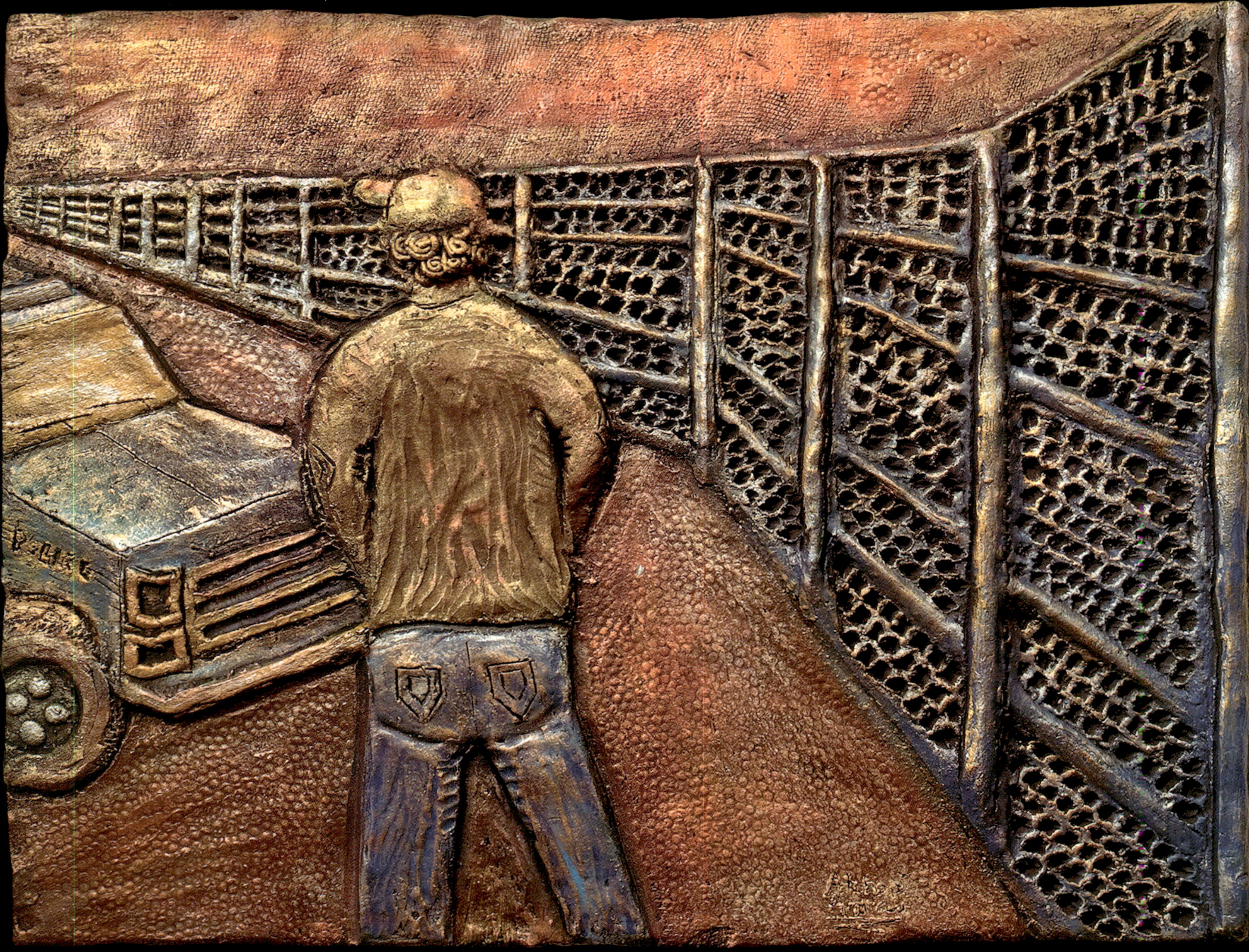

The Proud Son

Atshapi Andrew, Sheshatshiu

My image is taken from a photo of my father urinating on a police vehicle during the Innu protests of the early 1990's. At this time, NATO Allies wanted to set up low-level flight training over the land which we Innu call **Nitassinan**. The Innu are a proud and strong people. We stood together to protect our traditional use of that land by quietly walking on the airport runways, stopping all traffic. We did it many times. We would sneak through the fence early in the cold mornings: elders, children, mothers and fathers. It was always a peaceful protest: our elders made sure of that.

We were worried about the caribou and other wildlife; we worried about pollution of both land and water; we worried about the shock of screaming jets overflying our elders as they travelled inland; but we wanted most of all to honor our ancestors who passed this land and its responsibilities to us.

The young man who protests in this clay image still protests today. He is still bounded by a huge link fence of authority that continues to stretch before him. He is still defined by enforcement of laws and rules which do not always reflect Innu life. His protest is about land claims, taking control of health care and education, a place in the economy, keeping Innu values, language and culture strong.

I am proud of my father. I am proud to be Innu.

The young man who protests in this clay image still protests today. He is still bounded by a huge link fence of authority that continues to stretch before him.

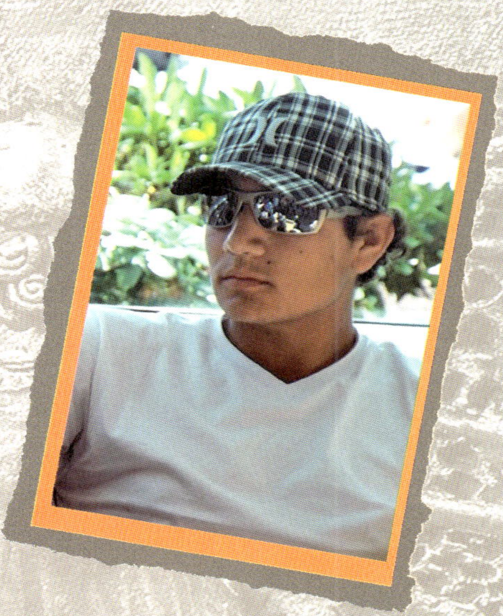

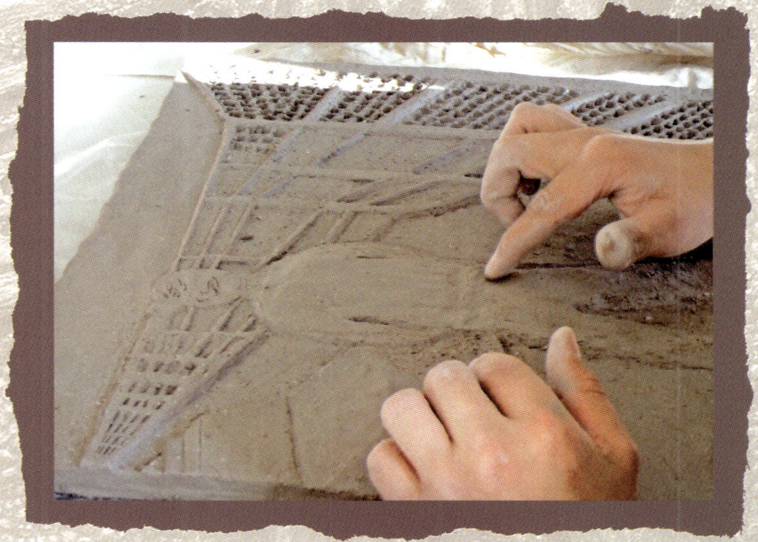

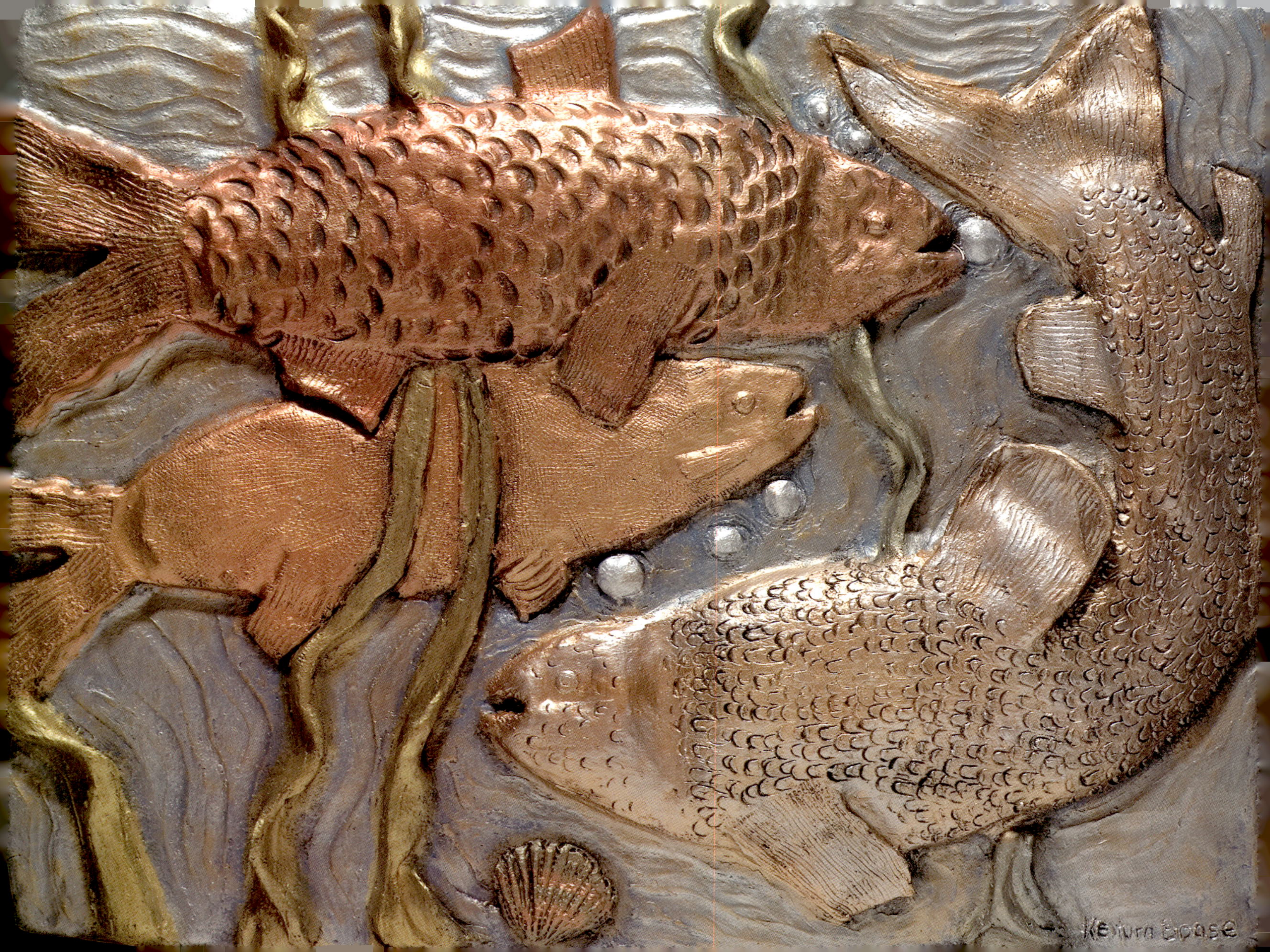

RICH WATERS

KITORA BOASE, HOPEDALE

Kitora's tile celebrates Labrador's once-abundant cod fishery. Cod was gold. For centuries, the cod drew fishermen from Europe, America and Newfoundland. It was a common practice for fishing vessels – first schooners, then motorboats, and later still long-liners and large trawlers – to ply the coastal waters and harvest cod. Newfoundland families and crews would come for the summer and live at fishing 'stations' scattered along the coast. Local families lived inland to hunt and trap during the winter, but moved 'outside' to haul the cod-trap and salt the catch, selling it to merchants who eventually distributed it throughout the world.

In 1992, a moratorium was placed on the cod fishery. It is now more a memory than a reality for Labradorians.

Kitora's piece is her legacy. Just as she celebrated the memory of the cod in her tile, we celebrate her memory, and her creativity, in this image.

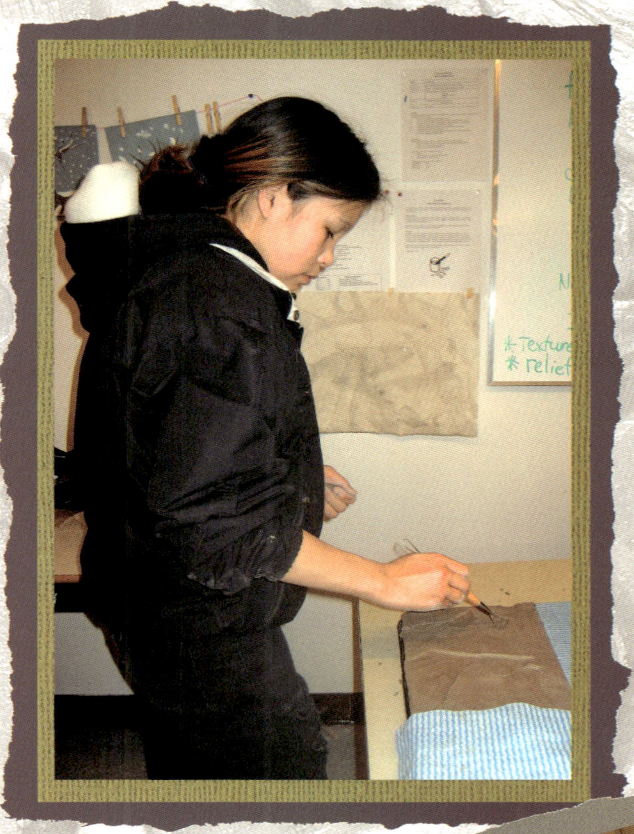

Kitora's piece is her legacy. Just as she celebrated the memory of the cod in her tile, we celebrate her memory, and her creativity, in this image.

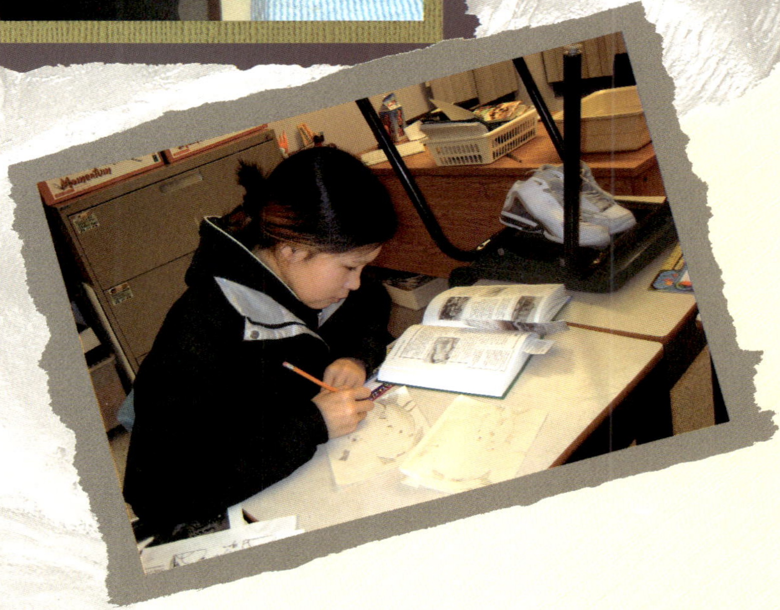

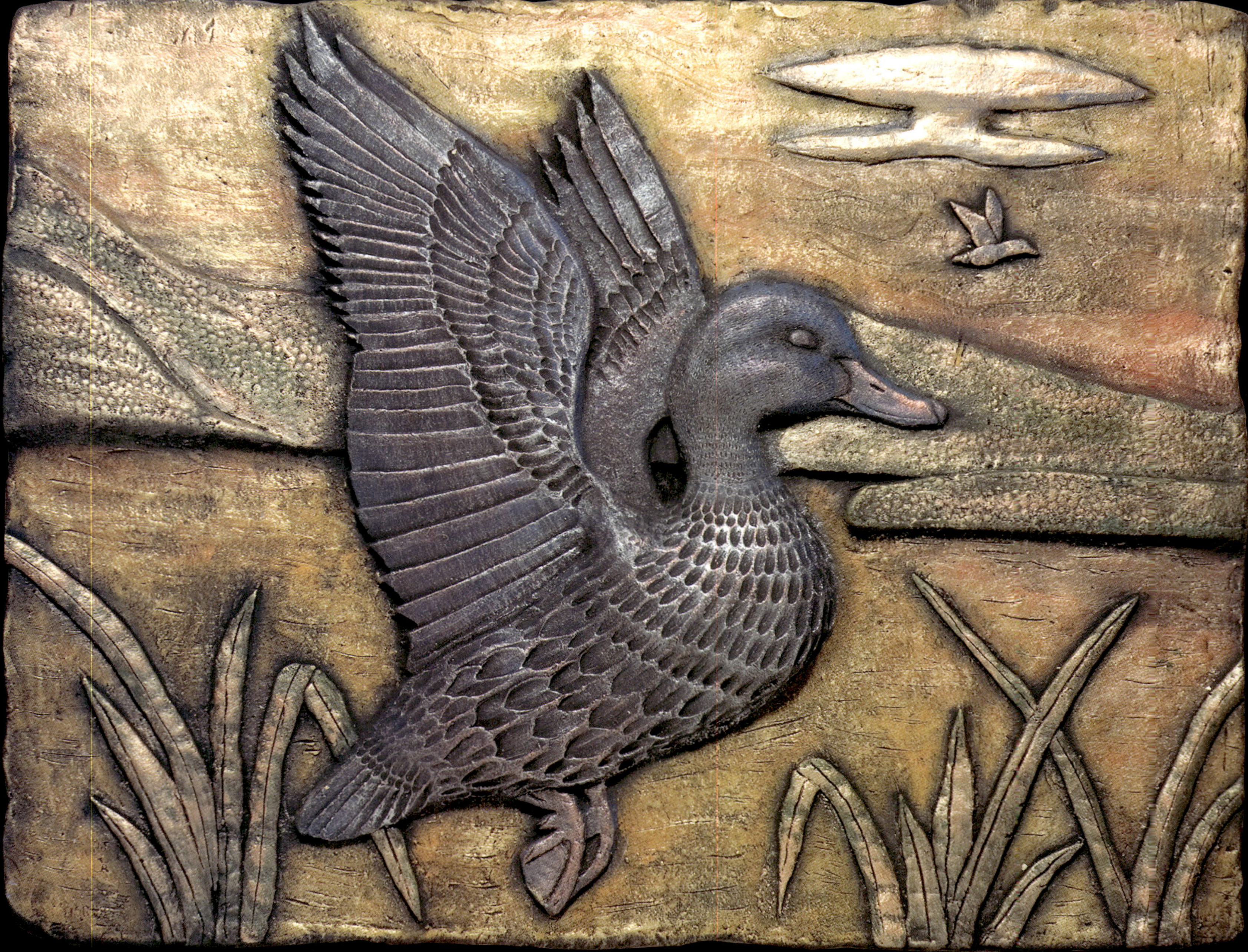

Labrador Black Duck

Herbie Jacque, Postville

I enjoy hunting especially in the fall, which is why I chose the black duck as the image for my tile. Hunting also holds for me many happy memories with friends. Hunting represents the freedom to do what you want; to use your wits and challenge the elements.

I wasn't too confident about working with the clay, as I'd never done that before. Once I got used to shaping it, I really enjoyed it. It turned out that three of us from Postville were using wildlife images, and I was actually able to help the others form details about their particular animals.

It means a lot to me to display my work for other people to see. Someday I'd like to make a career out of my art.

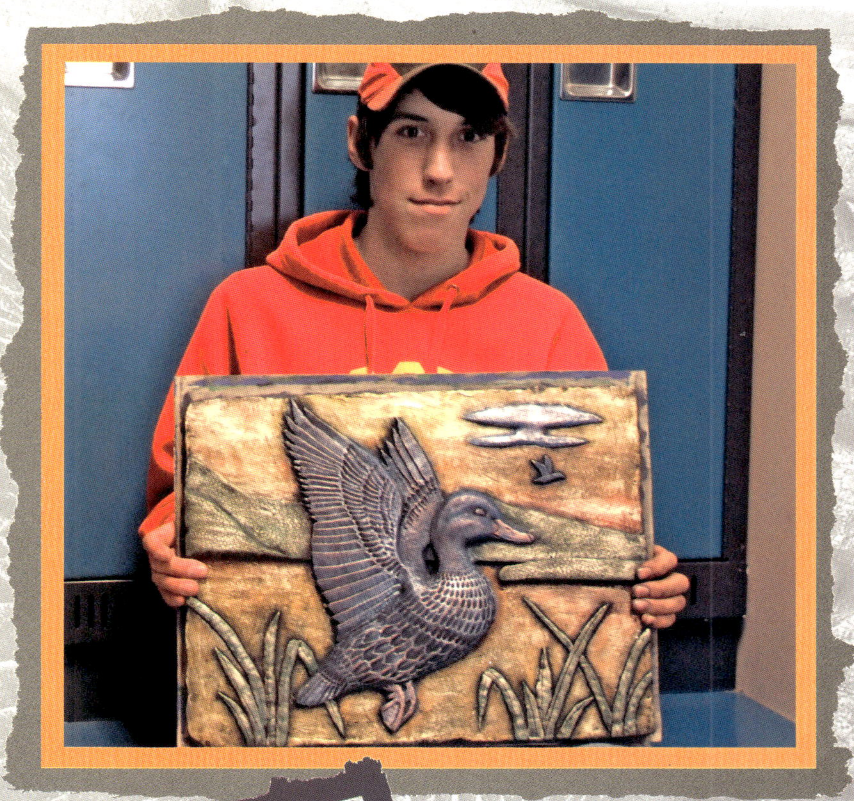

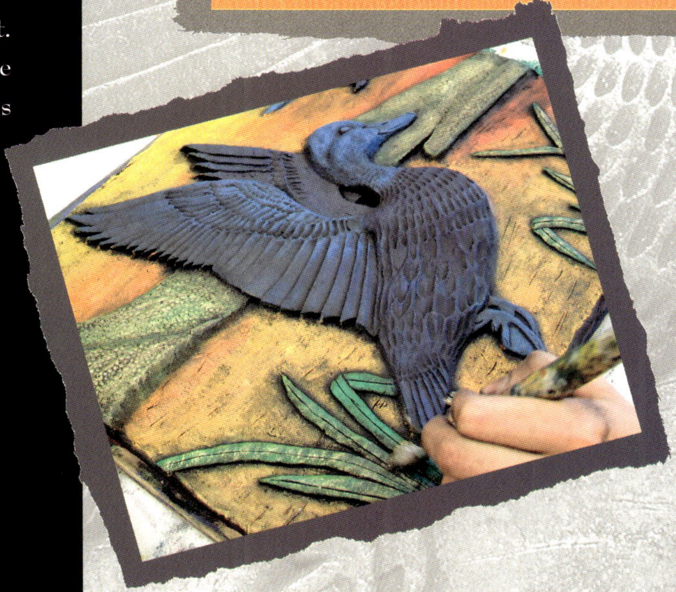

Hunting represents the freedom to do what you want; to use your wits and challenge the elements.

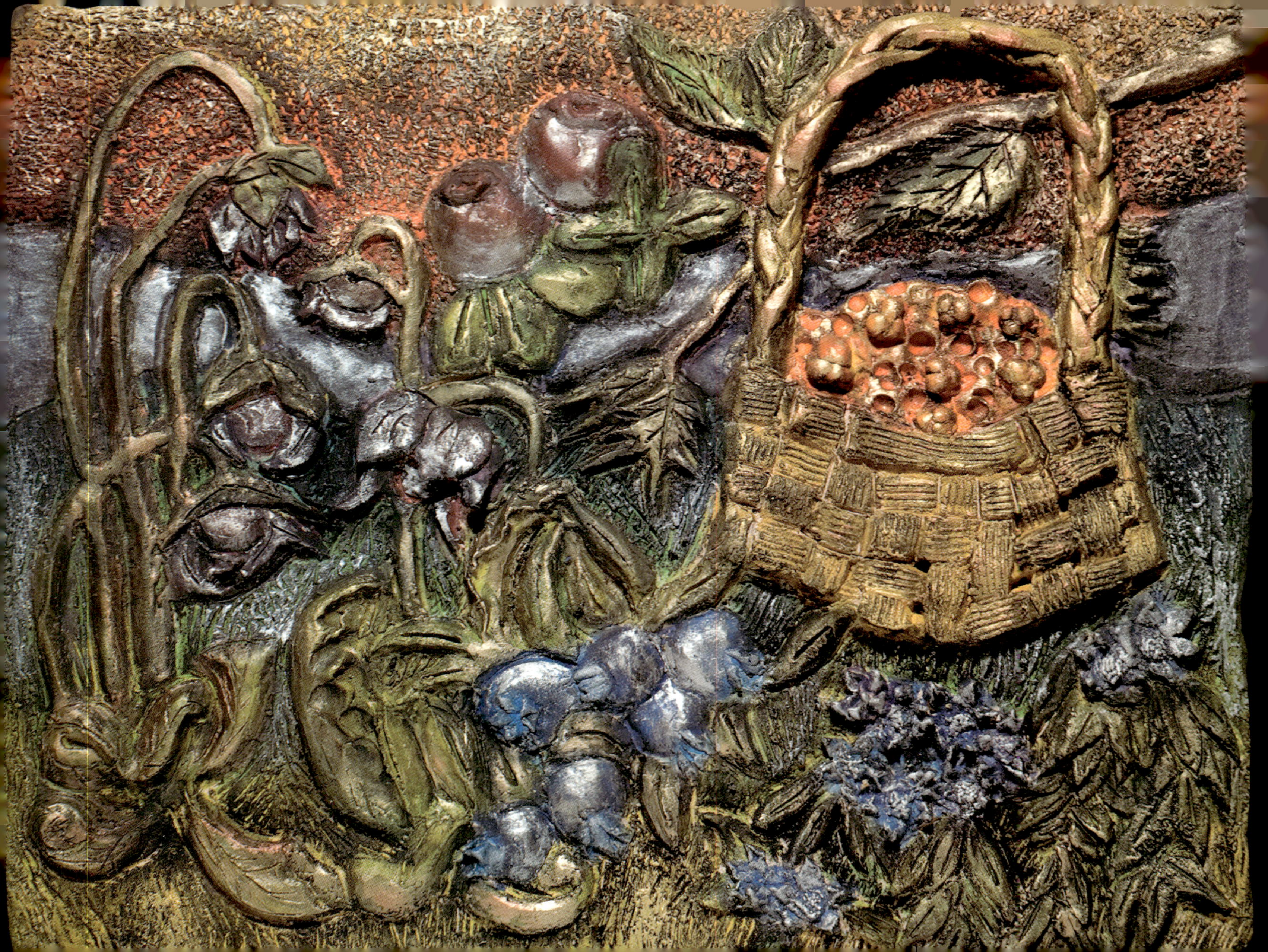

The Berries

Gabbie White, Happy Valley - Goose Bay

I've loved the excitement of the Labrador Creative Arts Festival since I was in primary school, so I jumped at the chance to be a part of the **Labradoria** Mural project. The four-day intensive workshop started with an extensive brainstorming session, followed by numerous sketches and iterations, and finally some very messy hands.

With each step, I found myself in complete awe of the results so far. At the end of the four days we laid the unfired tiles next to each other on tables; then stood on chairs so we could see what it would look like on a wall. I was amazed that twenty students were able to accomplish so much in so little time. After surviving the kiln, and a marathon painting session, our tiles were done.

It took a spectacular amount of dedication, creativity and inspiration to create this work of art, and I feel very proud of myself and the students I worked with to bring Labradoria into being. It is an incredible honor to have my work displayed in a venue I feel so passionately about. When I look at each clay tile in this mural, I am reminded of the beautiful landscape and rich culture that have surrounded my growing up. The narratives in these tiles continue to inspire my own artwork today and give me a greater appreciation of home. **(The year following her work on the mural, Gabbie went on to study art at Nova Scotia College of Art & Design)**

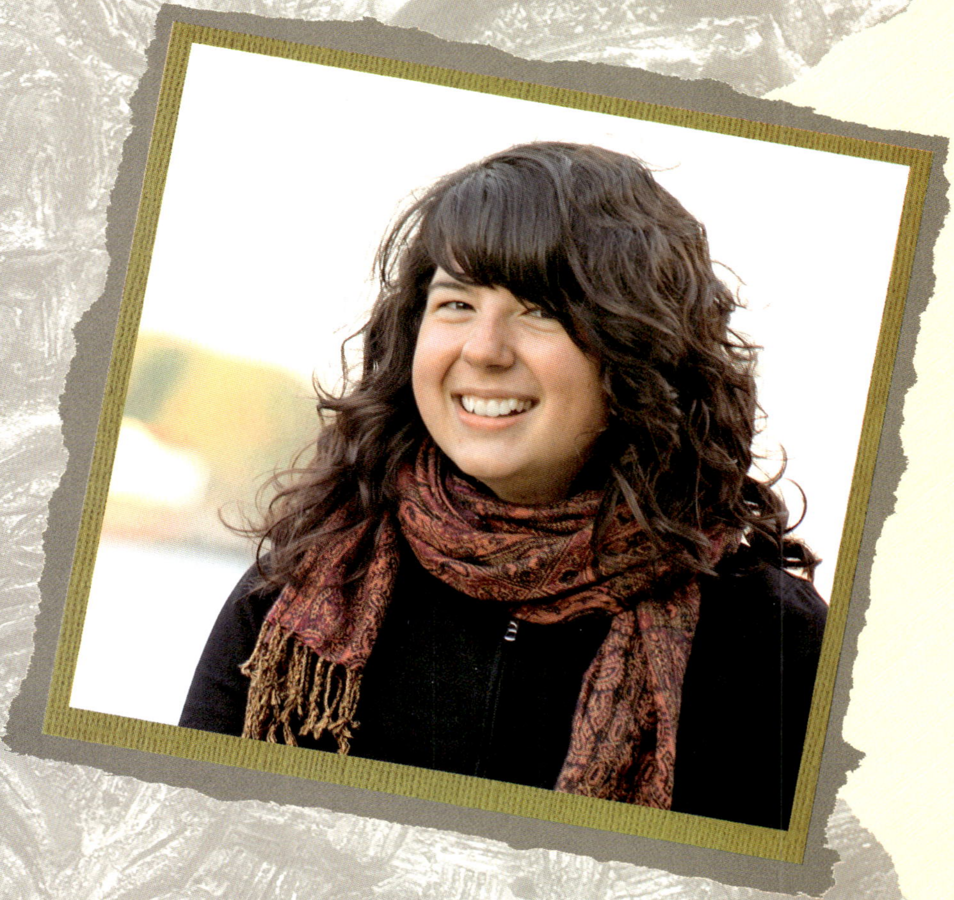

It took a spectacular amount of dedication, creativity and inspiration to create this work of art, and I feel very proud of myself and the students I worked with to bring Labradoria into being.

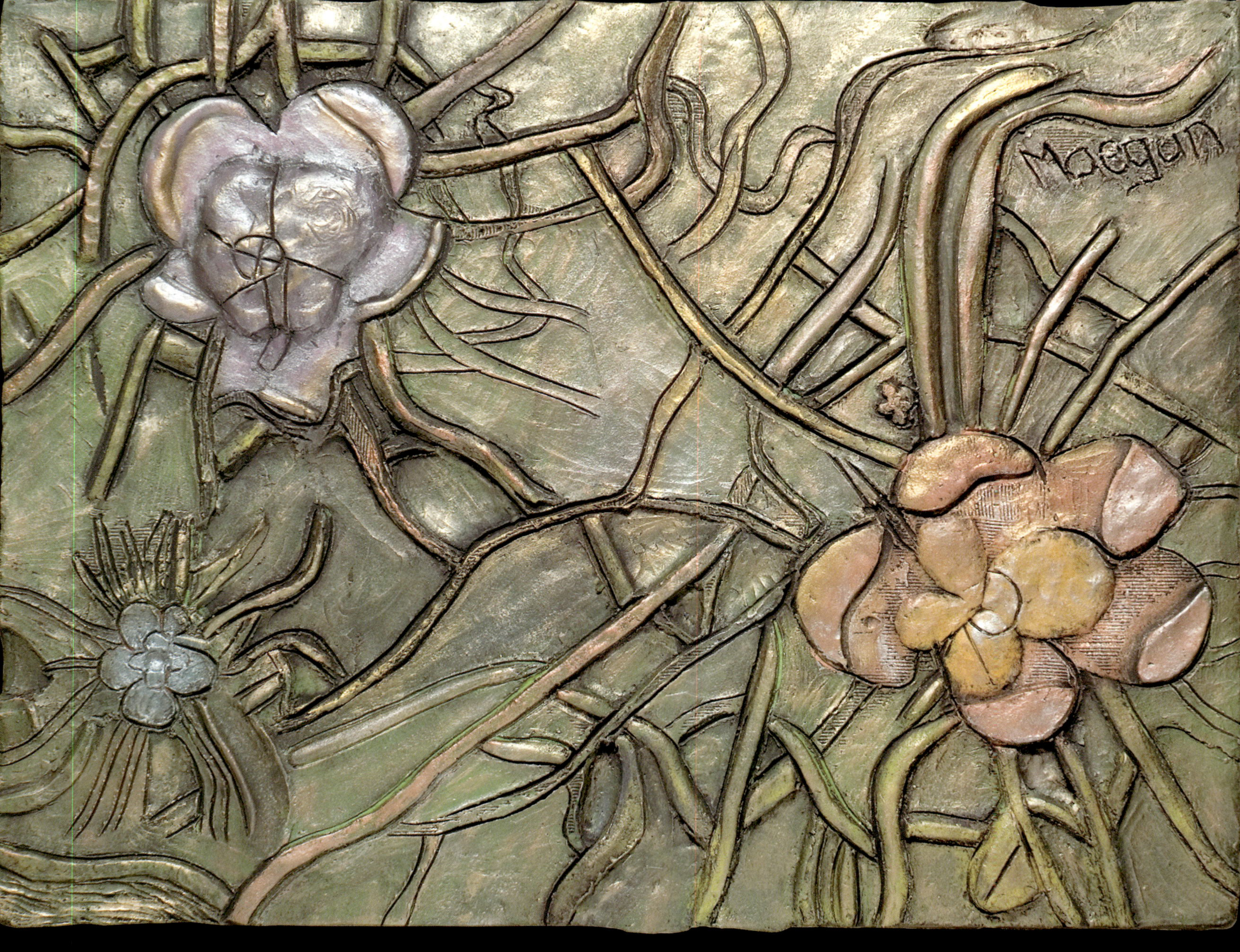
Maegun

Wildflowers

Maegan LeDrew, Happy Valley - Goose Bay

The growing season is short in Labrador, but things still grow, nonetheless. Many different flowers can be found in many different environments. On the marsh, bakeapple flowers quickly move on to form berries. Nestled in caribou moss, Labrador Tea's tiny pink flower-clusters are like short-lived miniature rhododendrons. On rocky outcroppings the redberry's tiny white blooms will become deep red fruit by September.

Labrador bog flowers grew plentifully right outside my cabin. They were what came to mind when I was searching for an image that represents Labrador. I knew this was what I wanted to create.

I was hesitant when I first looked at the mushy clay: how was I supposed to make that into something at all, never mind something beautiful and reminiscent? I worked; the images took shape; the clay hardened; we painted.....and I knew it was going to be great!

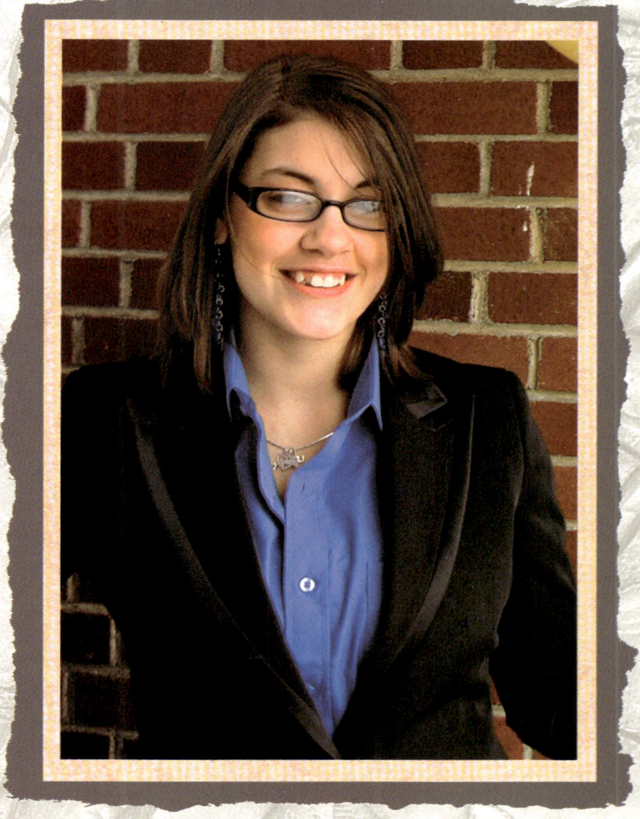

Labrador bog flowers grew plentifully right outside my cabin. They were what came to mind when I was searching for an image that represents Labrador. I knew this was what I wanted to create.

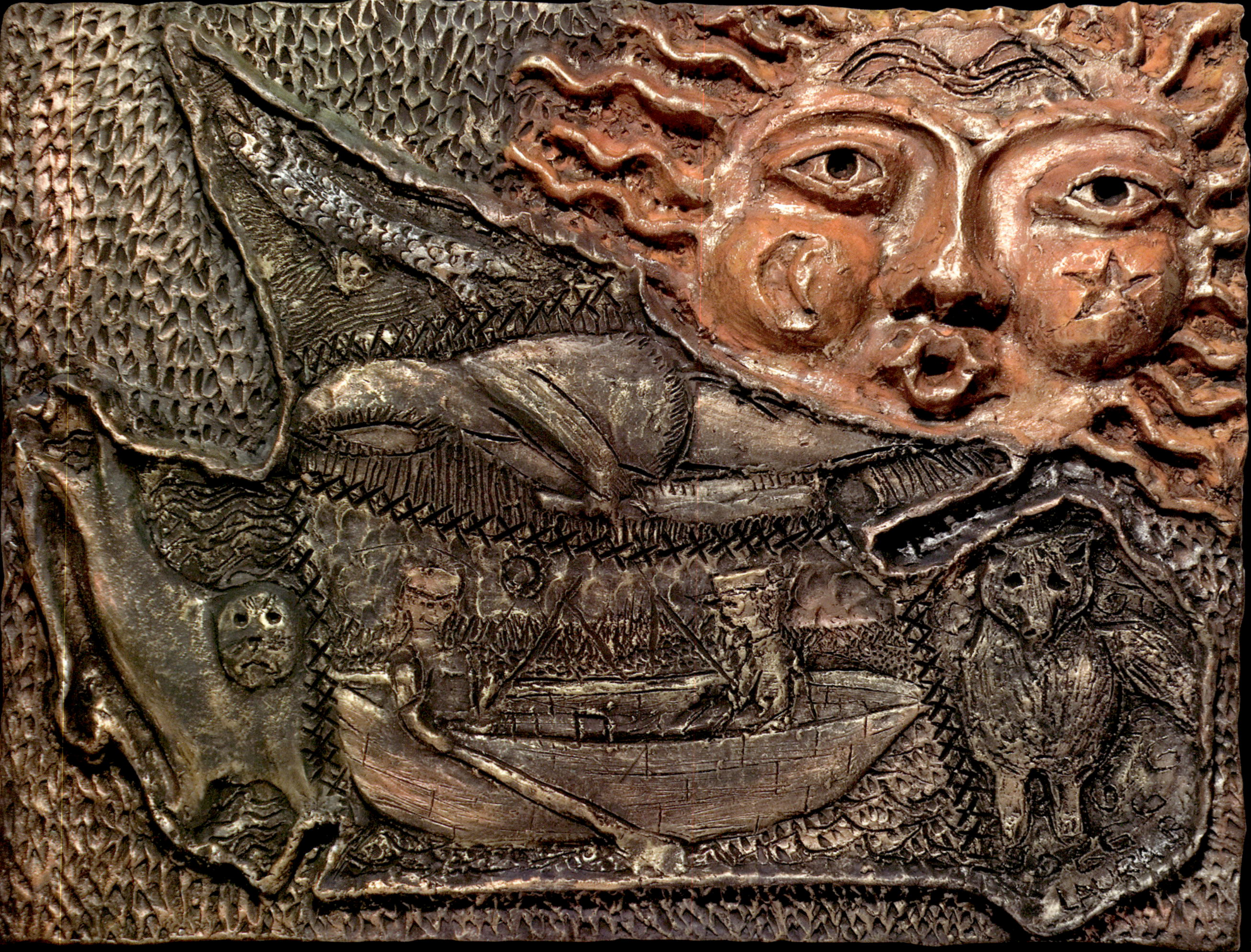

Labrador Images

Laura Bonnell, Churchill Falls

I could not sum up Labrador in one image, so I chose multiple images 'sewn-together' within a map of our land. You will find a boat with fishermen, an Inuit hunter, a fox, a fish and a seal. Outside the boundary, riding the cold Labrador current, a giant sun blows the North Wind onto the land. Many cold faces in Labrador end up looking ruddy like that sun, once the wind scours their skin!

This image, like the mural itself, shows how diverse and unique Labrador is.

I was not confident when working on my tile. I had zero experience and felt I could not accomplish the task. Once the project was complete, I was astounded by what everyone had created. I am so proud to be a part of Labradoria. My piece in the mural will always be in Labrador, even when I am not. This makes me extremely happy. I am so glad I did this.

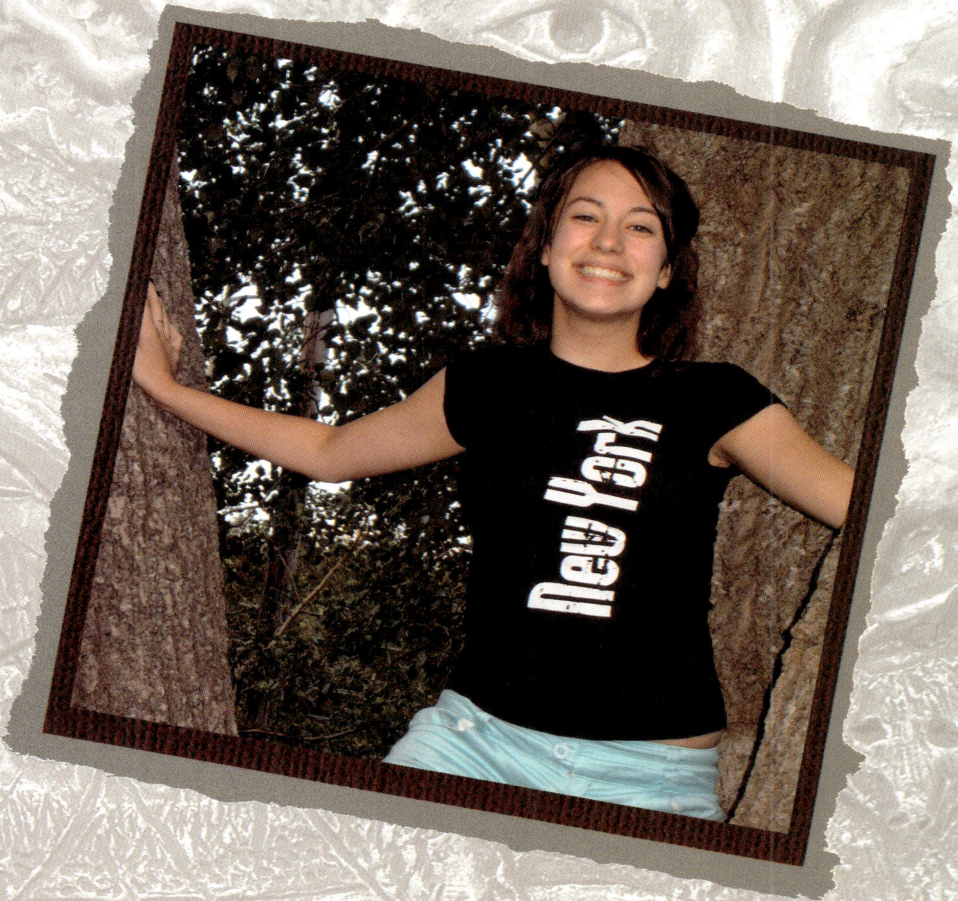

I am so proud to be a part of Labradoria.
My piece in the mural will always be in
Labrador, even when I am not.
This makes me extremely happy.
I am so glad I did this.

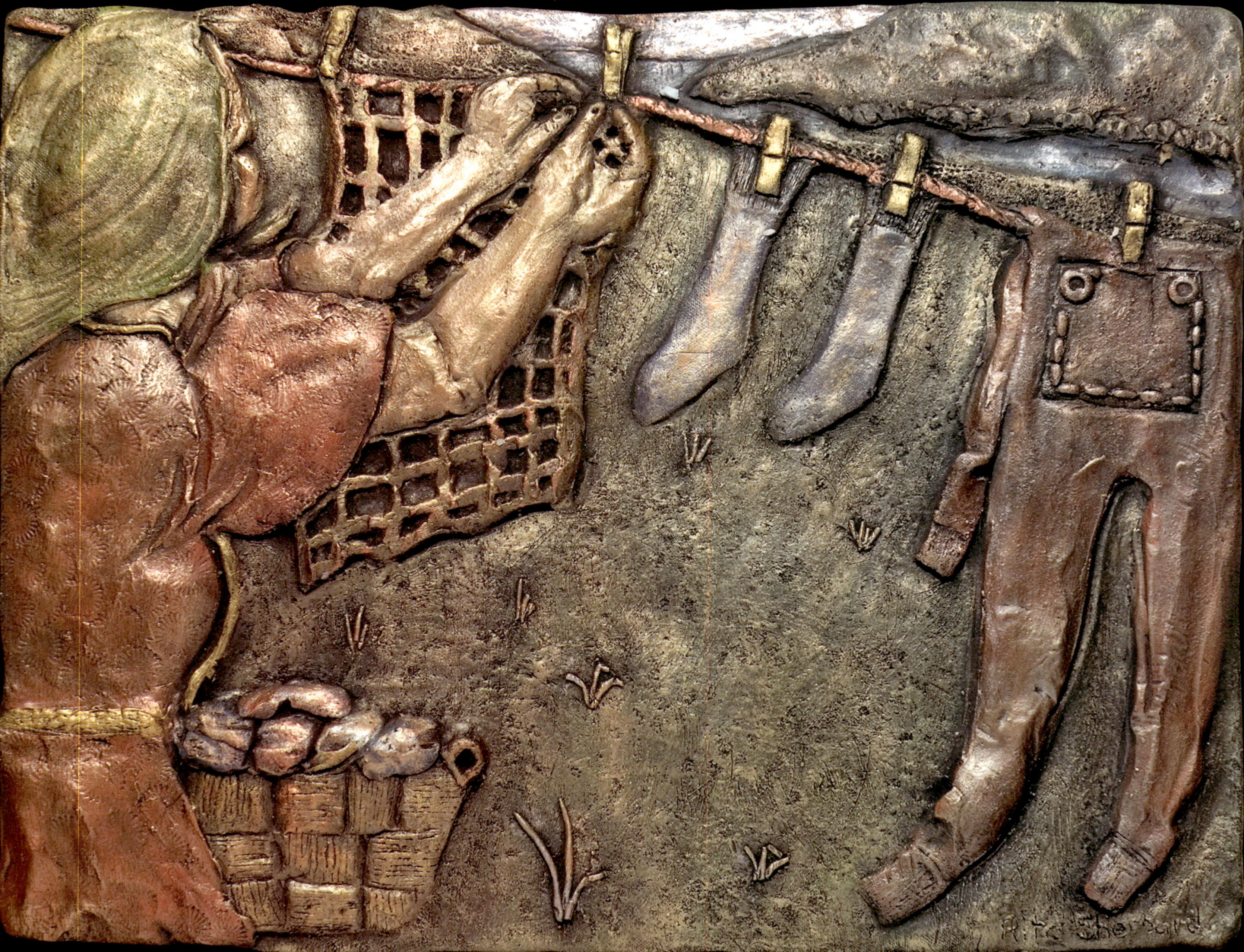
Rita Sherrard

Woman of Labrador

Rita Anne Sheppard, Postville

When Europeans began to arrive in Labrador, many of them stayed, having married Inuit or Innu women. The women brought with them their traditional skills and tools for living off the land. These families have forged lives together over generations, blending lifestyles and are today known as Labrador's Métis.

My late grandmother, Violet Flowers Sheppard, was one of these Inuit women. I never met her, but I have chosen, nonetheless, to celebrate her life of hard-work and commitment to family. I am inspired by all of these Inuit women; by what they endured; by their strong work ethic as providers; by their efforts to pass on Inuit heritage and values to my generation. My tile is a tribute to all of these women.

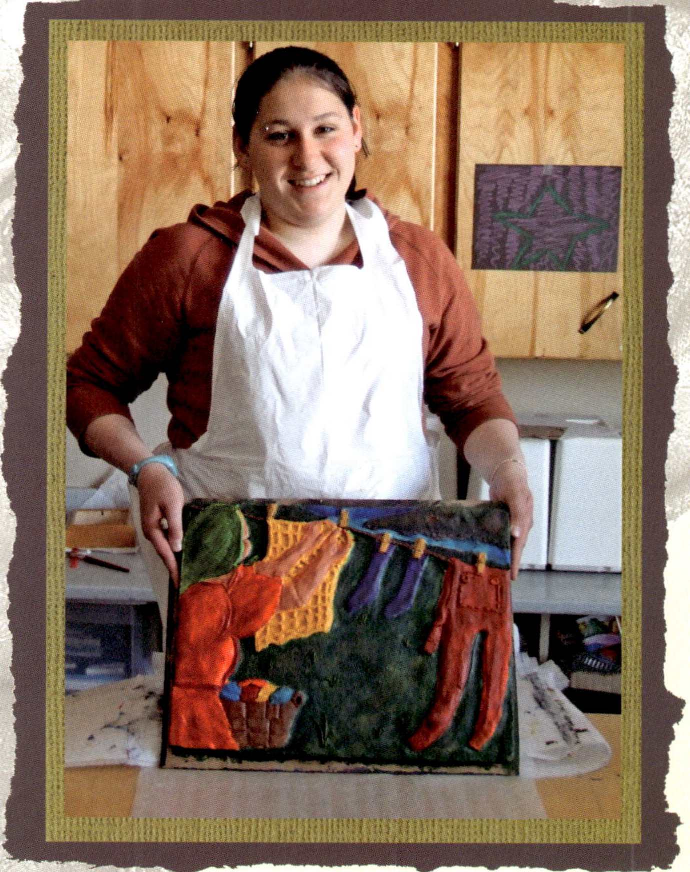

I am inspired by all of these Inuit women; by what they endured; by their strong work ethic as providers; by their efforts to pass on Inuit heritage and values to my generation.

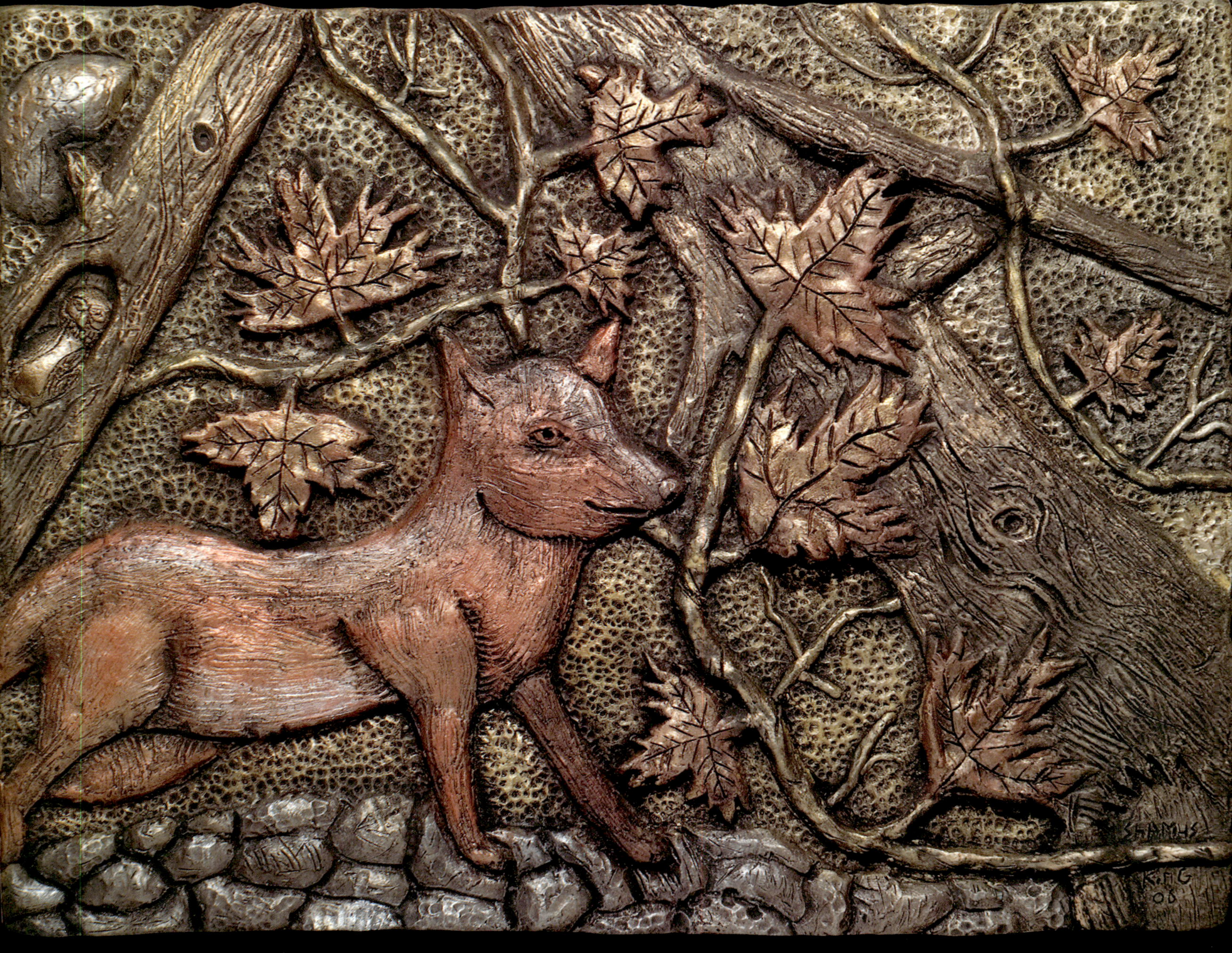
SHAMUS
K.A.G
08

Fox in the Fall

Shamus King, Happy Valley - Goose Bay

I like the fall. I like the wild colours. Often, in Labrador, the fall comes early and stays late. Birch trees will begin to turn yellow as early as late August. Then, once the frosts are visiting regularly at night, the maples turn loose their scarlet fury and the woods are in riot.

A fox is well-camouflaged during this change-season, which made it easy for me to choose which Labrador animal I would place in a fall scene. It is easy to relate foxes to Labrador, for trappers relied heavily on them for their livelihood when trapping was king.

Working with clay was a new experience for me. Watching the image evolve was really something. The step-by-step process made the work feasible for me, as my starting skill-level wasn't very high, but I am impressed with the finished product.

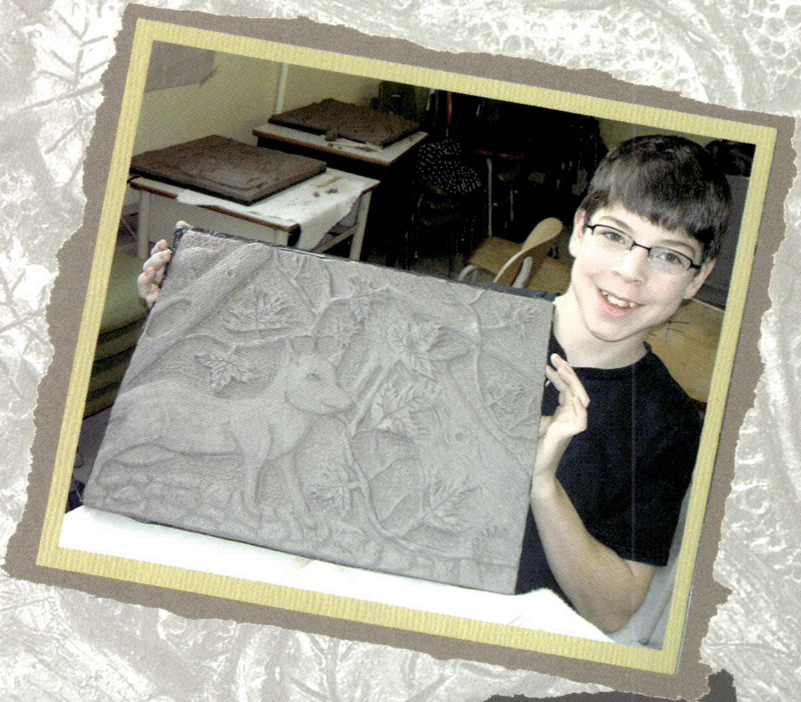

Working with clay was a new experience for me. Watching the image evolve was really something.

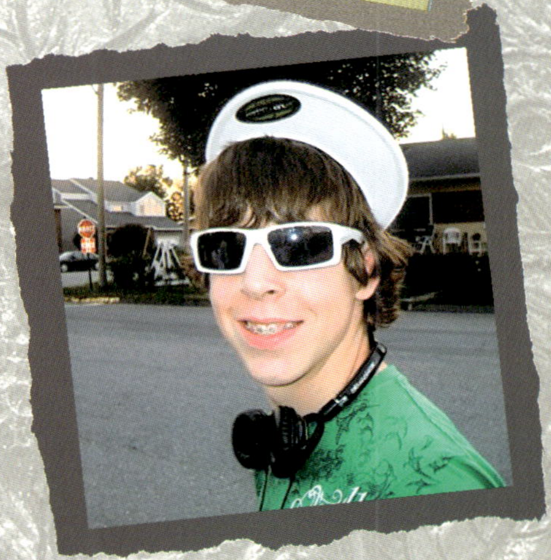

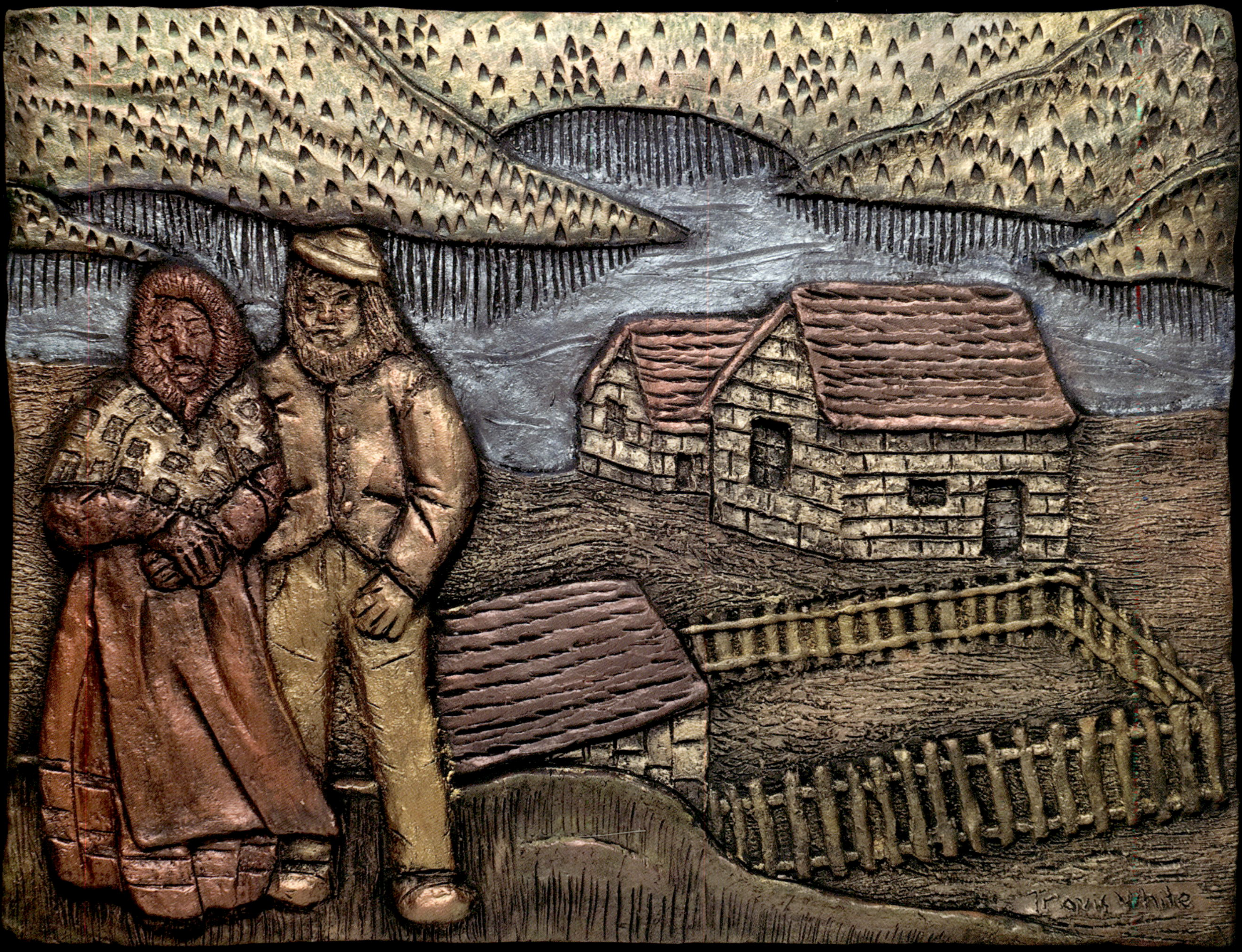
Travis White

Hannah & Mersai Michelin

Travis White, Happy Valley - Goose Bay

I got my inspiration from a photograph in a **Them Days** magazine. Hannah and Mersai Michelin were early settlers in Labrador. Hannah was sister to Lydia Campbell, Labrador's first diarist, whose family was an example of the literal marriage of two cultures: Inuit and European. Hannah & Mersai Michelin and Lydia and Dan Campbell are forbearers to many, many of today's Labradorians.

In my tile, I honor their history as early settlers – the landscape from which they took their living, the buildings, gardens, and clothing that characterized their lifestyle.

It is significant that our mural is made up of contributions from all over Labrador that examine, display and celebrate our varied cultures and environments.

It is significant that our mural is made up of contributions from all over Labrador that examine, display and celebrate our varied cultures and environments.

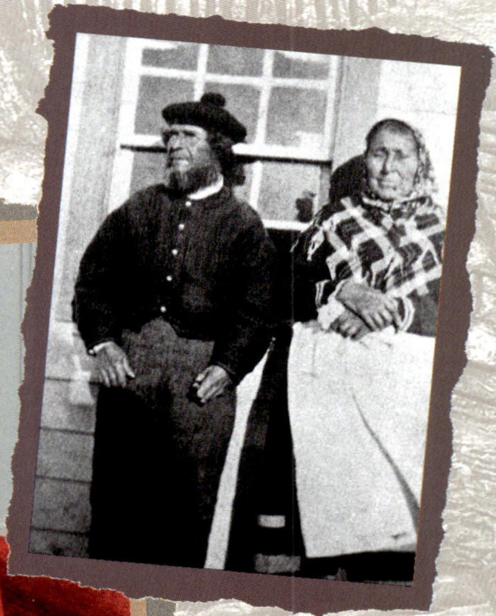

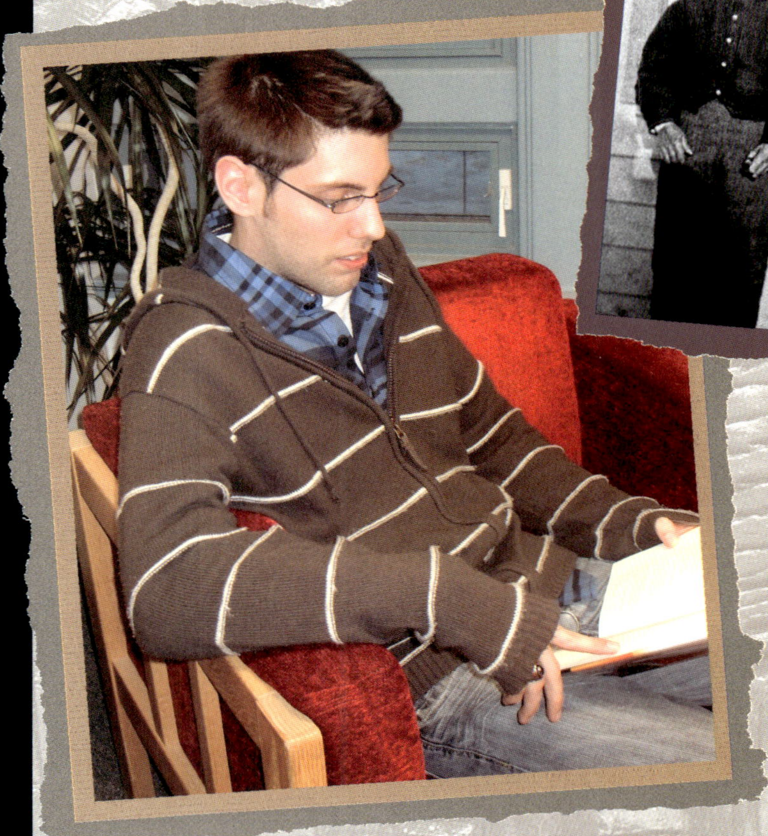

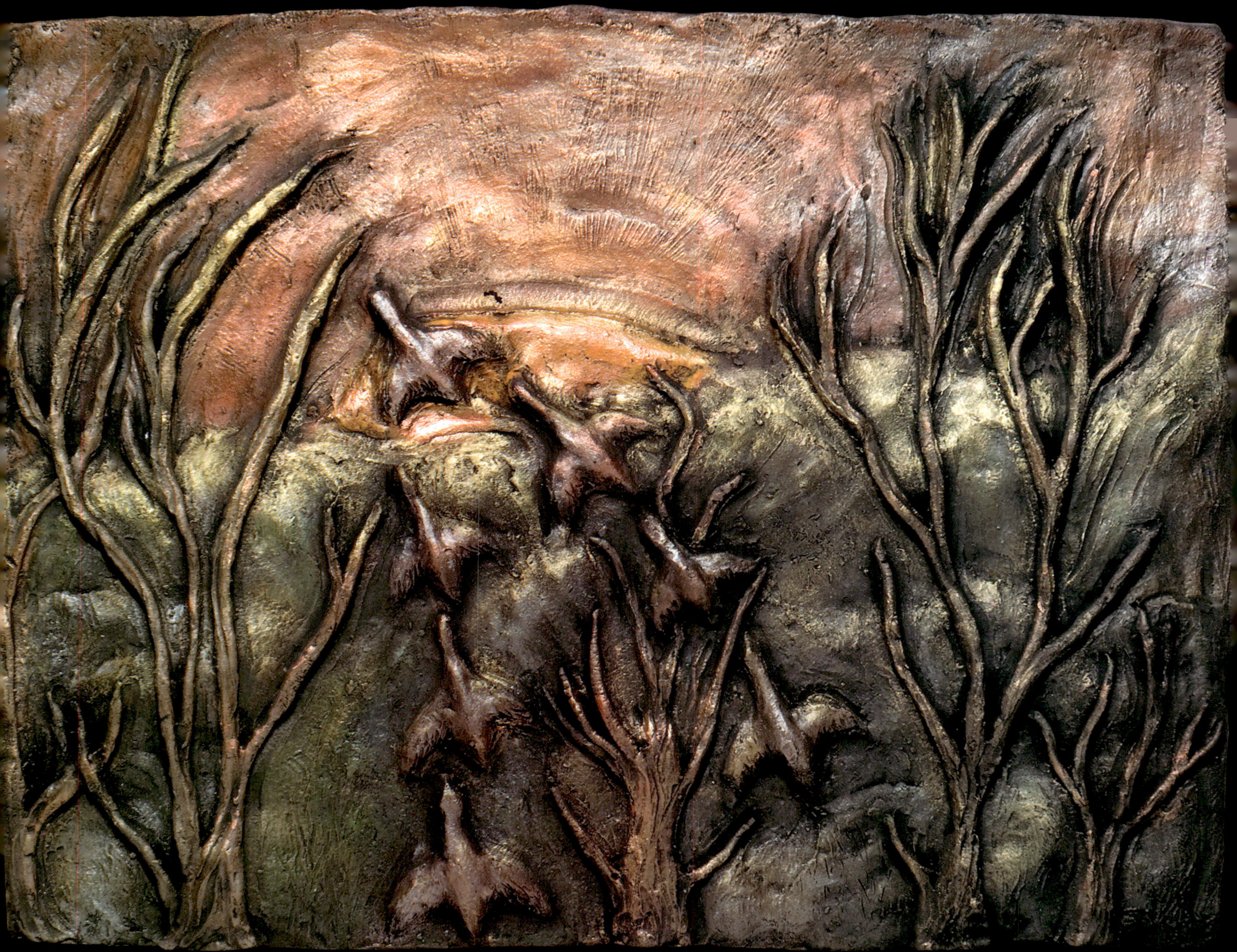

Open Season

Sandra Hollett, Happy Valley - Goose Bay

I enjoyed digging in the clay and getting messy. Here was a new experience, and an interesting one. I don't think my tile met my expectations, in the end, but the project is wonderfully creative, just the same. It gave me the chance to work with my good friend, Lissa, and to make new friends in Mud Lake. I had never been to Mud Lake before, and riding over early each cold morning in an open boat was a genuine Labrador experience!

My image is inspired by migrating geese. I love to see them flying in 'V' formation; it makes me think of freedom and grace within organization. They are the ultimate team; the ultimate community.

Isn't this what the mural is, too?

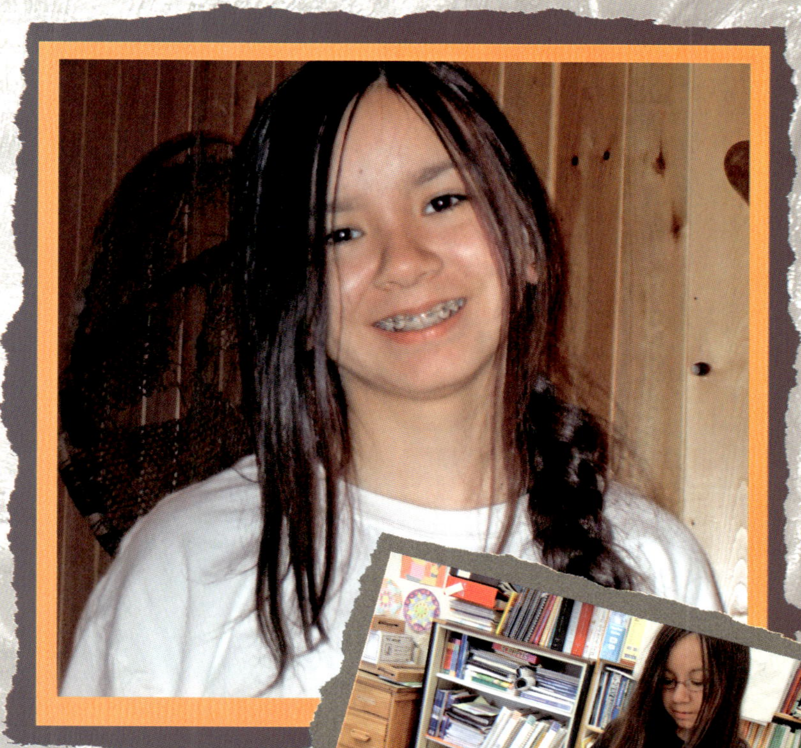

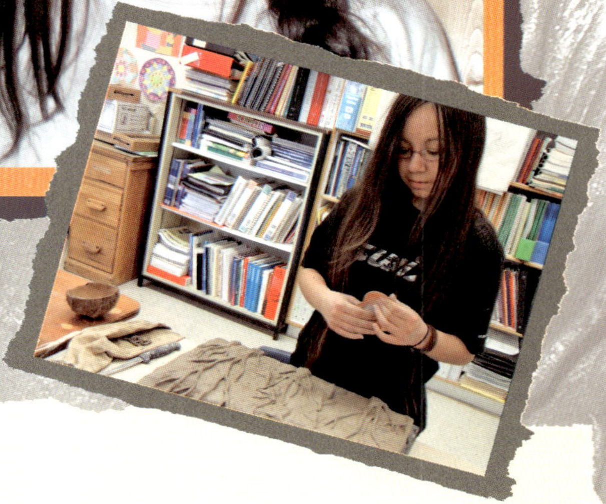

Geese are the ultimate team;
the ultimate community.
Isn't this what the mural is, too?

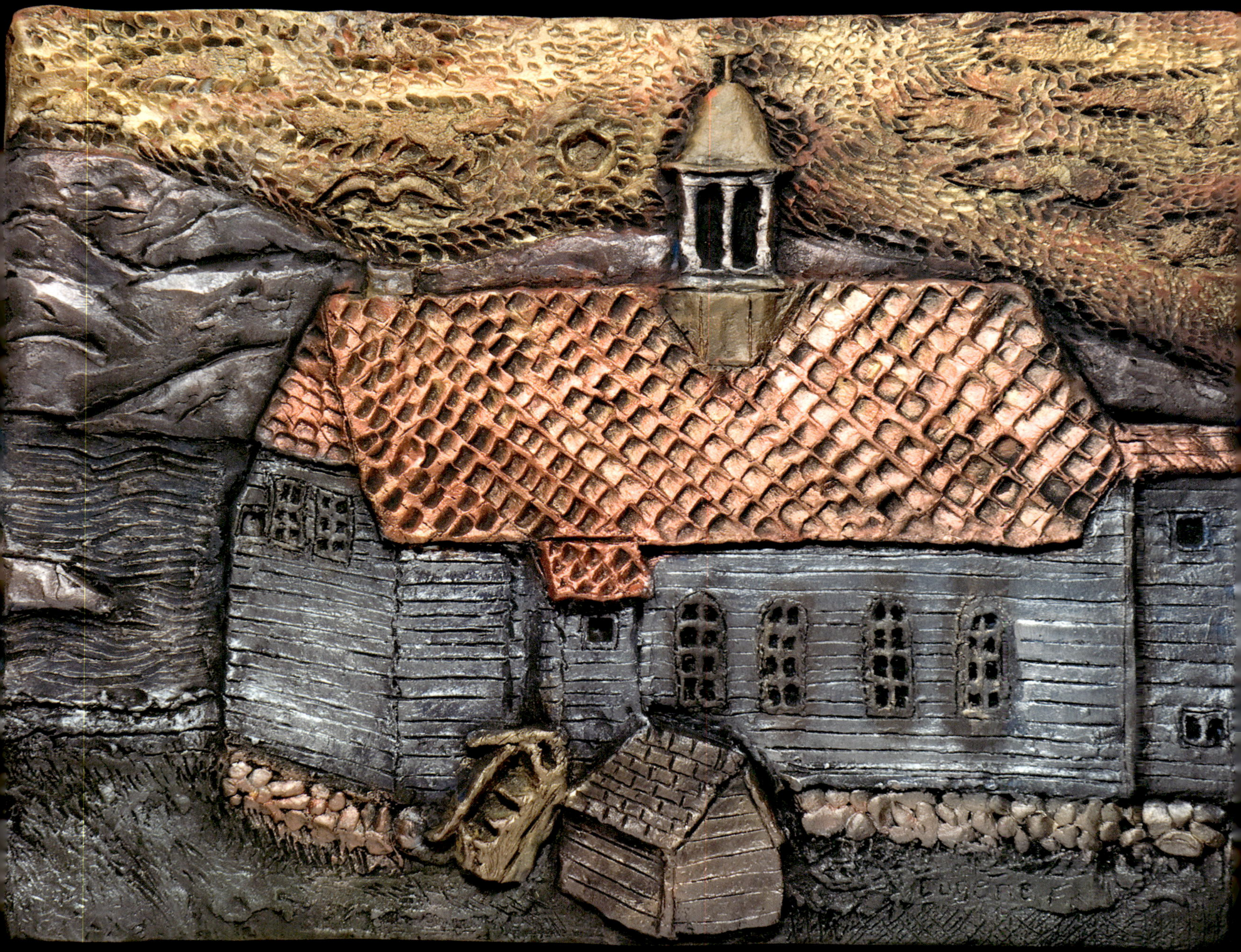

Hopedale Church

Eugene Frieda, Nain

There is much to say about my image....this mural means a lot to me and my past.

I chose the Hopedale church as my subject because it is the first thing that comes to mind when I think of home. I was brought up around it. The first thing I would see when looking out my livingroom window was the Moravian church. There wasn't a day when I didn't play around that church. My friends and I had picnics beside it, and sometimes we would pick (Icelandic) poppies from the garden.

The main reason I chose this image, though, is because I really missed my home in Hopedale at the time I made the tile. I was living in Nain, and I pictured this view in my mind whenever I wanted to go home.

(P.S. There's no place like home!)

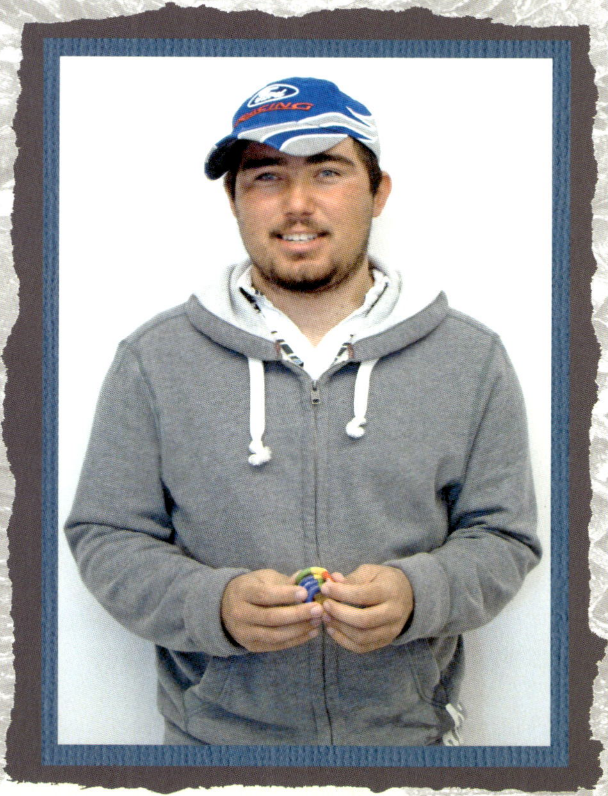

I chose the Hopedale church as my subject because it is the first thing that comes to mind when I think of home. I was brought up around it.

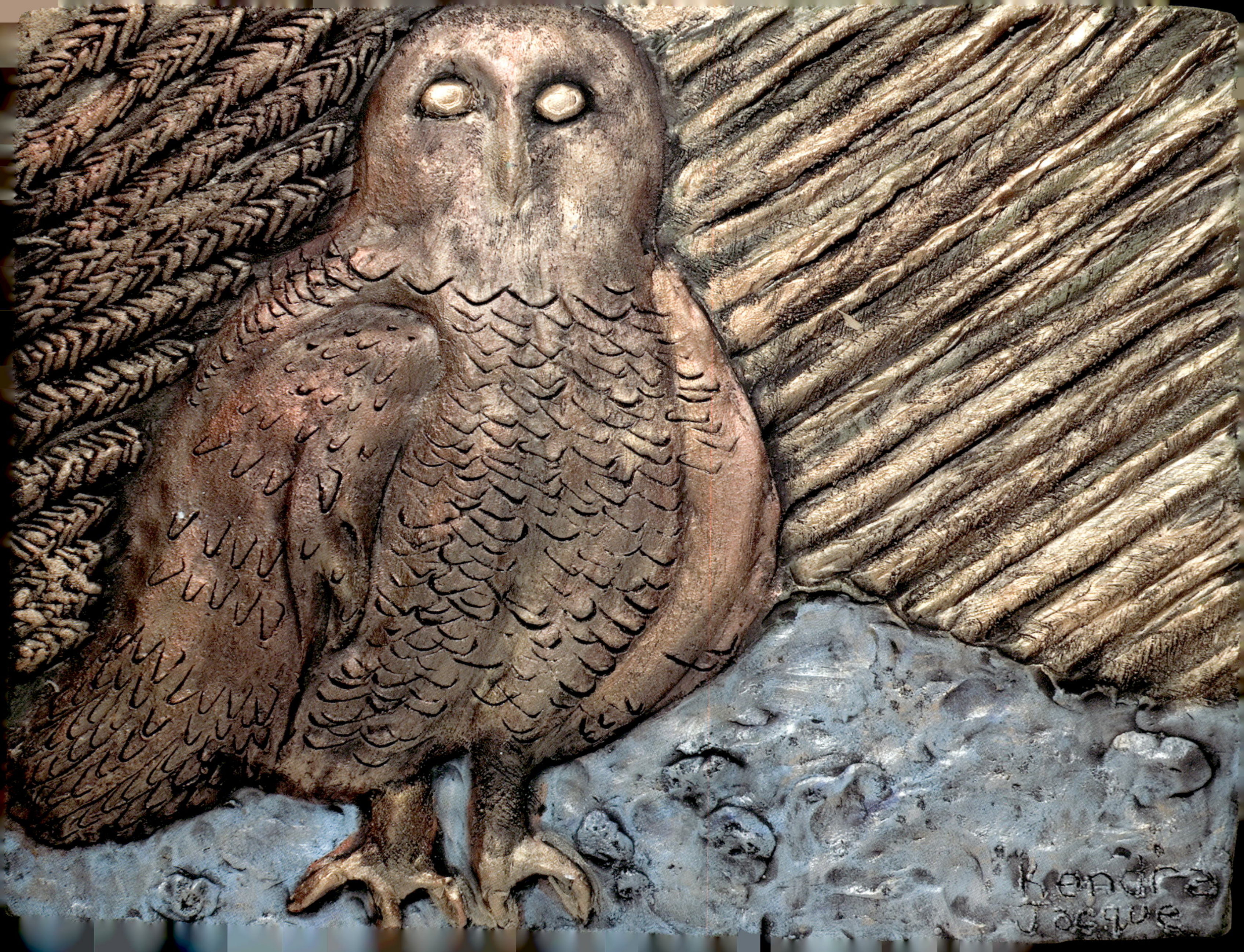
Kendra
Jaque

Snowy Owl

Kendra Jacque, Makkovik

The Snowy Owl is my favourite bird, even though I rarely see one. This is because they breed north of the treeline in Labrador, and move south in our region only when northern food supplies are scarce. Wildlife is important as a food source in Labrador, and while the Snowy Owl is not eaten, it is still part of the delicate balance of nature. Snowy Owls feed on mice, voles, ptarmigan (partridges), arctic hare, but mostly on lemmings. The male is almost completely white; an elegant "King of the North".

It was interesting working with clay. I gained confidence as I worked, and was pleased with the piece when it was finished. Making an owl in the clay was, for me, a way to show how much I have always loved this silent, watchful hunter.

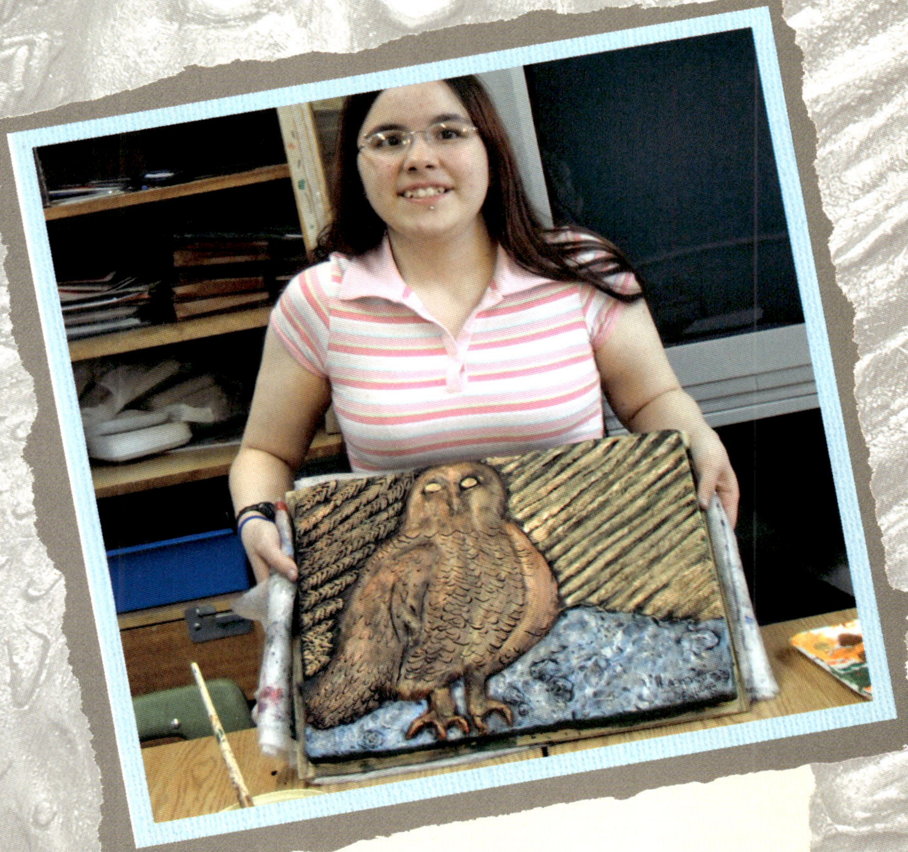

Making an owl in the clay was, for me, a way to show how much I have always loved this silent, watchful hunter.

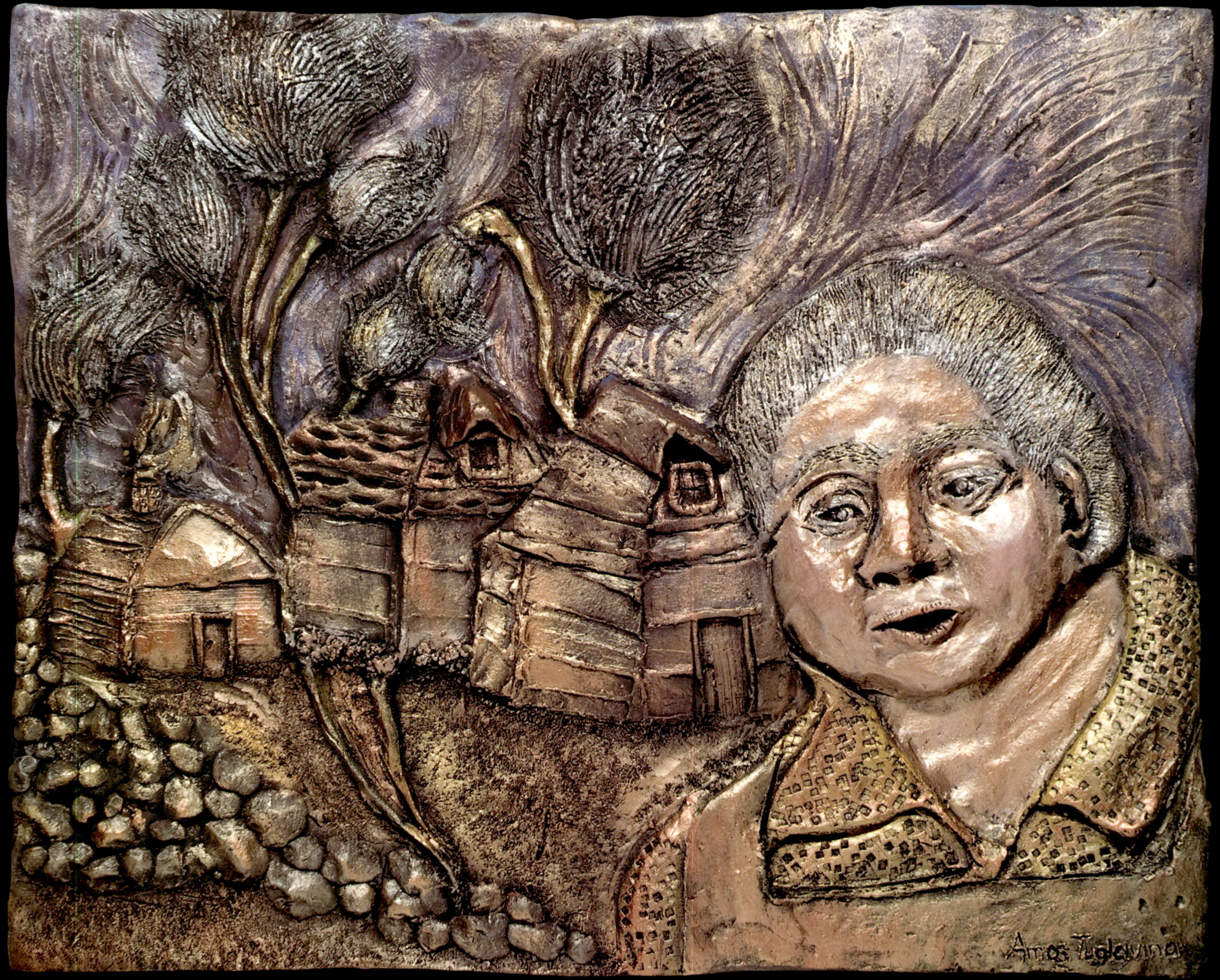
Amos Tuglavina

Moving From Place to Place

Amos Tuglavina, Hopedale

I really did not know where to begin with an image for the mural, but I did know that I could draw, and others encouraged me to get involved. So I did. I piled into stacks of nature magazines, Labrador books, old photos and **Them Days** magazines to look for ideas and inspiration.

And I sketched.... I sketched, and I sketched! I like drawing, so maybe this was the best part for me. And everyone came to see what I was doing, and they said it was good.

Aunt Flora Baikie's picture was on the cover of a **Them Days** issue, so I started to draw her face. Then I found a picture of the old buildings at Hebron and started to draw them. Miss explained that the three small buildings that I drew were the last three houses still standing there. And then we talked about how families used to move around a lot in Labrador, following good trapping or hunting, and setting up for awhile in different places. And that's when these ideas came together.

Arctic cotton was used to line kamiks (skin boots) as insulation against the cold. This grass placed across the middle of the image joins the 'home' (houses) to the 'family' (woman) because when families moved, they found different vegetation; different conditions; different resources wherever they went.

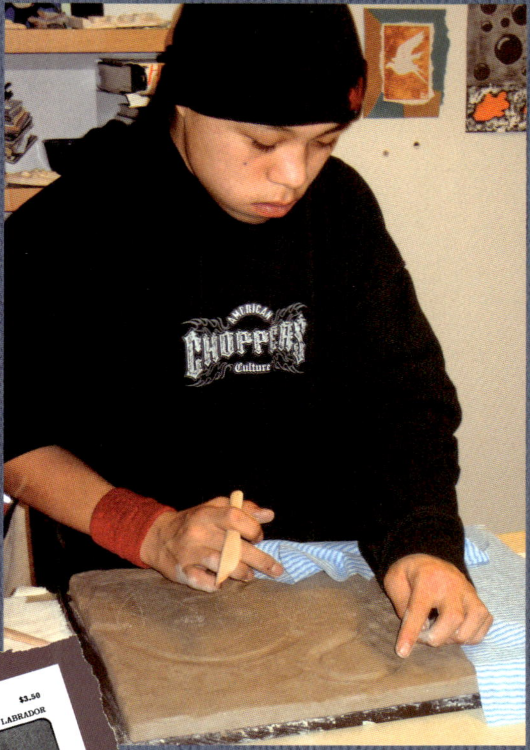

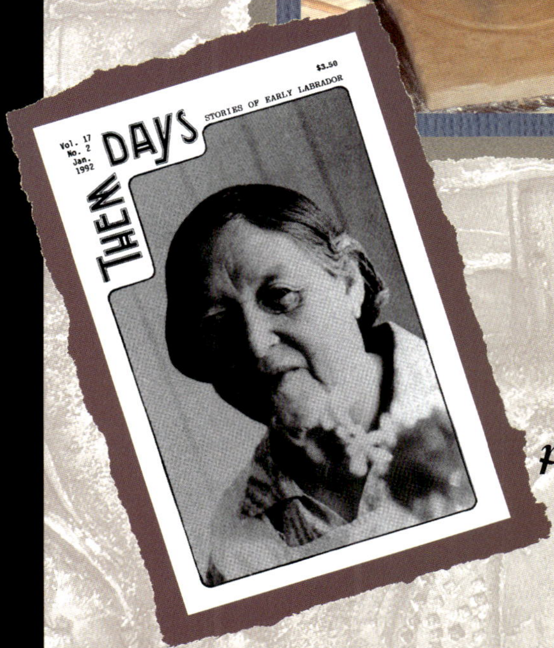

I piled into stacks of nature magazines, Labrador books, old photos and Them Days magazines to look for ideas and inspiration.

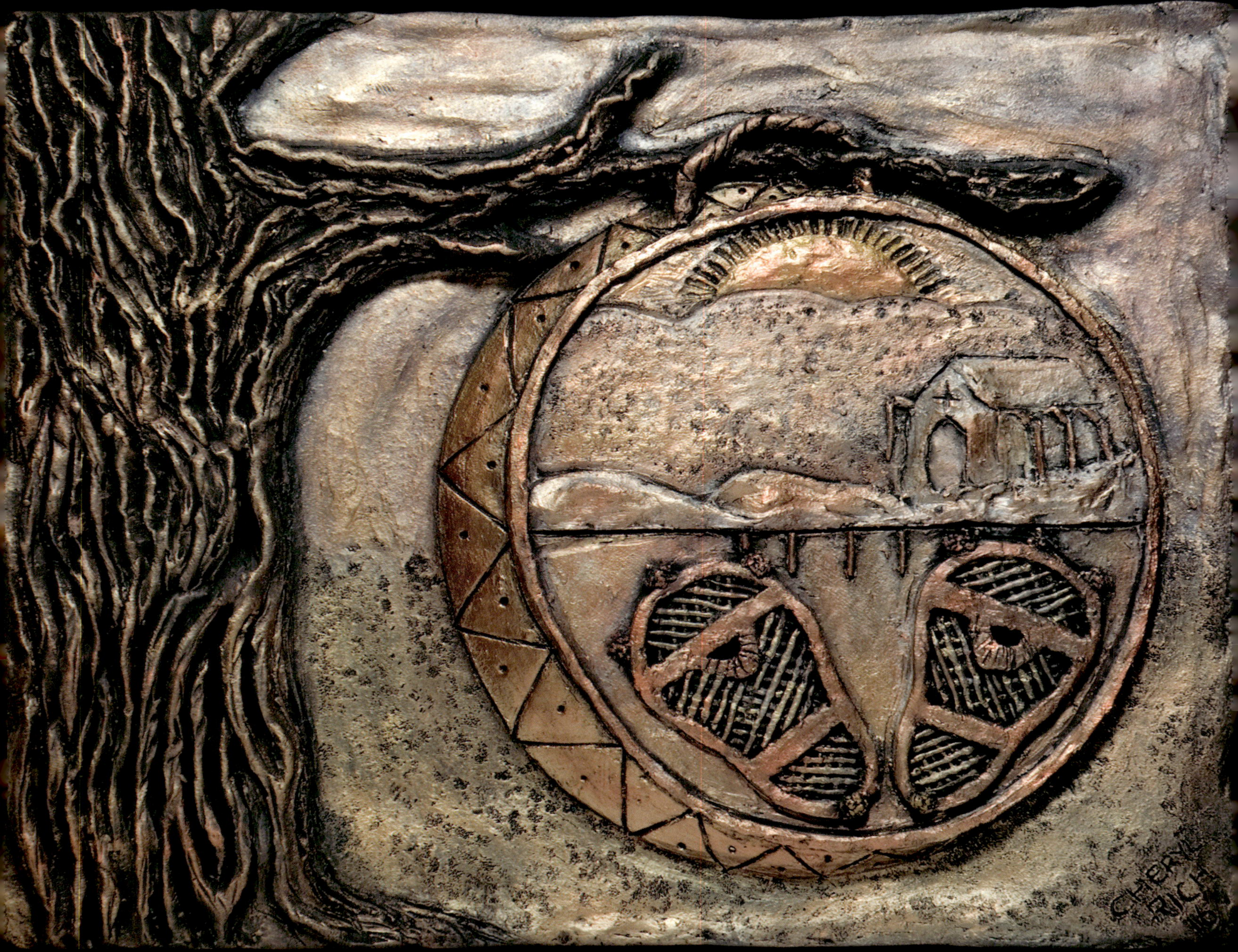

CHERYL
RICH

Numushum mak nukum eshaniuts/ Way of Life

Cheryl Rich, Natuashish

I have a cousin who is a very good artist. I was inspired by his artwork. Instead of seeing his artwork on paper though, I wanted my piece to look real, and this was a good way to try it.

The image I've created shows how my grandparents lived years ago. Snowshoes and tents were what they used most when they were in the country. I have placed these things inside a drum, which holds the heartbeat and spirit of the Innu. The other things are used less today than they were in the past; we do not live off the land like we once did.

But the drum is still very important to us today.

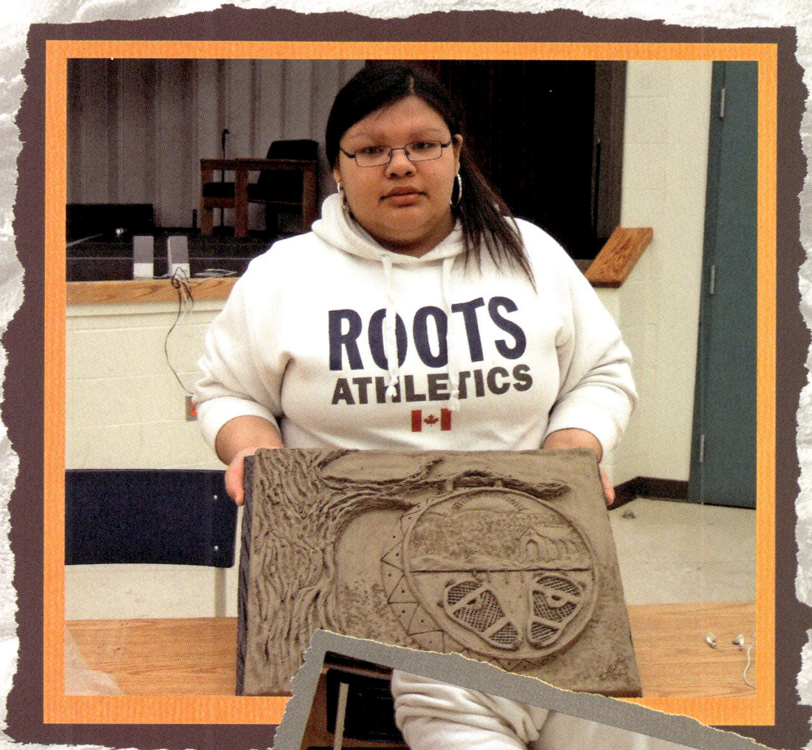

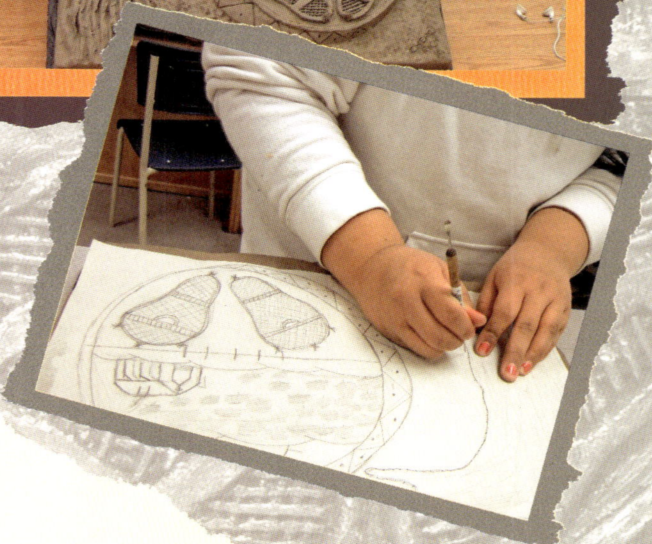

The image I've created shows how my grandparents lived years ago.

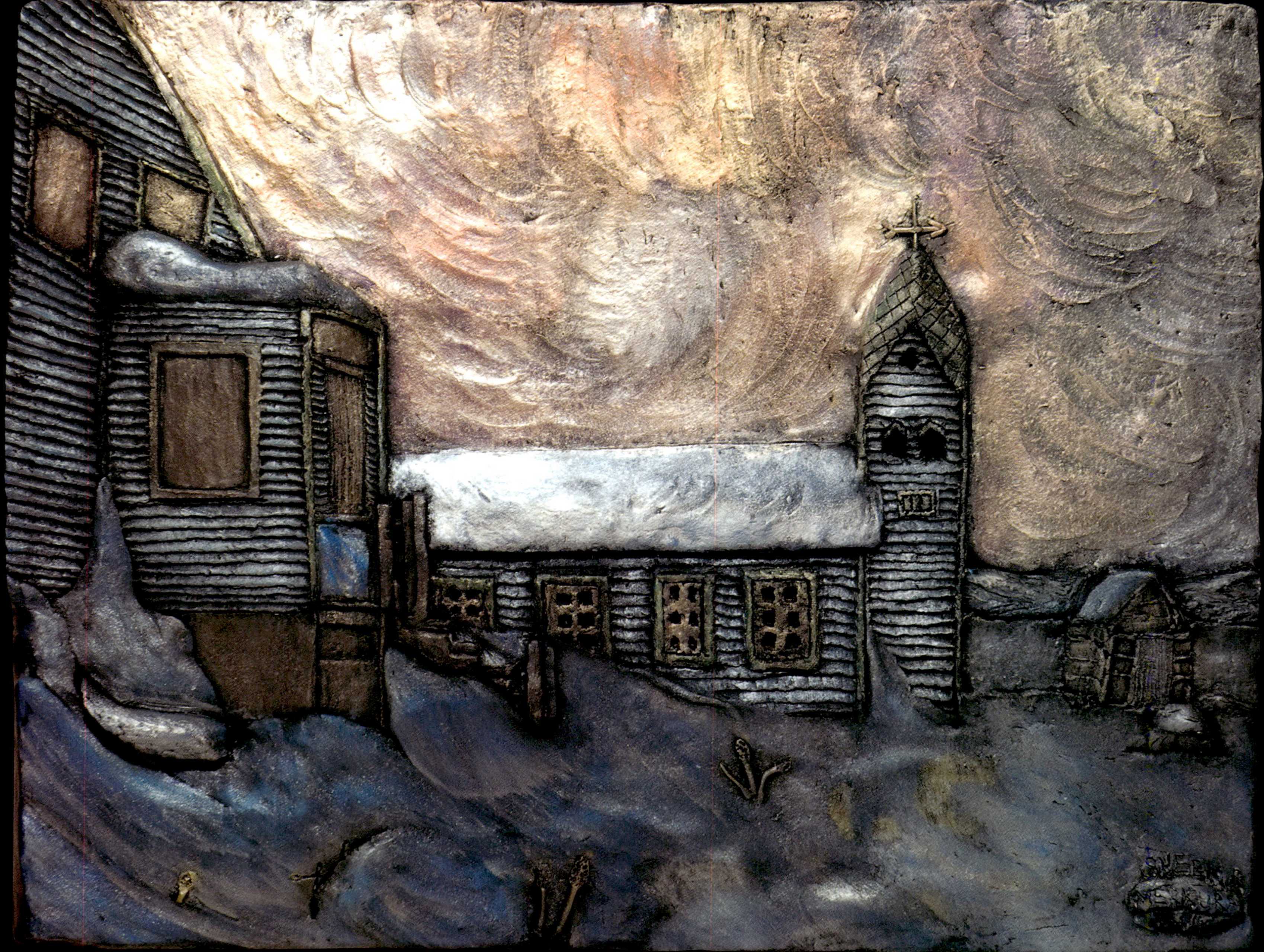

KATIMMAVIVUT

SHEENA MERKURATSUK, NAIN

Katimmavivut means 'my church' in Inuktitut. I chose the church of Nain because it is a defining landmark. My family, and most of the town, always go to the Moravian church at Christmas and Easter for as long as I can remember.

The first Europeans who came to stay in Labrador were Moravian missionaries, arriving in the 1770's. They brought their architecture with them; in fact, their buildings were 'pre-fabbed' in Germany and reassembled when they reached Labrador. Each community can be recognized by its church, as each one is slightly different from another. Because Moravian buildings can be found all along the coast of Labrador, I thought it would be fitting for the mural.

It was fun to work in clay – a different medium for me. Students from all across Labrador put the mural together in a short time; it shows many different images of Labrador culture and lifestyle.

It's great that the mural will be on display for everyone to see. It would be even greater if more students in the future get to have the chance to make a tile like we did. They are all very beautiful.

I chose the church of Nain because it is a defining landmark.

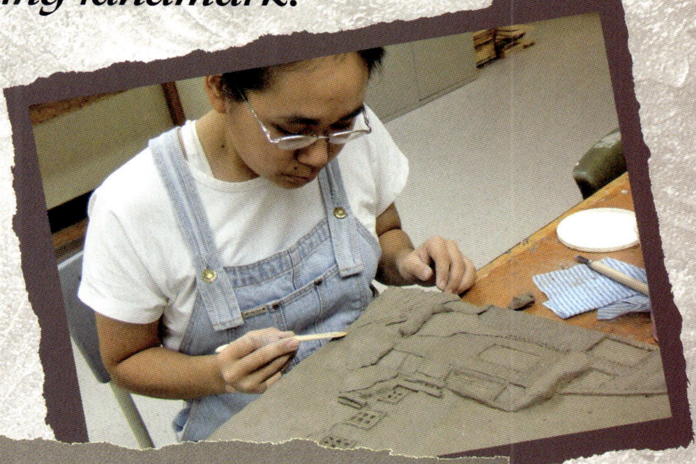

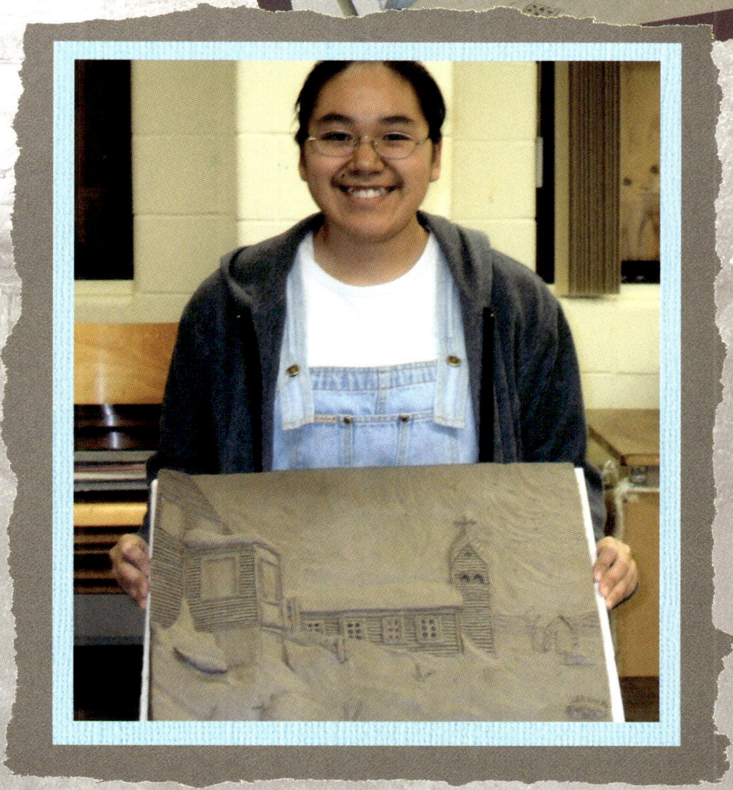

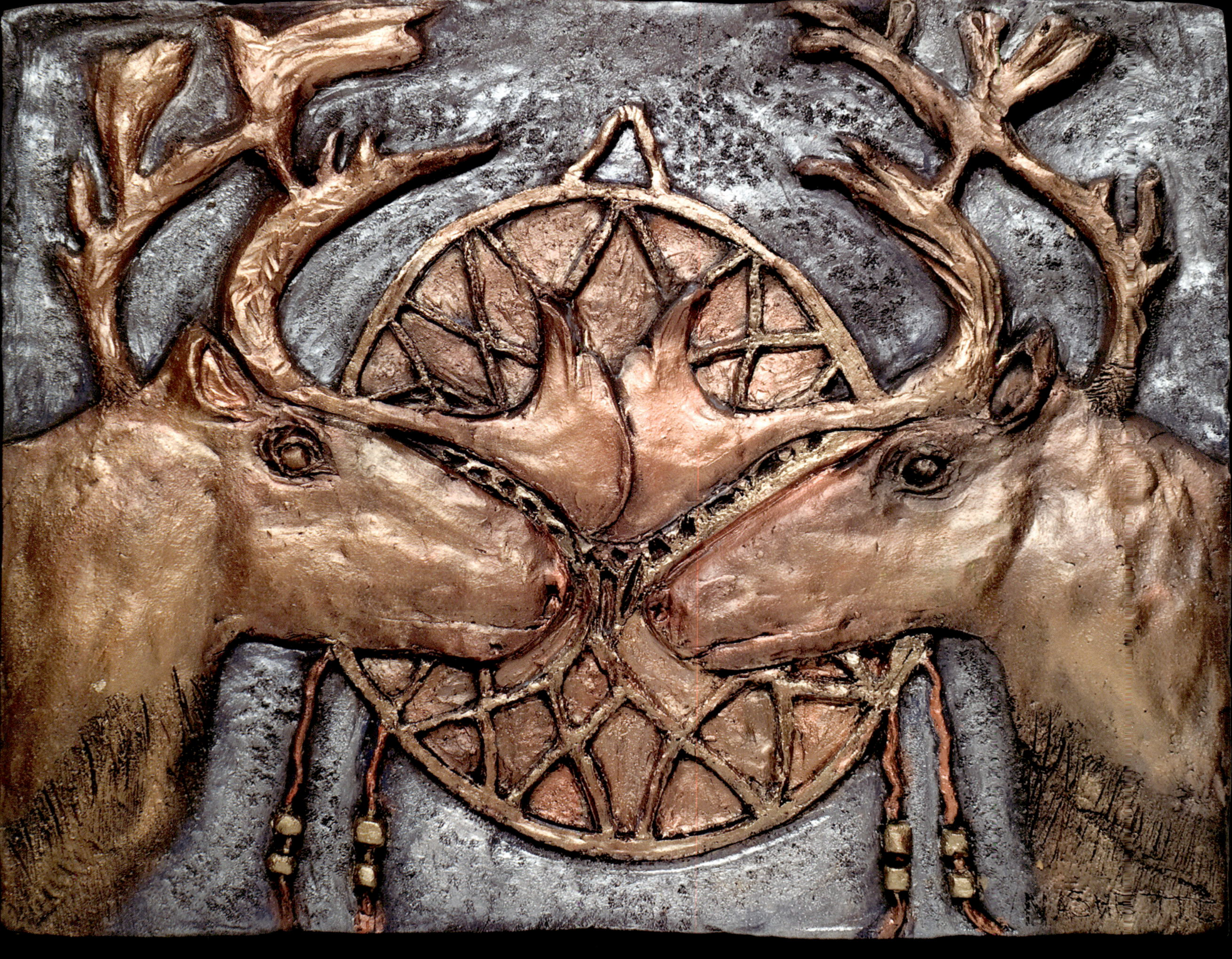

Kauitshinits nete nipuamunish/ My Dream Leads Me

Nashette Piwas, Natuashish

My idea came from a dream I had about an elder, who I later found out was my grandfather. One caribou represents my grandfather: **the past**. The other caribou is me: **the future**. The dreamcatcher binds us, the past and the future, together.

It came about as I made it: the caribou came first, and then I added the dreamcatcher. It was after I finished the piece that I discovered the connection between my dream and my grandfather.

The piece is about family connections. It is very touching that my grandfather and my own children and grandchildren will see my tile someday, and I am proud to have something to leave for them.

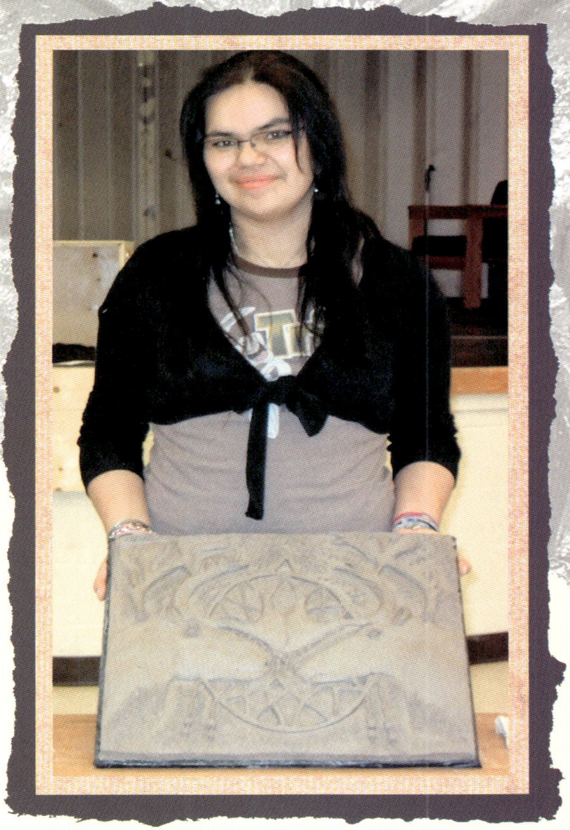

Kauitshinits nete nipaumunish

Anite nipuamunits nutinen ume etenitaman katshi puatik tohishennu, kie aishkats patush tshessenimik nimushum ni puatashipan. Peik "ne atik", niimushum nitashinuau; ueshkats nete. Eku ne kutak atik", eukun nin: aianishkats nete. Puamun mamu nitanukunan, nete ueshkats kie nete aianishkats, mamu.

Ne eshi, puamuian, miam nituten ne puamuna ka petauimakati ka anipikatati ka tutakanita: atik" nishtam tau, kue anipikataman. Patush katshi tshishtaian eku tshessenitaman eshinikuat nipuamun, nimushum ka puatek.

Mamu uikanishimaun ka takuat eshi-tapitik. Ni mishta ishpitenitenimau nimushum kie nituassimits kie
nitanishkut - apanits tshe uapatakau umuennu ka tutamuk, kie ni minuatamuan tshetshi nikatamukau.

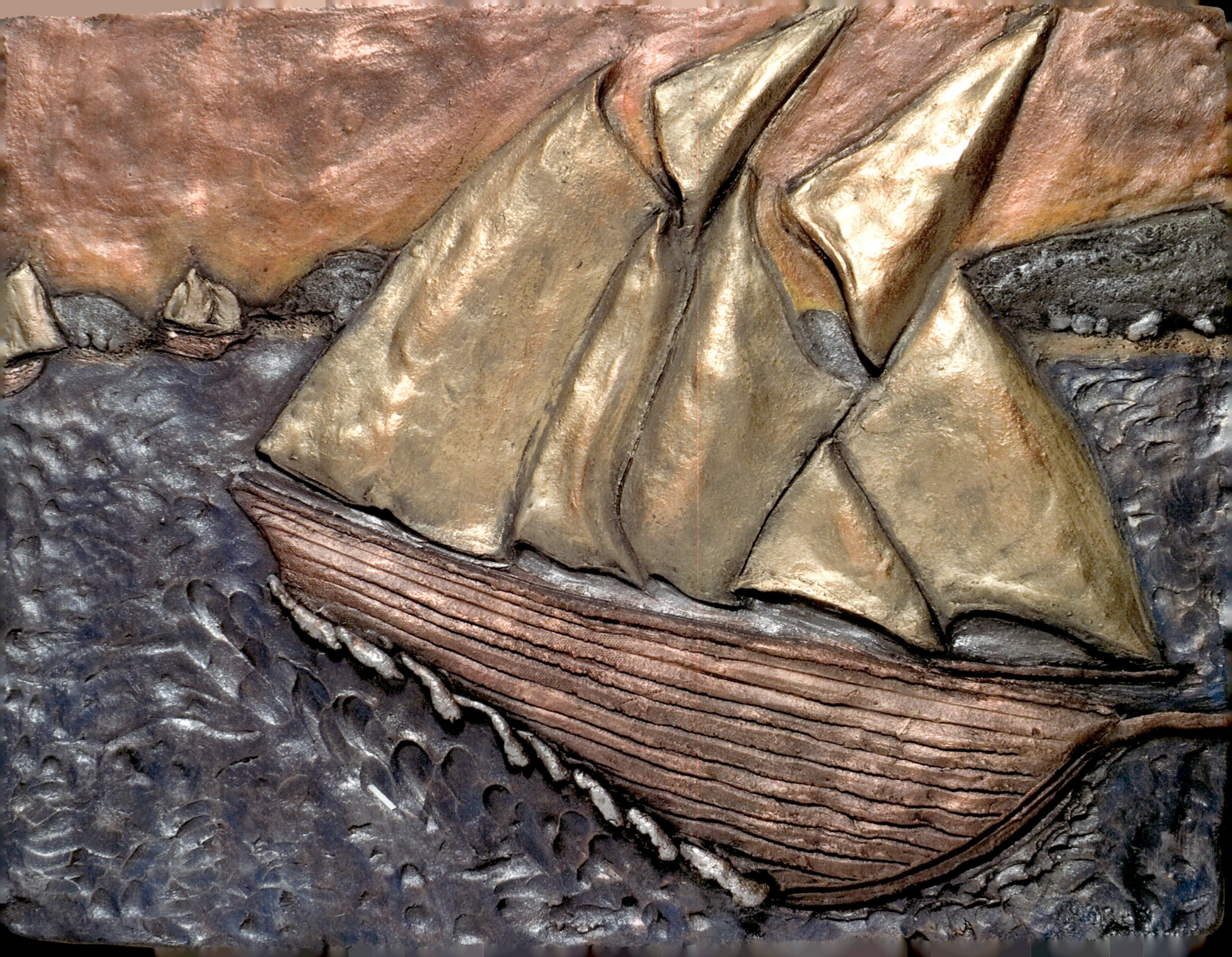

The Schooner, Geneva Herridge

Chelsea Morris, Cartwright

It was common for Newfoundland schooners to ply the waters and even choke the harbours of Labrador in pursuit of the cod fishery as late as the 1950's. In 1899, fifty-two vessels carrying 1500 crew sailed from Carbonear alone.

The **Geneva Herridge** was such a schooner, captained by my great-grandfather. It used to sail each summer from Harbour Le Cou, Newfoundland to Labrador's coast, to fish. In 1918, the Geneva was carrying a load of freight between Port-aux-Basques and North Sydney when it was mysteriously lost in the fog. Nothing was ever found of the ship or the crew.

When I was first asked to make a clay tile, I told Dorrie that she asked the wrong girl. I was the least-artistic person in the school, but she told me that there was an artist in everyone....you just had to find it.

I've never been so proud or confident of a piece of artwork in my life, as I am of this tile.

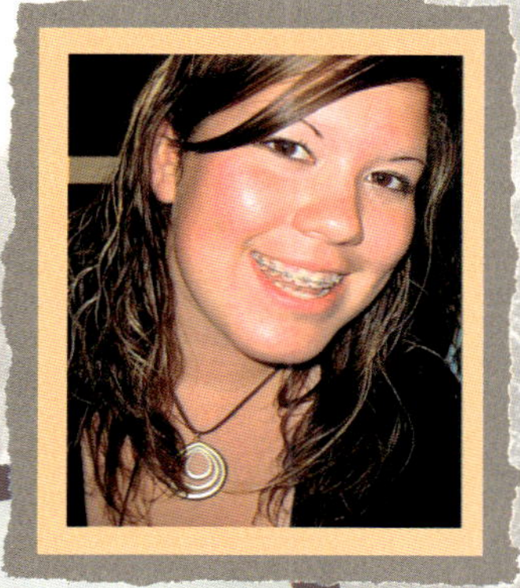

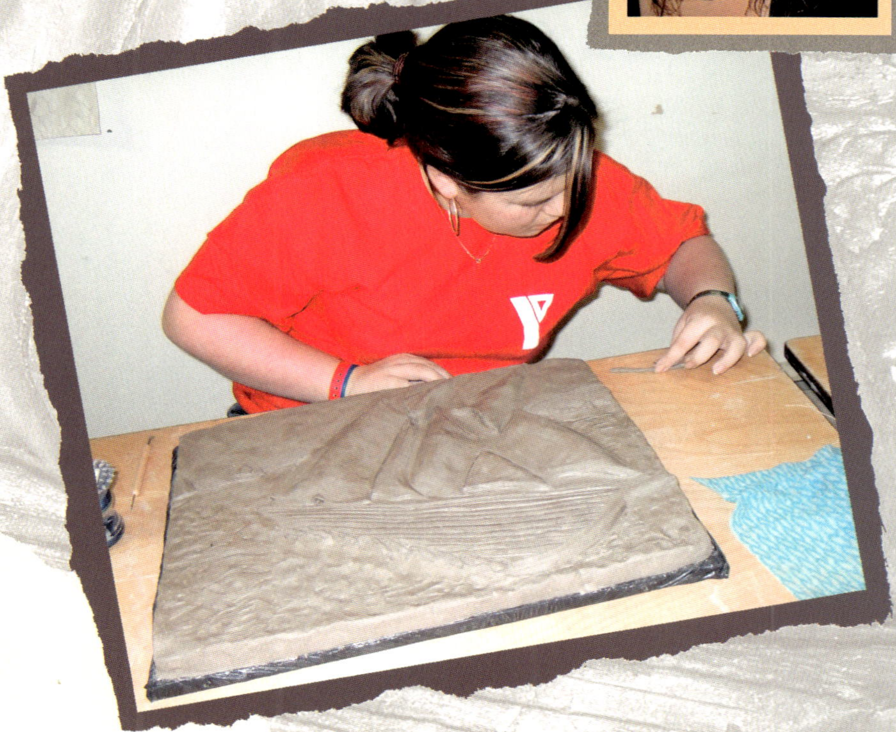

I've never been so proud or confident of a piece of artwork in my life, as I am of this tile.

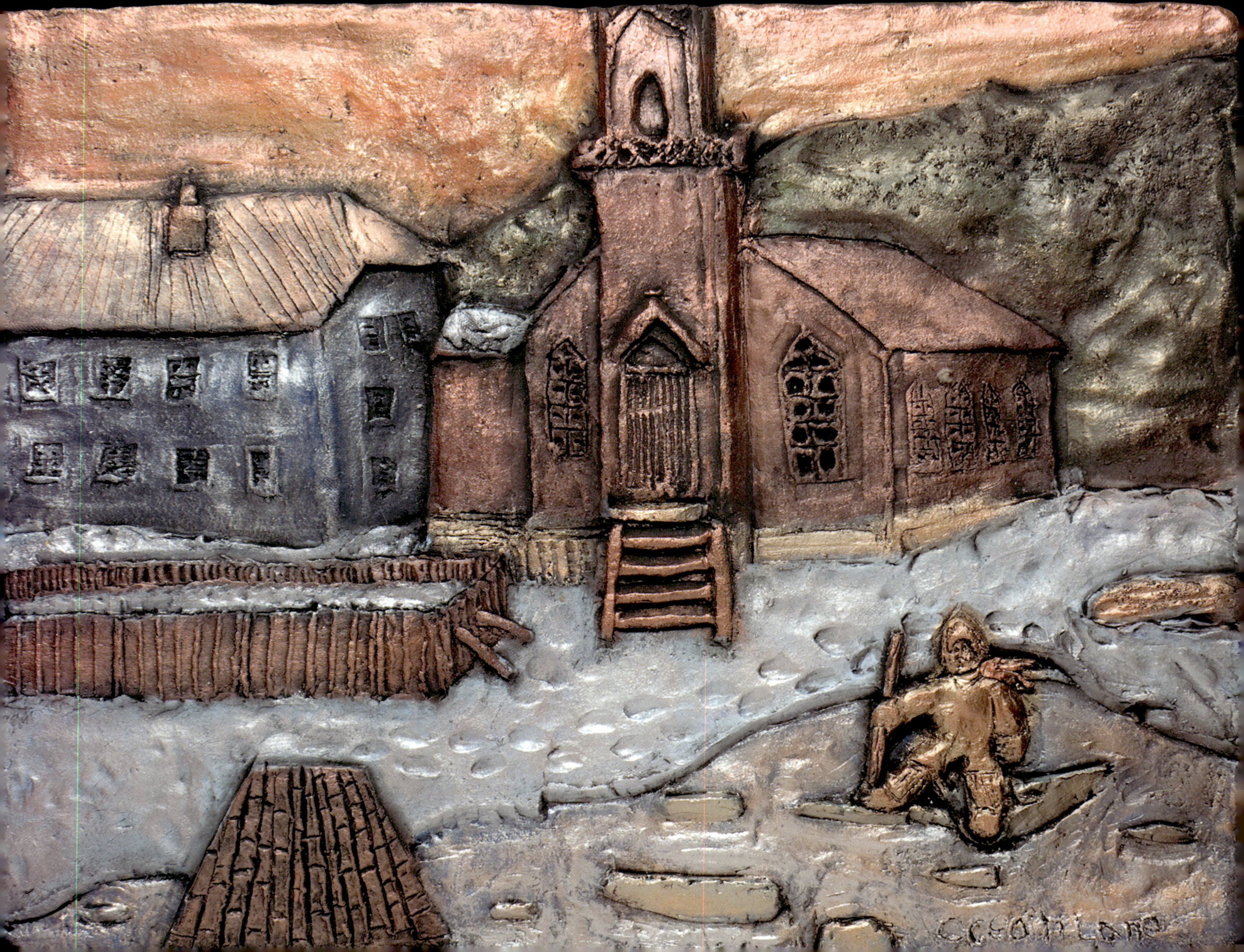

Old Makkovik Church, Burned 1949

Ocean Lane, Makkovik

I found a photograph of the old Makkovik church and thought it would be a good image for my tile. Mrs. Brown asked me what I knew about the church, and all I could tell her was that it had burned. She said I should find out whatever I could about it, so I asked my grandmother, and she said, "This sounds like a visit to Uncle Jim". Uncle Jim (Andersen) knows all the old stories and especially all about the church in Makkovik.

I found out that the church burned in 1949. I wanted to use this image because the church was important in uniting and building community. I wanted to show how much it means to the community.

Doing something creative that would be seen by all who attend the arts centre, only made me want to do it more. It's great that so many communities are involved in the mural, representing the cultures of Labrador.

Doing something creative that would be seen by all who attend the arts centre, only made me want to do it more.

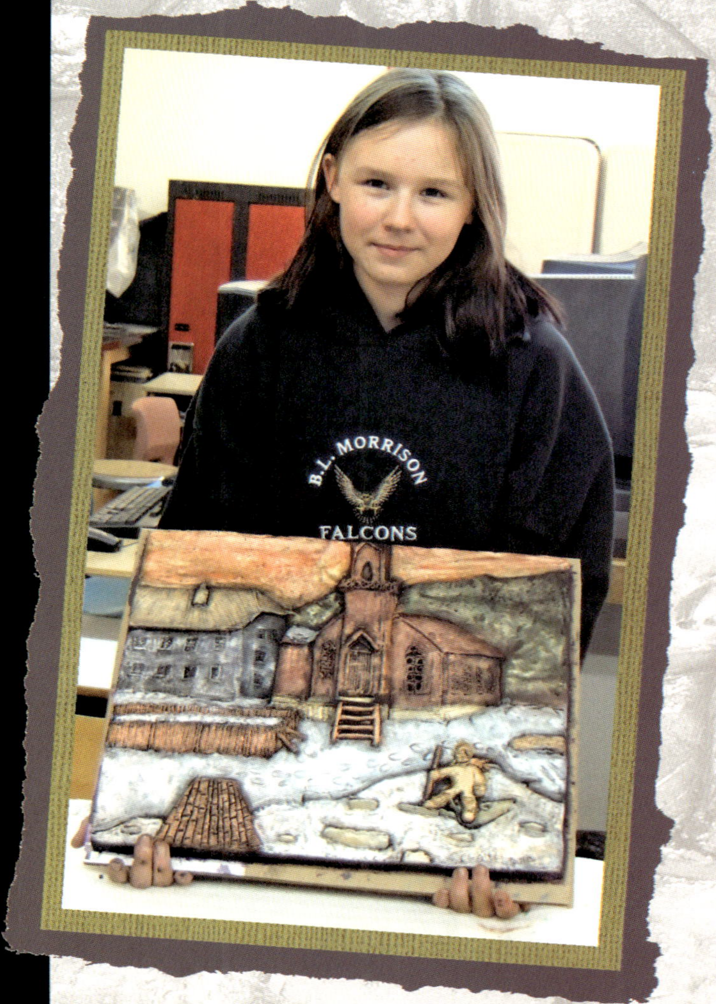

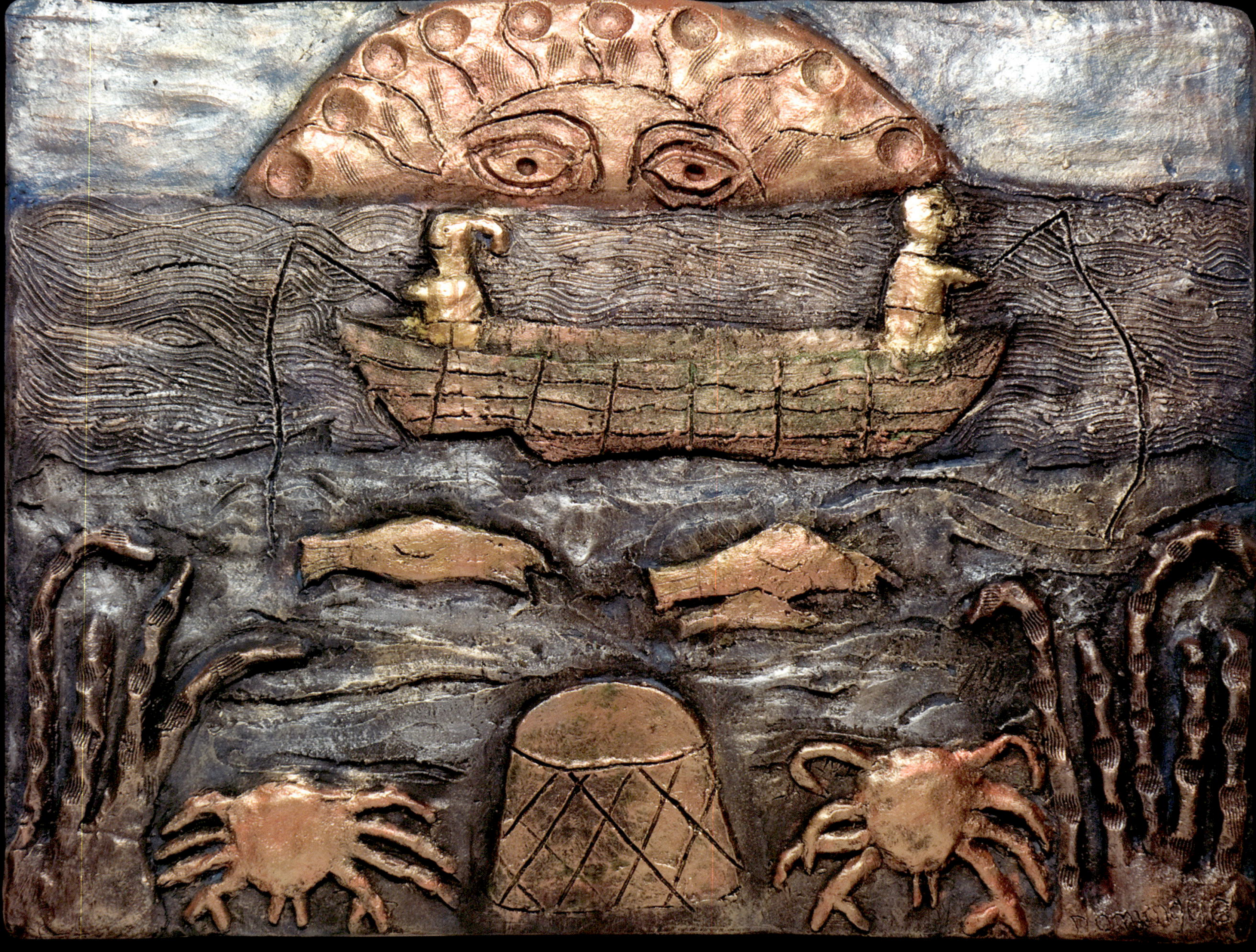

Harvesting Crab

Dominique Keefe, Black Tickle

My friend Nikita and I started the mural work by talking about our community: what makes it 'home', and why we love it so much. We came up with some great ideas and became even better friends through the experience.

And, as a result, what you see in my tile is first, my grandfather and me fishing for cod from a speedboat. My Pop loves to fish but I don't – or, at least my stomach doesn't! I get seasick easily, but I also love spending time with my grandparents.

Below the boat are fish – not just any fish, but codfish: the best fish that ever swam the ocean. My community of Black Tickle was known as the Cod Capital of the World, and it is only natural to love eating such a tasty creature. Cod can be good, made into traditional 'fish and brewis' or the simple 'fish, fat and potatoes' for Sunday supper.

At the bottom of the sea are crabs and crab-pots. Crab is my absolute favourite shellfish and has replaced cod as the staple of our fishery.

I am not a very crafty person but I feel that my tile is an accomplishment. It is a proud way to say, 'I love where I came from.'

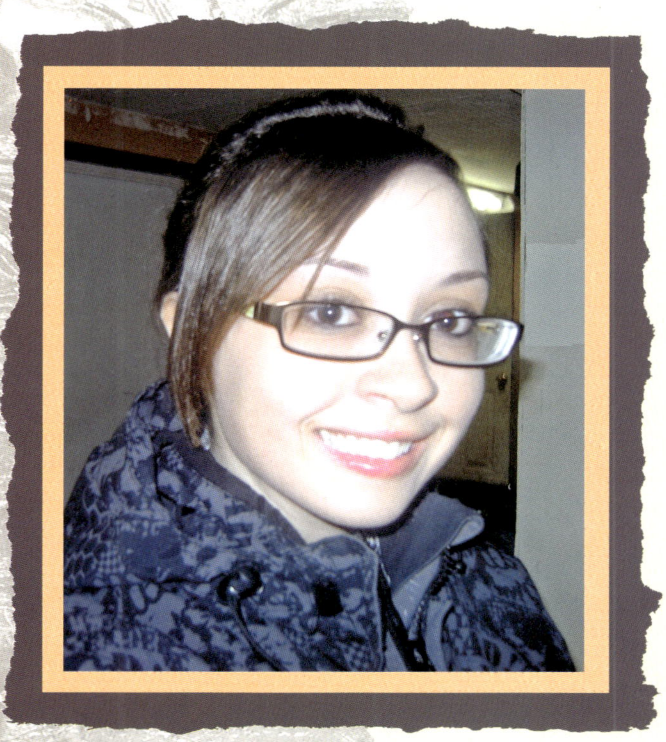

I am not a very crafty person but I feel that my tile is an accomplishment. It is a proud way to say, 'I love where I came from.'

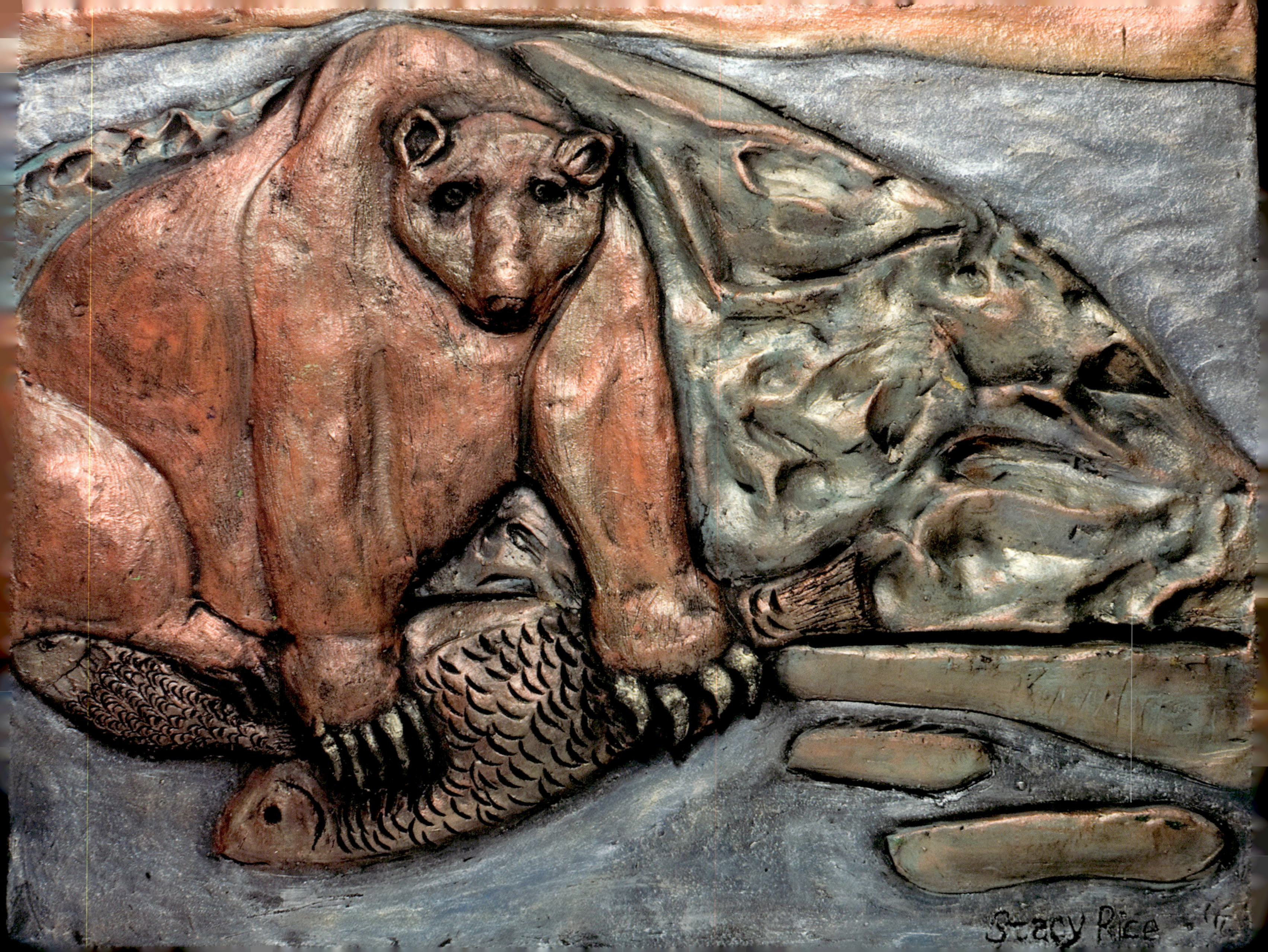
Stacy Rice

Labrador Beauty

Stacy Rice, Makkovik

Polar bears have traditionally been important to the Labrador Inuit culture – **my** culture. They have been hunted to provide food and clothing. Polar bears usually arrive along the Labrador coast on floating ice pans in the spring.

In recent years, the polar bear has been recognized as an endangered species. Though we have been hunting them for hundreds of years, only a few licenses are now granted each year, to protect them

Not only are the bears threatened, but so is their ice! Global warming is causing the polar ice cap to melt, which in turn endangers the polar bears' environment.

I want to preserve the polar bear and its ice in my clay tile. I just wanted to create that image. I would like to preserve this small piece of my Labrador Inuit culture in clay.....**forever**.

I want to preserve the polar bear and its ice in my clay tile. I just wanted to create that image. I would like to preserve this small piece of my Labrador Inuit culture in clay.....forever.

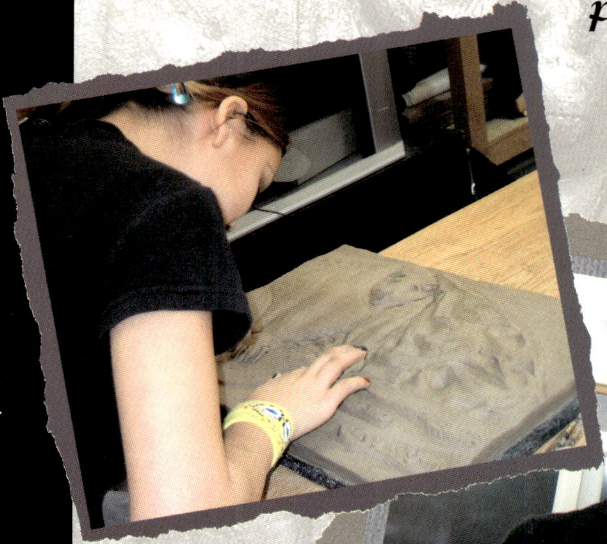

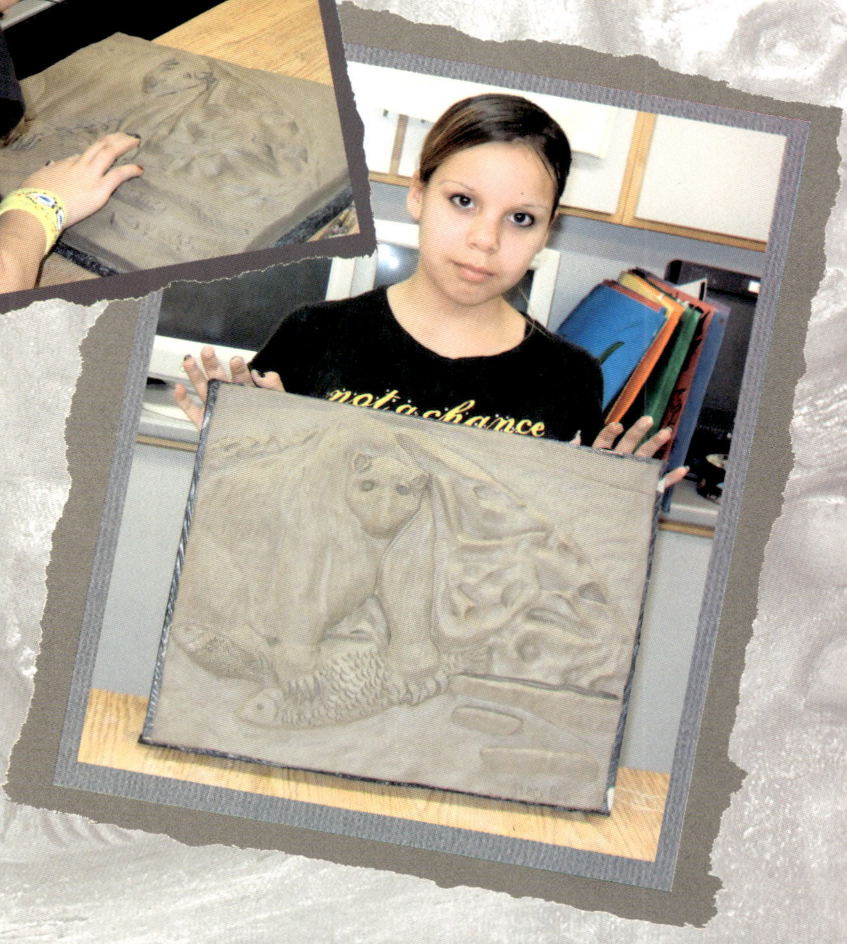

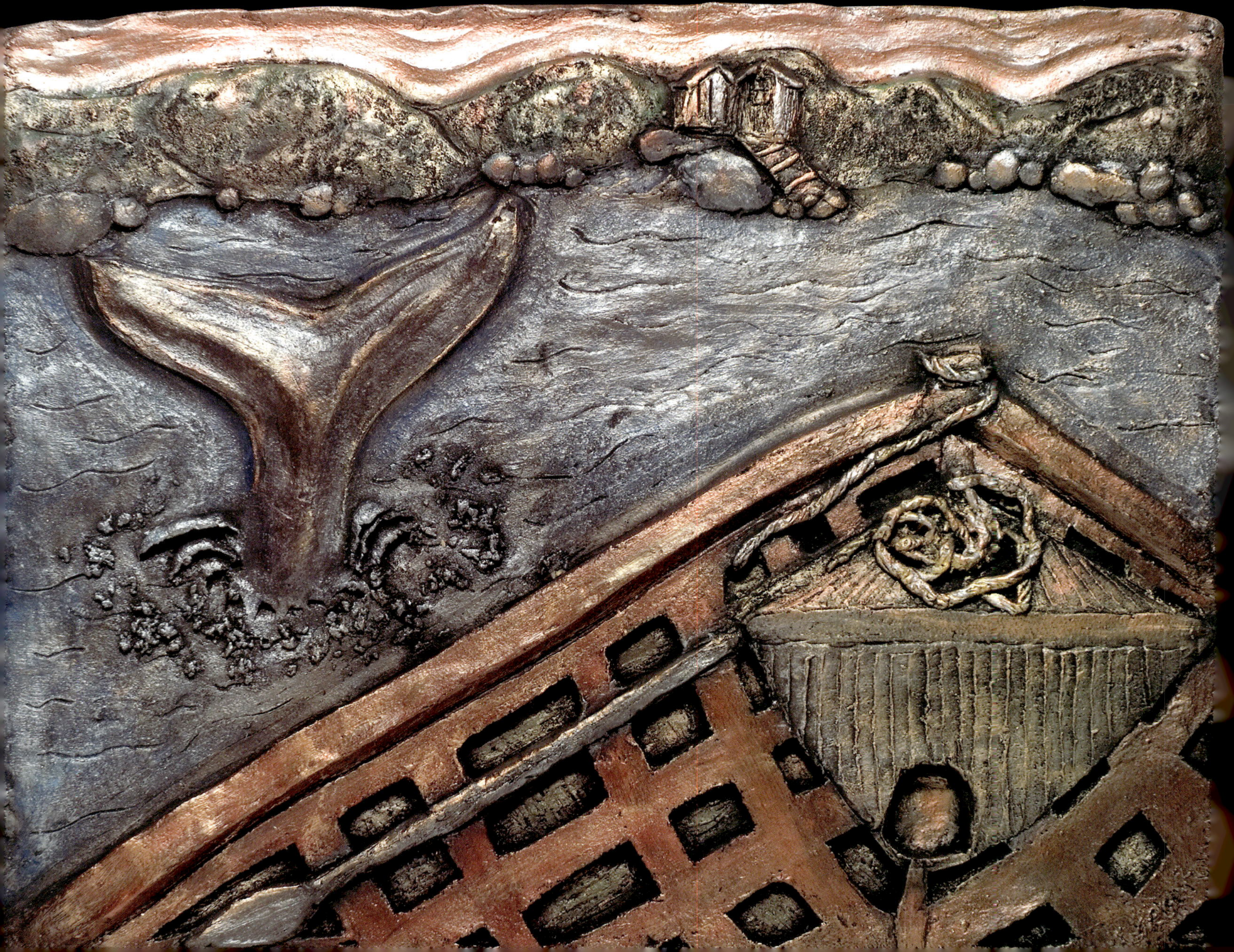

Comin' Into Cutthroat

Chelsea Dyson, Cartwright

I had an uncle who passed away. I have a picture of him riding in a speedboat. It is the only photograph we have of him smiling. I designed an image where the speedboat is prominent, to dedicate my tile to him.

Speedboats have been a way of life – and certainly of transportation – ever since outboard motors replaced the 'old putt-putt' or the make-and-break engine. Speedboats and motorboats have always been distinguished by their engines.

I actually started my tile based on my uncle's photograph, but it was a difficult image to create in clay. Dorrie always told me, "An artist never has one set idea and keeps to it; an artist's mind is always open and changing." So I changed the image somewhat, and my confidence grew. When I made a mistake I turned it into something that belonged in the image. When the tile was almost done, I looked at it and thought, "How did I do this? I can't draw!" But I discovered that with a bit of confidence, anything is possible.

Now, when anyone asks me why I chose this image, I have a million reasons.

When the tile was almost done, I looked at it and thought, "How did I do this? I can't draw!" But I discovered that with a bit of confidence, anything is possible.

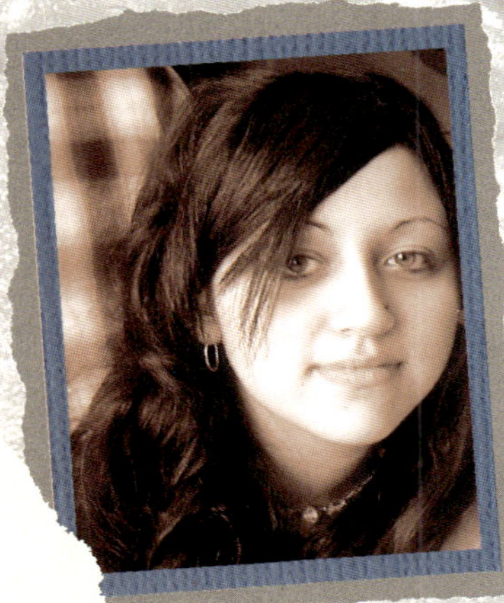

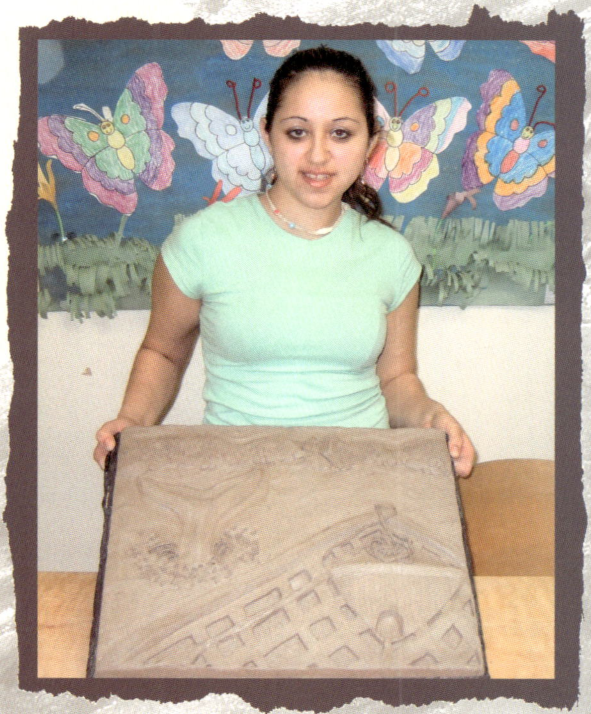

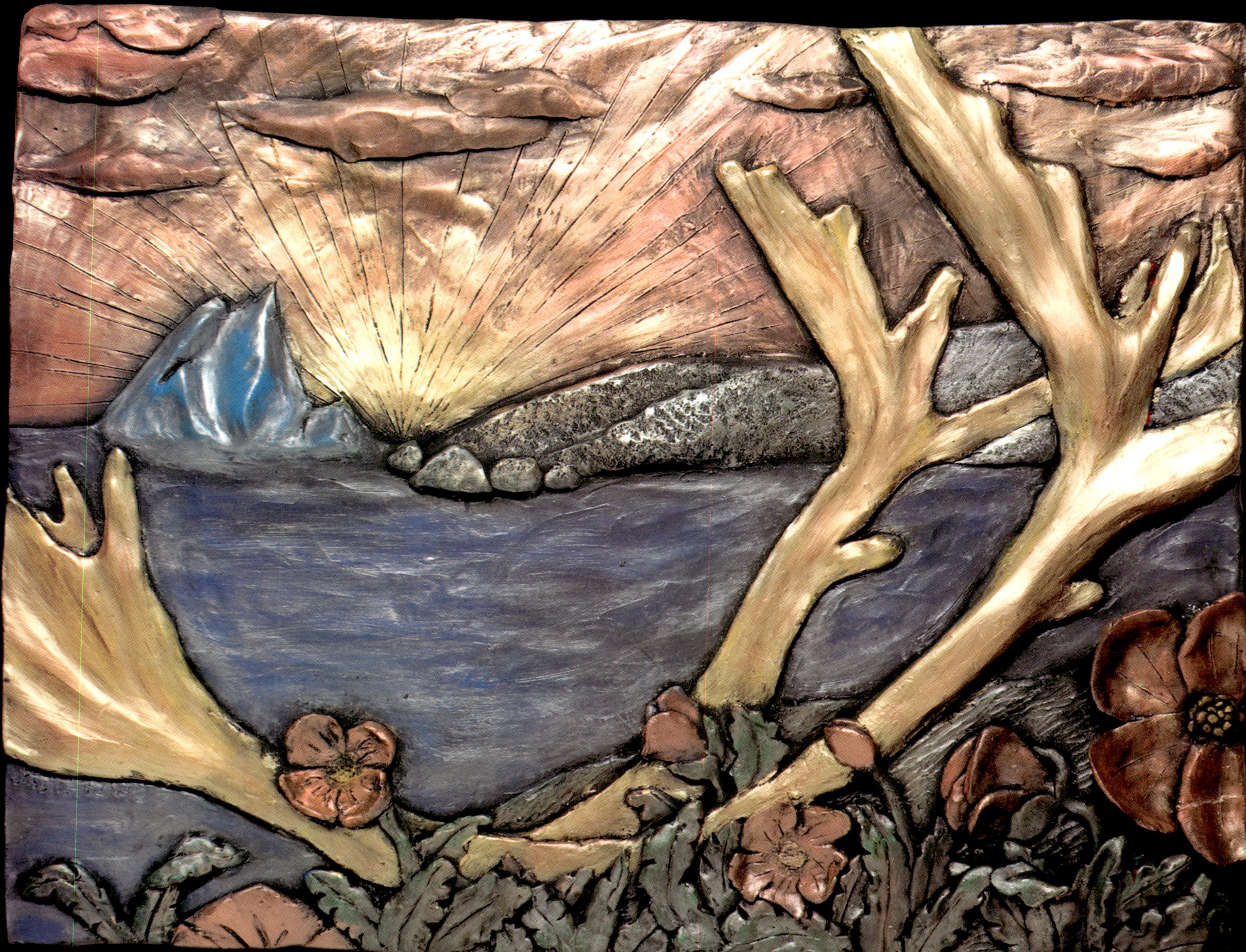

Natjut Piguttuilu

Jessica Dawe, Nain

The title of my piece translates as 'Antlers and Wildflowers.' In fact, the 'wildflowers' are Icelandic poppies, but there is no Inuktitut word specific to the species.

The tile shows a typical landscape in northern Labrador — it could be almost anywhere. Predominant in my image are a set of caribou antlers and the poppy; in the distance, an iceberg. The antlers are a haunting reminder of the past, bare and white on the green tundra, a reflection of heritage. The poppy is not native to the area, but was introduced by European missionaries. The flower has become so abundant that it now is a part of Labrador, much like myself. I've grown up in Nain and have become as much a part of Labrador as someone whose family goes back generations.

The mural is a showcase of talent, offering a mosaic of views and ideas that make Labrador such a unique place.

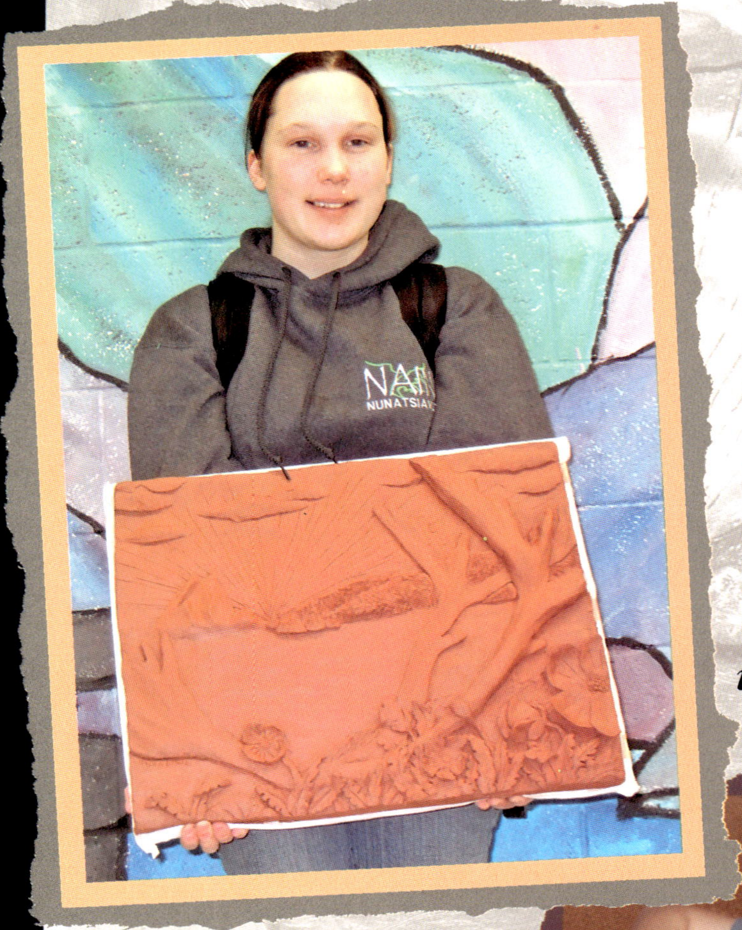

The mural is a showcase of talent, offering a mosaic of views and ideas that make Labrador such a unique place.

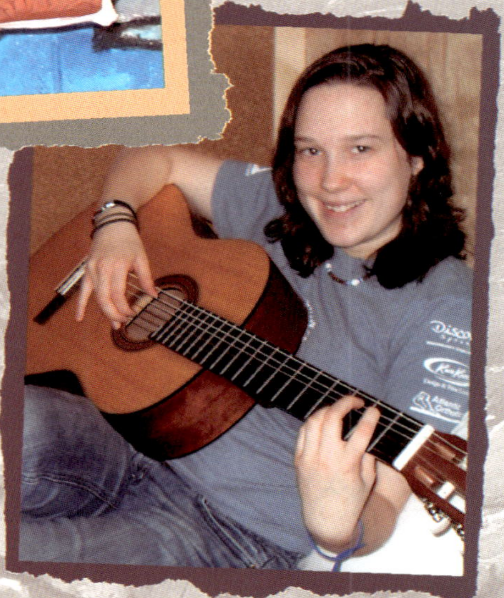

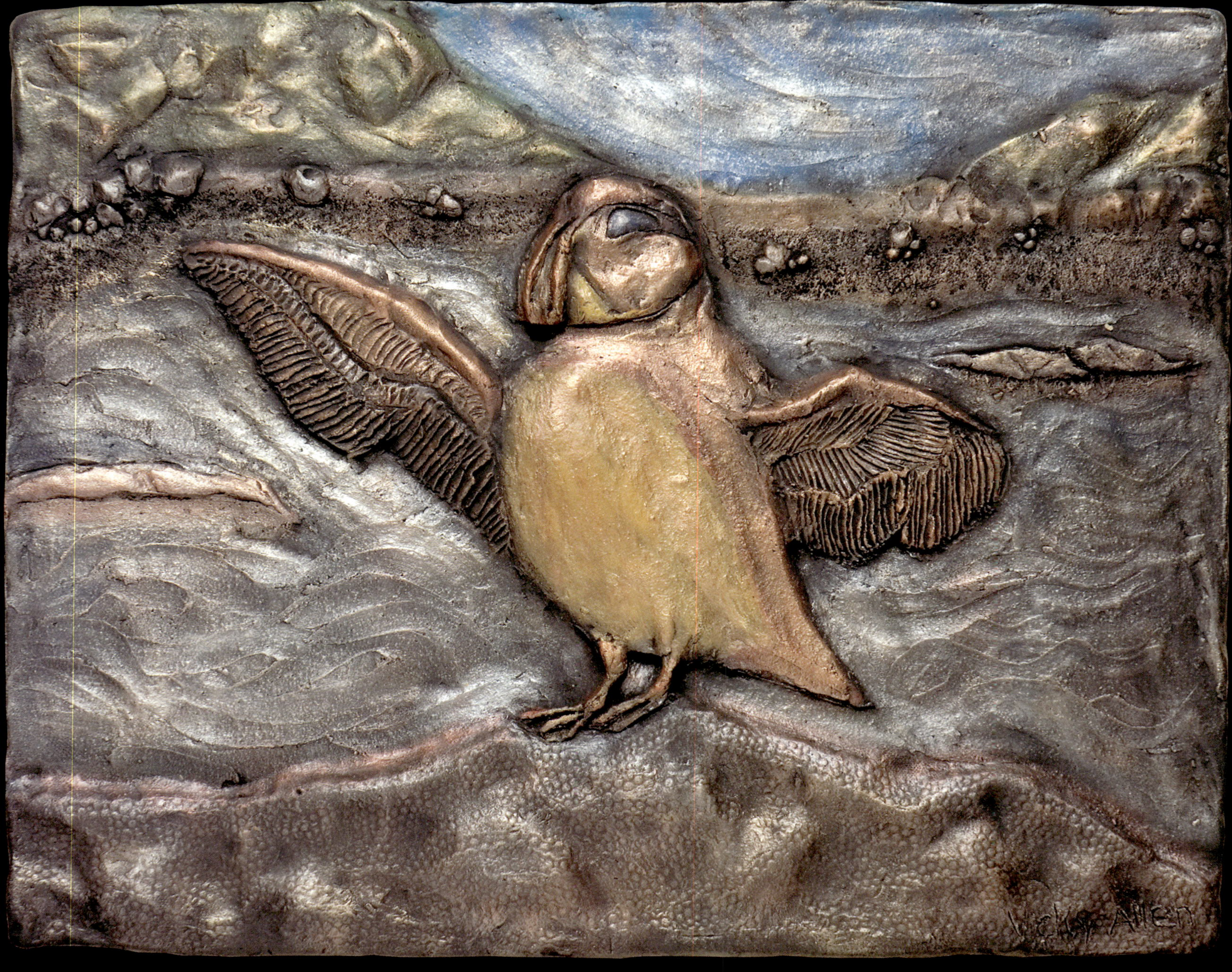
Vicky Allen

UNCLE PUFFIN

VICKY ALLEN, RIGOLET

My Uncle Sam is nicknamed Puffin. He's been called that name ever since he was a boy.

He is a very special person to me; I knew I wanted to dedicate my tile to him, for he is a man of Labrador, and our mural is all about this wonderful region and what it means to us.

As I was searching for ideas for my tile, I thought of the puffin, which can be found off the coast of Labrador. It spends most of its life on the water, resting by riding waves when not flying or hunting.

So, in my tile, you will see these two ideas put together. Although the process was strange to me, as I believe that I have little or no artistic talent, I love my finished piece. The time I spent learning from Dorrie – Oh! What a time we had! – what can I say?

This: that I dedicate the work to Mr. Sam "Puffin" Williams and Mrs. Dorrie Brown. Thank you to you both for inspiring and pushing.

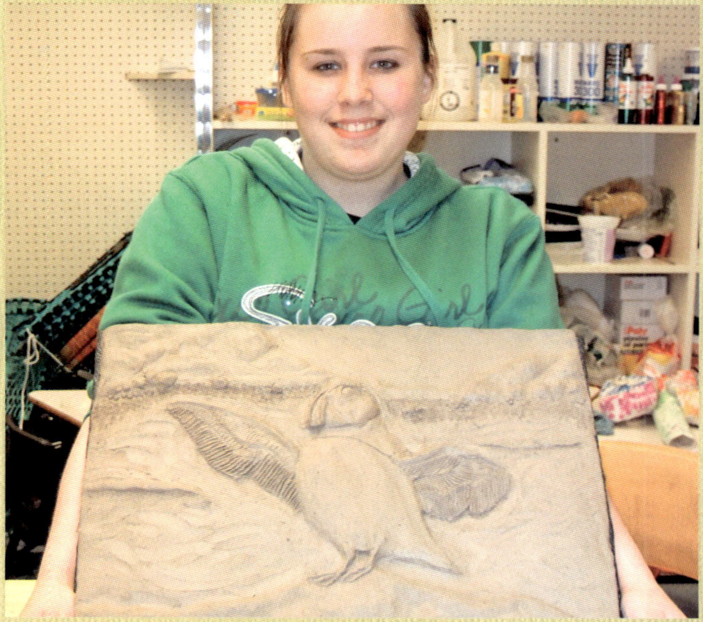

Although the process was strange to me, as I believe that I have little or no artistic talent, I love my finished piece.

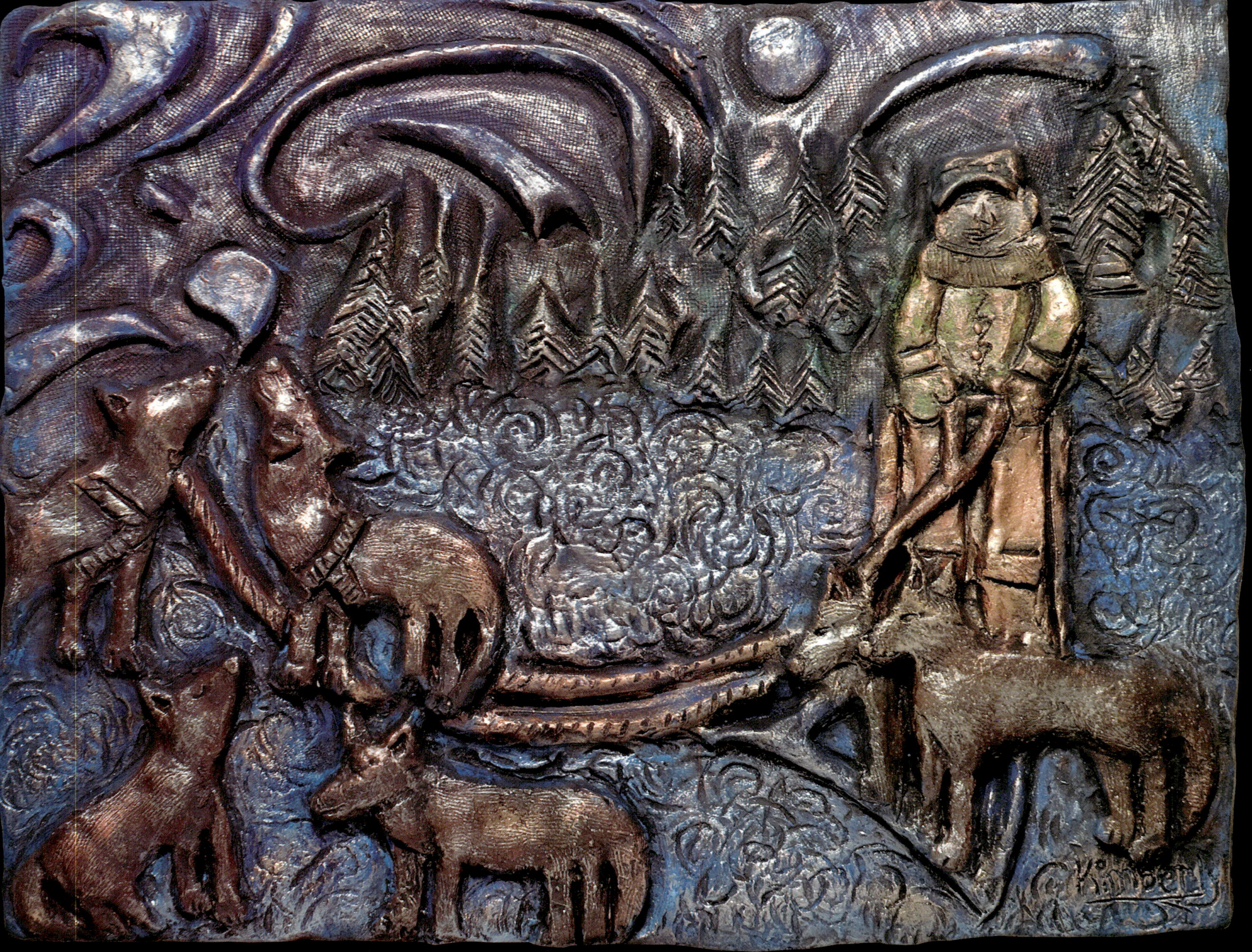
Kimberly

Northern Lights & Dogteam

Kimberley McKinnon,
Happy Valley - Goose Bay

I wanted to combine two images: the dogteam, which I believe accurately represents an important part in the transportation history of Labrador, and the northern lights, which fascinated me the first time I saw them – maybe moreso, because I am not native to Labrador.

I felt compelled to bring these two images together, to show how spectacular the lights might be, when seen while riding with the dogs on a clear night.

I was unsure what the clay tile mural project would entail, but I was willing to try it. After sketching my design, I had no idea how difficult it would be to convey my original idea without losing detail. I later learned it was extremely difficult.

Having my tile displayed permanently in the new arts center gives me a sense of pride, especially considering how young I was when I made it, and how unsure I was about how it would turn out, and what would become of it.

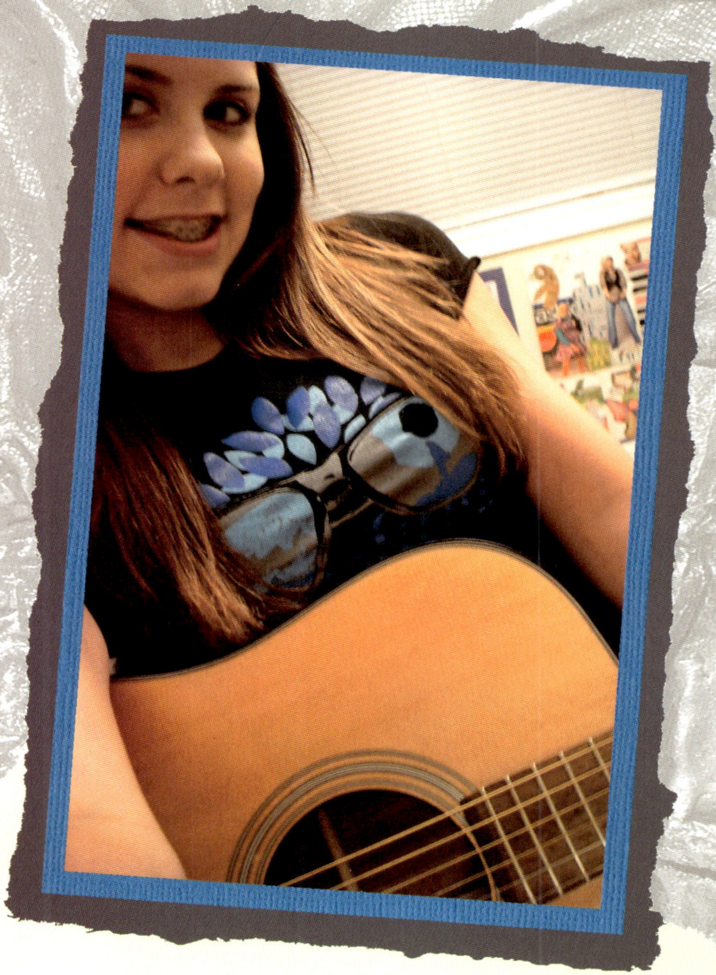

I felt compelled to bring these two images together, to show how spectacular the lights might be, when seen while riding with the dogs on a clear night.

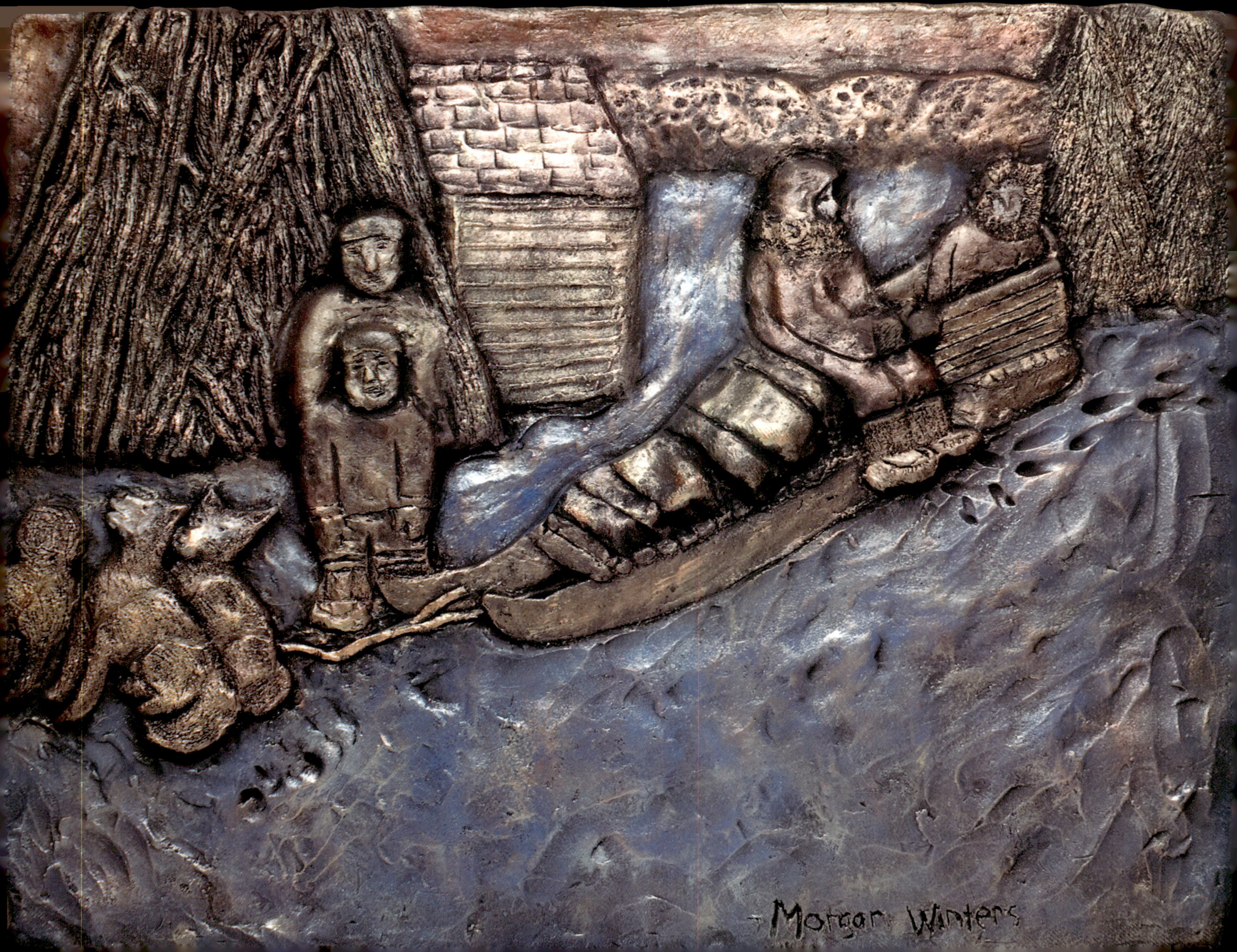
Morgan Winters

Makkovik, 1929

Morgan Winters, Makkovik

My tile is based on a photograph taken near Makkovik in 1929 that shows a group travelling by dogteam. I loved the dogs, the woodpile and the family with their **Komatik**. The scene shows the way people lived back then, relying on dogs and living close to the land. I knew even before I started on my tile that I wanted to include dogs in my clay piece. When I saw this picture, I was inspired: I knew this was the one!

Working in clay was difficult and at times, frustrating. I thought I got the hang of it near the end, though. I am honored to have my clay tile displayed in the new arts centre; to see it there in years to come and say "I did that when I was 13!". I am very proud and thankful.

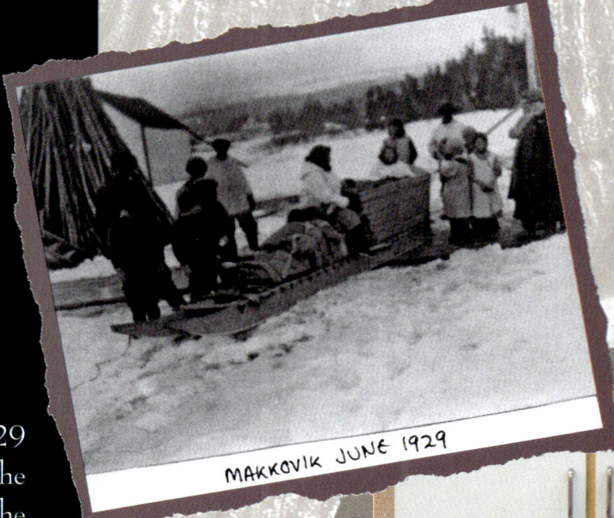

When I saw this picture, I was inspired: I knew this was the one!

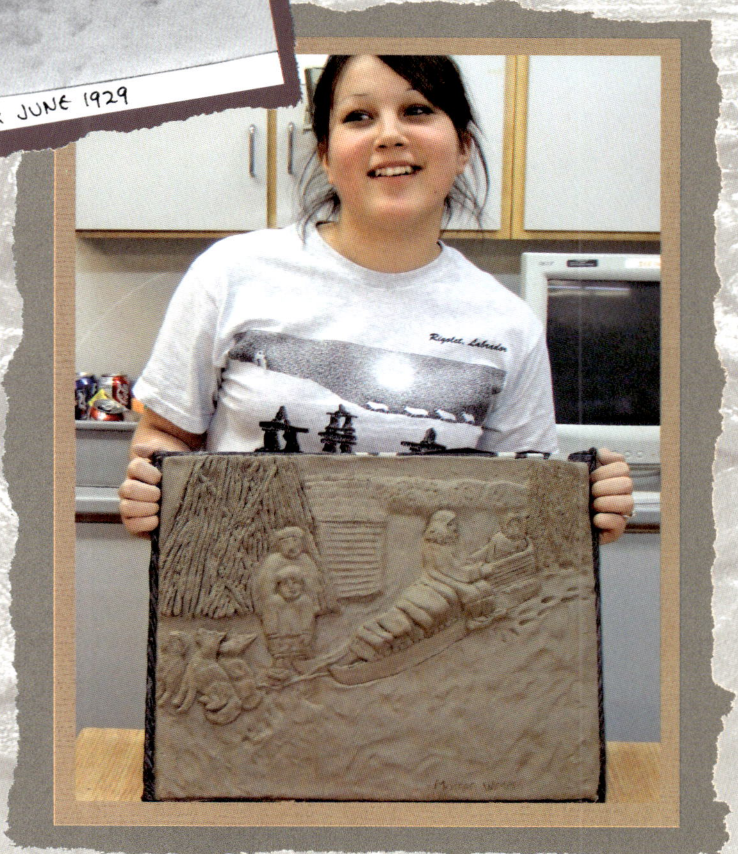

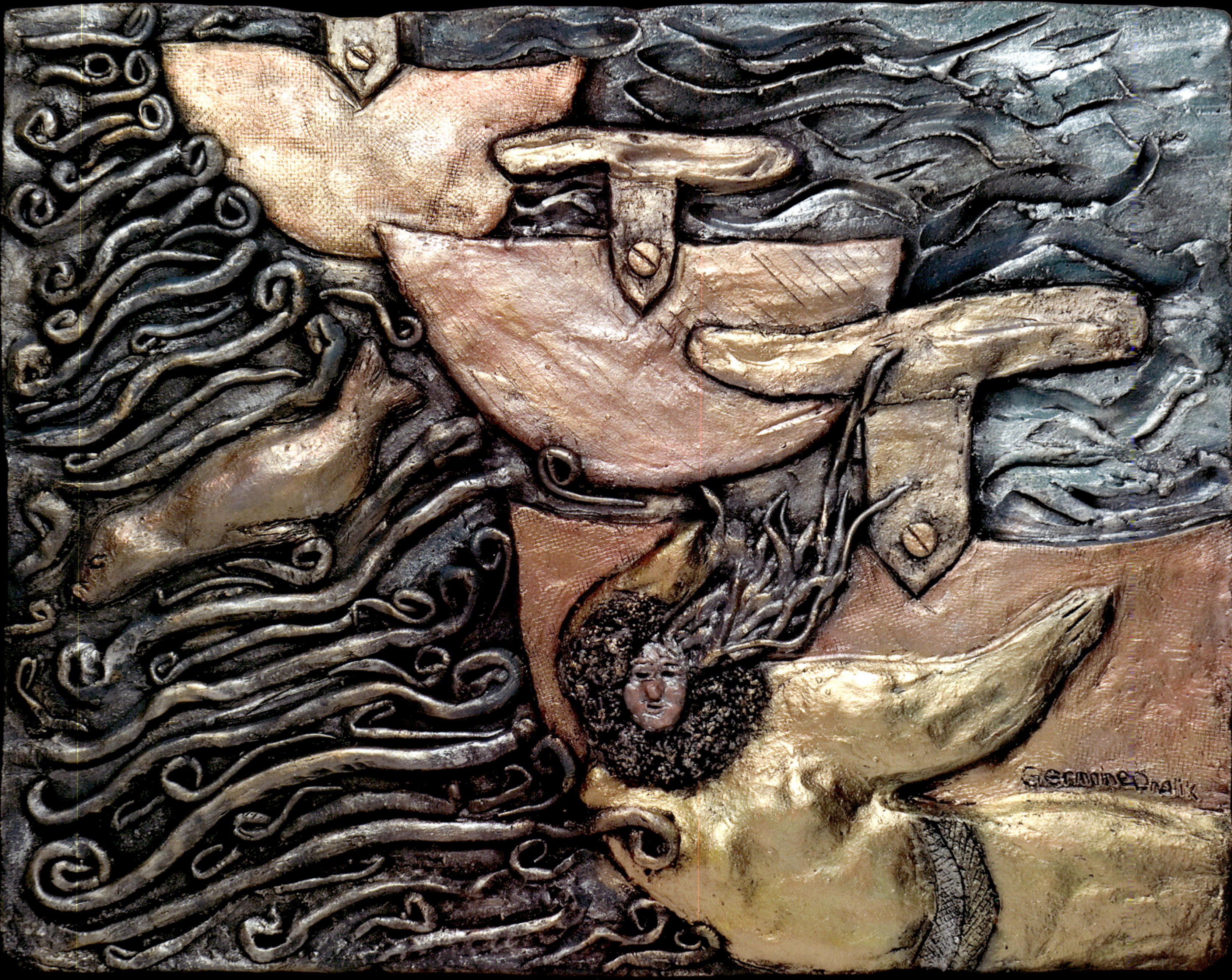

Sedna

Germaine Onalik, Hopedale

Sedna was a young woman who married a shaman. She did not know he was a shaman, until the next morning when he appeared as a raven. She was frightened of him and ran back to her father. He told her she must go back to her husband. She didn't; instead, she hid in the bottom of her father's boat, and when he and her brothers headed out to hunt, they discovered her. A storm blew up; they knew that the shaman had caused it, and they must give Sedna back to him. They threw her overboard, but she clung to the side with her hands. They cut off her fingers and she floated away to become the first seal. This explains why the seal's flippers look like hands without fingers. Her fingers sprung up to become all the other creatures of the sea. Sedna is sometimes called the Mother of All Sea Creatures that now feed the people.

There are different versions of this story. Everyone brought me to it and I enjoyed finding the differences. I love mermaid-looking people. I drew Sedna beautifully swimming with a very large ulu (women's knife)

At first I thought, how would we get this carved? But we used our hands and useful tools. I had fun, especially with the others and the helpers. Dorrie was very helpful and the best! After a few strokes, the picture came along and when we painted it black, I thought it was ruined! But painting it with metallics afterwards brought out the story once again.

Having my tile permanently installed means everything to me. I am proud of myself to be part of something so huge! I get to be famous and I can see it when I'm old. I can show my nephews and nieces, children or grandchildren: "When I was young."

We are recognized. We are emotional that we had friends to help us and we helped them. It makes me happy and joyful.

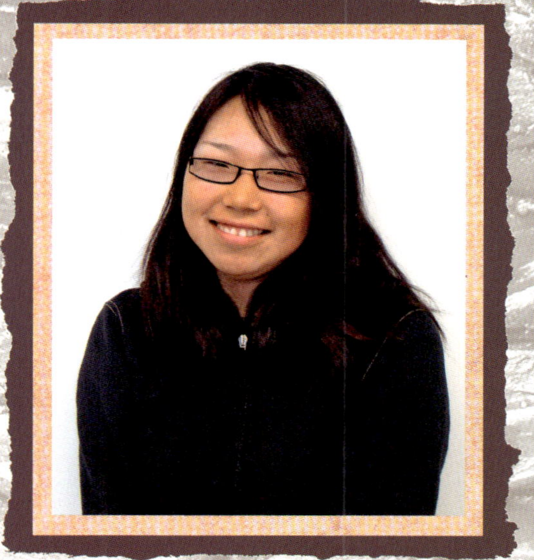

UiggasuKalautsimavuk Sednamik atilimmik Kaujimalugani angutittâsimajuvinik angakkumik. Ullâk angutinga tulugautluni itimmat Kaujivuk angakkoninganik, kappiasumut Kimâvuk atâtakkuminut. Atâtangata utiKuvauk angutinganut. Sednali ijigiattuvuk atâtangata motangata atânut. Sednali motaup atâni ijisimavuk nagvâvauk pinasuagiasimatlutik anikkungita atâtangatalu. Anugitsuamut tikikallaviuvut angakkuk angakkumat, taitsumani Kaujivut Sednamik utittisigiaKanniminik angutinganut. Sednamik imânut igijauvuk, igijaugami motaup sininganut aggaminut Kangatasivuk. Aggâgita inugiangit nakatlugit sakkutitauvuk motamik. Sedna puijinguvuk imâni puttaligami inugiangit siammativut imappimut omajungutlutik imammiutait. Sedna unikkausigijauligami imaup omajunginnut anânagijauningâttauKattavuk.

IsumatsasiuliaKilaukKunga Kanuk sananguanialimmangâmma atullunga sanakKutinik? Atuligama ilakkalu sanakKutinik aggakatinut Kuvianak ikajuttigetluta pijagetlugu. Dorrie piunippaulaukKuli ikajutsialaummat uvannik! Sedna sanatlugu Kinnitamut minguagiaKalauttaga usemmalu sujutlatuinnalimmijaga! Ukkusitsajamut mingualigakku sakKivallialimmat unikkausiliusimajaga ommatojânialitluni.

Sanguasimajaga sakKijâttitaulimmat pijugiutigivâtlataga angijualummut ilitlugu sakKijâttitausongulâlimmat piulimattauvimmi. Pimmagittumik pigiasittitauKatausimagama inutuKauliguma takugiattusogilâligakku. Sugusitsagilâttaka ingutatsagilâttakalu ujugukkalu, Kangiakkalu takutigiattusogilâligakkit. IkKaumallunga, "Inosuttotlunga."

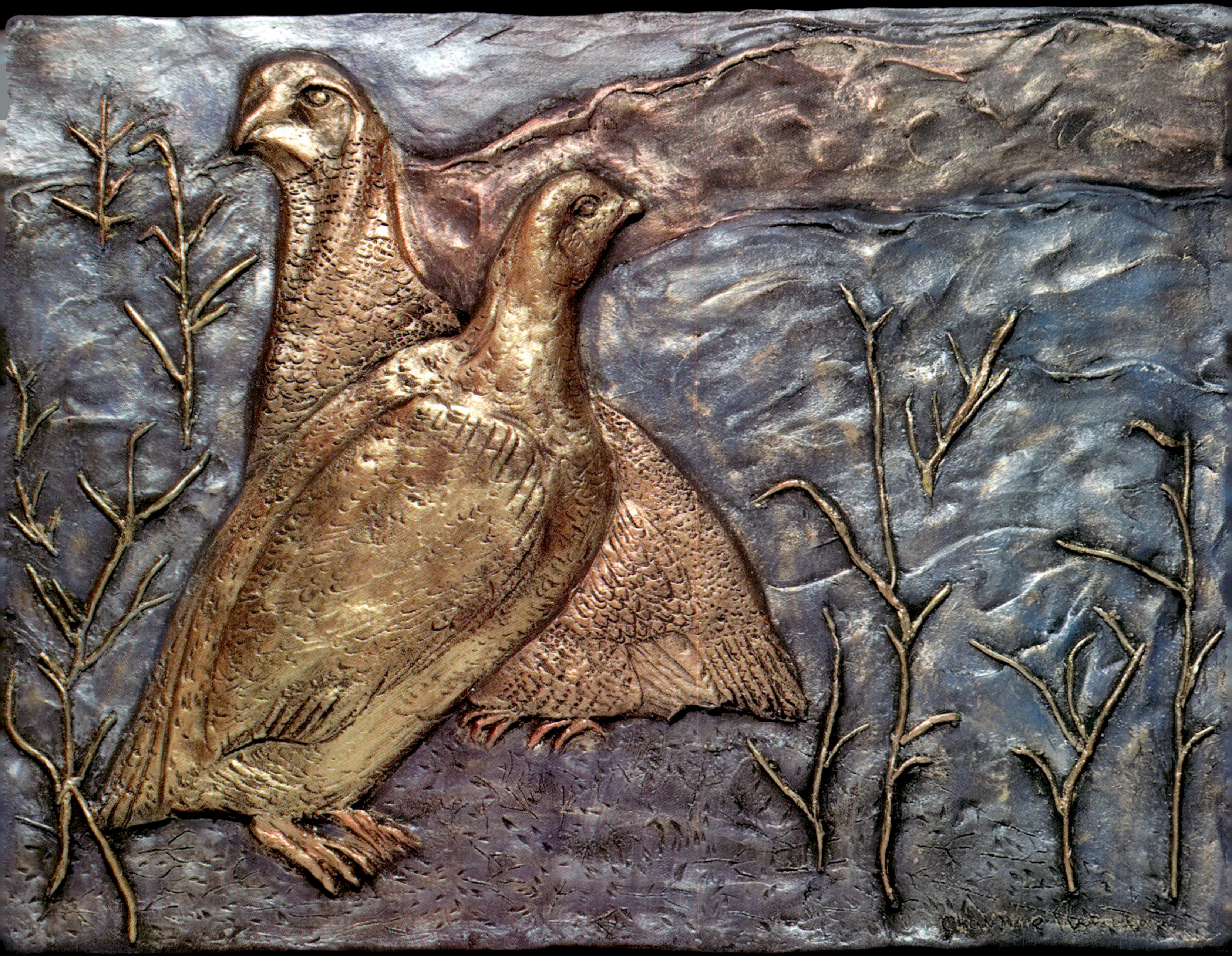

PARTRIDGE PAIR

CHANTELLE WILLIAMS, RIGOLET

Partridges are beautiful to look at and wonderful to eat. Labrador is home to spruce partridges that feed on buds of spruce trees where their mottled brown color hides them in the shadows. White partridges (ptarmigan) feed on willows and change color with the seasons, turning white as winter sets in so that they blend into a snow-covered landscape.

The smooth curve of their bodies made me think that partridges would shape nicely in clay. I put a lot of hard work into the clay work – especially rolling the thin willow pieces that would often break off before I could place them! It means a great deal to me, knowing that everyone who visits the arts centre will see my little 'piece of Labrador.'

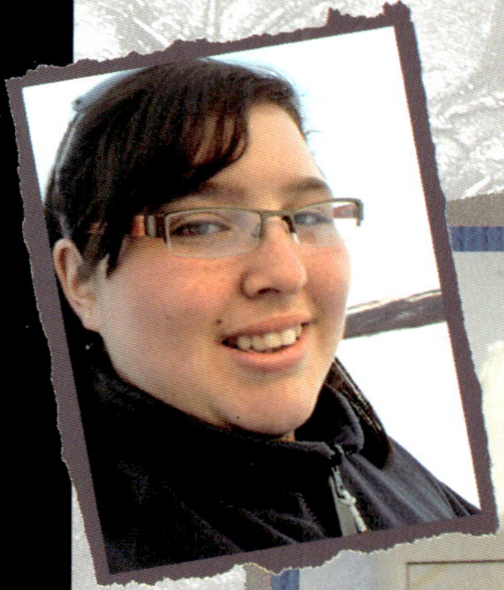

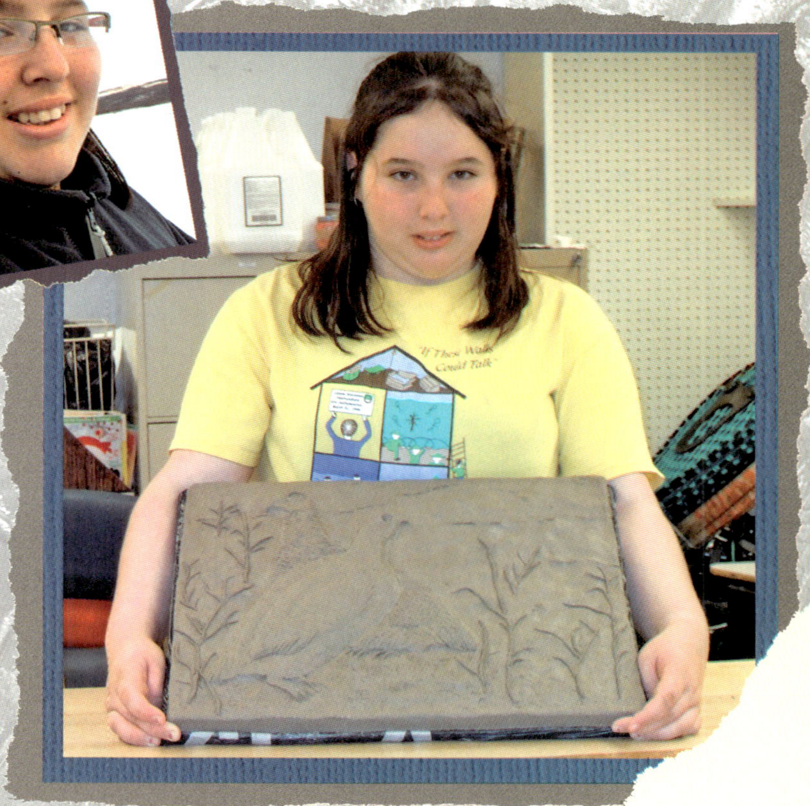

It means a great deal to me, knowing that everyone who visits the arts centre will see my little 'piece of Labrador.'

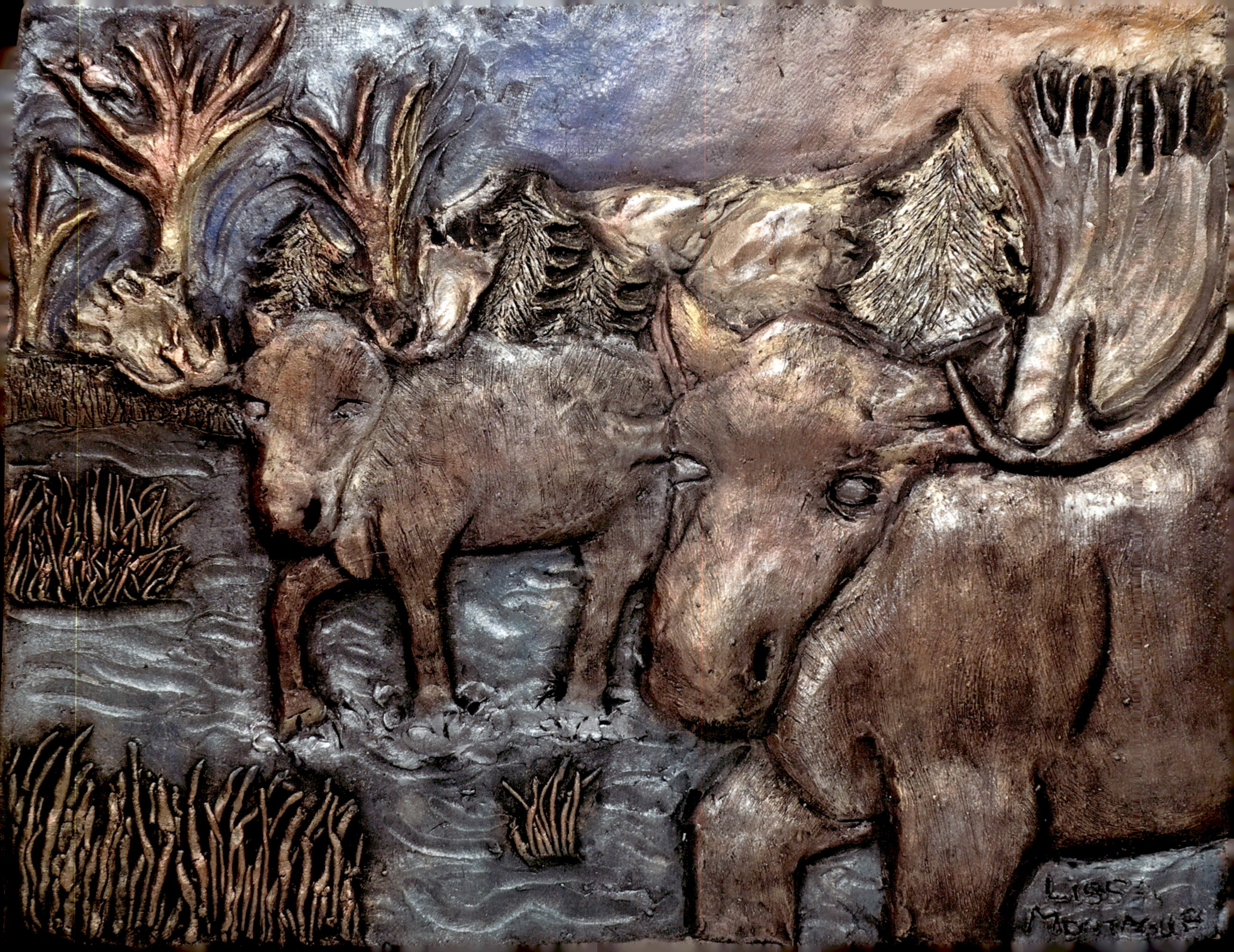

Moose Luncheon

Lissa Montague,
Happy Valley - Goose Bay

I knew I could draw, but I didn't know I could work in clay. At first I thought that I would do fish images and I spent a lot of time trying to learn to draw them. Mr. Hicks, my teacher, took much pride and put time into my mission, taking me to the Fisheries Office to do research; he was very helpful.

In the end, I chose to work with a moose image instead. I like hoofed animals. Mine is a picture of a moose with its head enlarged, mostly to take up space and to create depth. I love how big the moose are, and I like the bell that hangs from the moose's throat. I thought of calling the piece "Reflection", because of the bog in which the moose is standing; it just seemed fitting, but "Moose Luncheon" was my final choice.

My friend, Sandra, and I travelled by boat (br-r-r-r!) each morning to Mud Lake during the week we spent making our tiles. We worked together with the four students at Mud Lake School. It was our first time in Mud Lake; we met new people and made good friends.

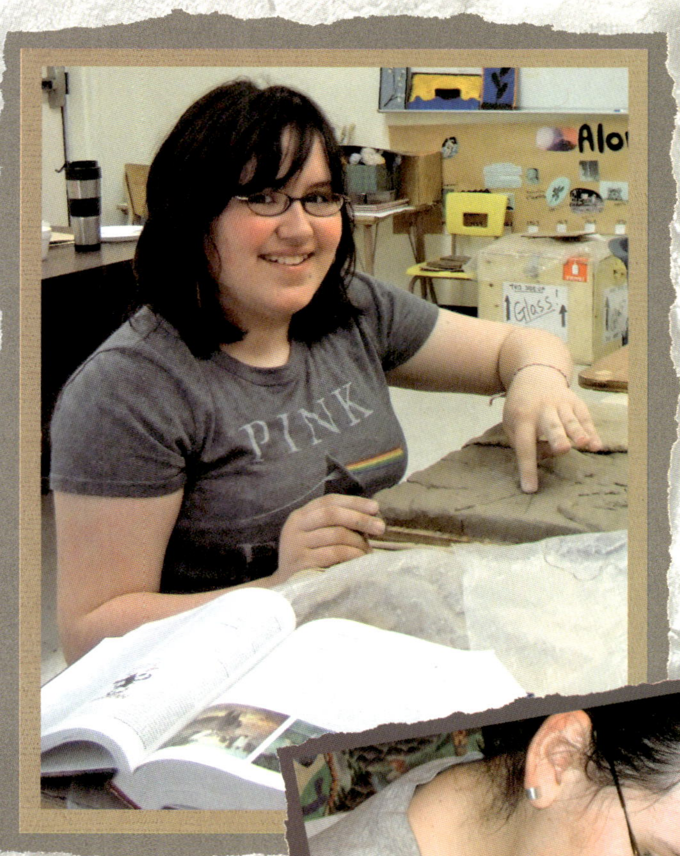

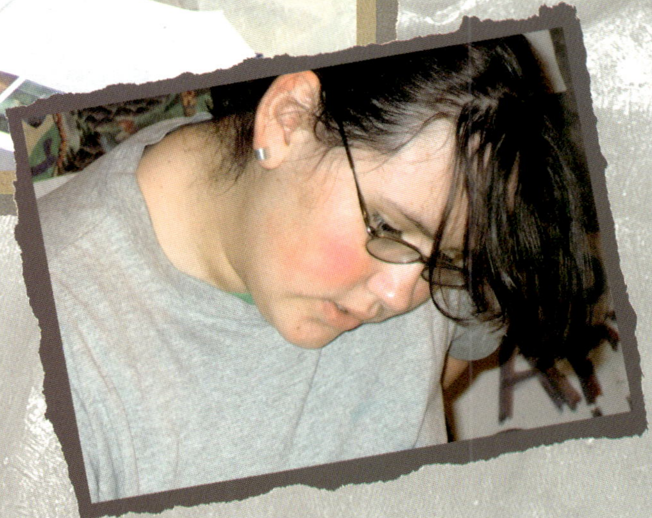

It was our first time in Mud Lake...
we met new people and made new friends.

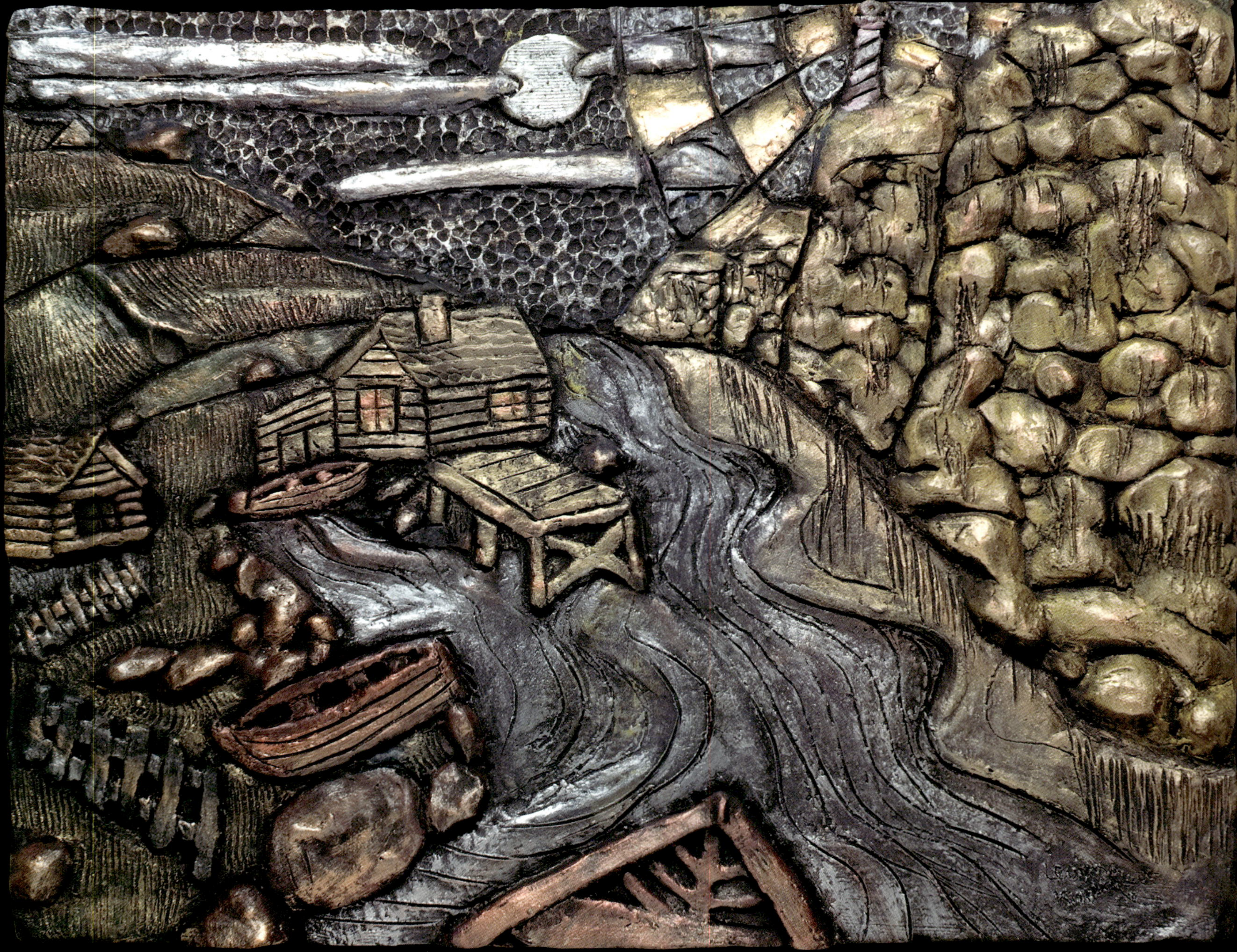

Fishing Station

Leanna Kippenhuck, Happy Valley - Goose Bay

Of all the tiles in the mural, my tile reaches the furthest south along Labrador's coast. I got the idea for this scene from a magazine photograph, which I adapted to show something about the fishery in The Straits region. My tile shows a fishing station, similar to one which might have been found at Square Islands near Charlottetown, where my father comes from. It would have been populated by *liveyers*, who moved out to the outer coast in fishing shacks for the season, and moved back inland to be better sheltered and to trap during the winter. Stationers were fishermen who came to the fishing stations for the season but returned to their homes in Newfoundland for the winter.

I enjoyed making the tile. I had not worked with this type of clay, and I learned more about sculpting techniques.

I enjoyed making the tile. I had not worked with this type of clay, and I learned more about sculpting techniques.

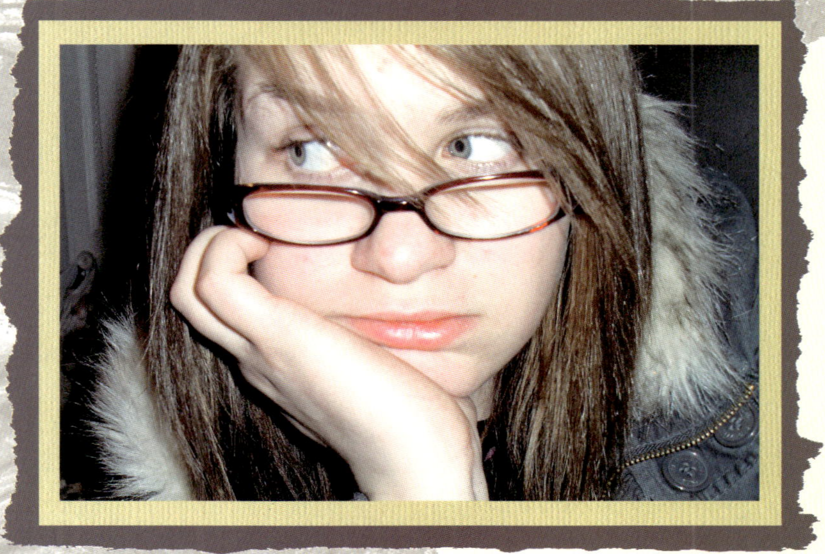

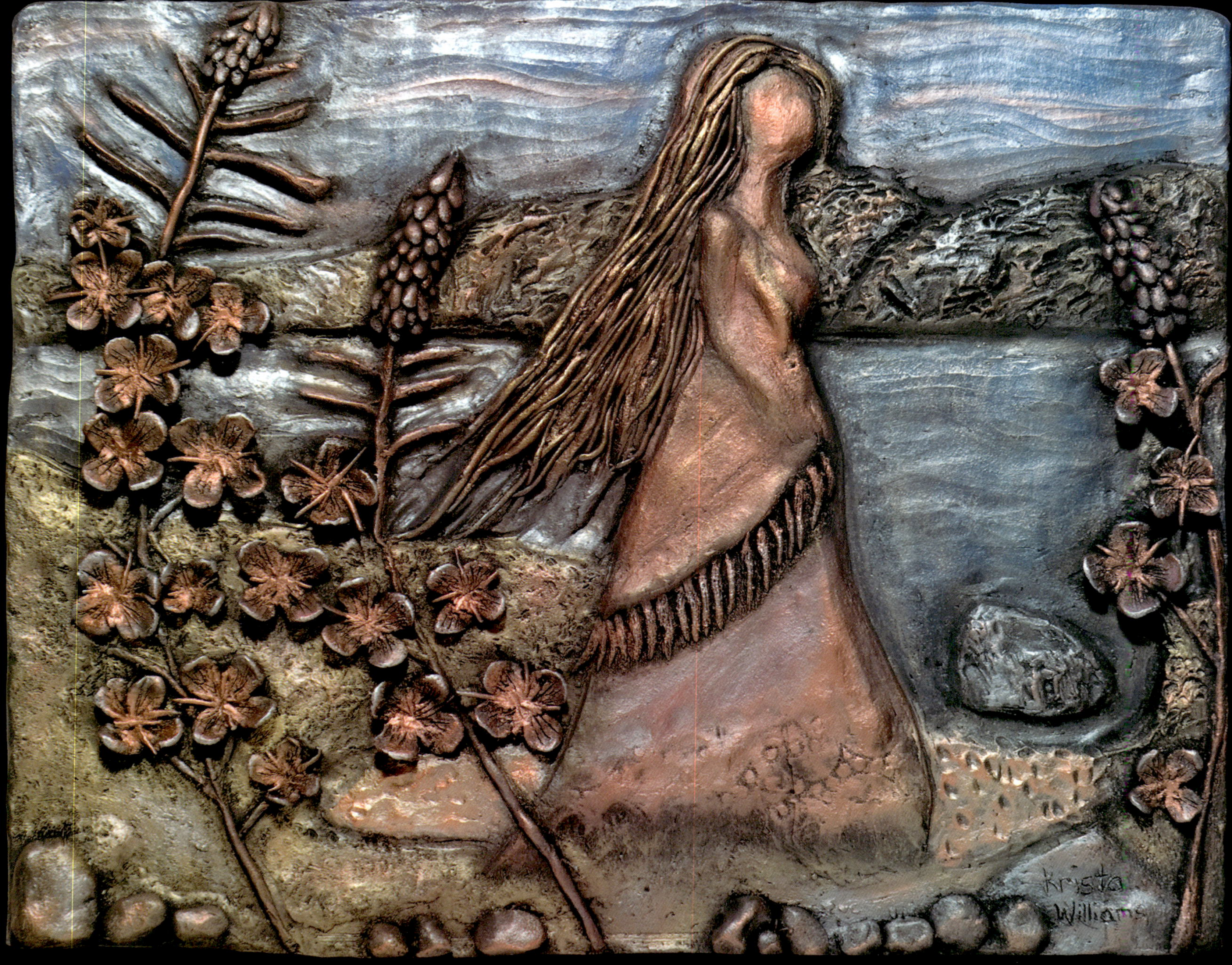
Krista
Williams

Betty Drokum's Gulch

Krista Williams, Cartwright

I created this image of Betty Drokum because it reminds me of my summer home in Spotted Islands. This tiny place holds much importance to my family as well as all the others who fished from there over the years.

The scene in clay is inspired by a photograph of my family having a picnic in the gulch.

There are many different stories about Betty Drokum's Gulch. My favourite version tells how Betty ran from her abusive husband, and hid in the gulch, refusing to return to Newfoundland after the summer fishery, as was the custom. She perished there, never to be seen again. Children were warned by their parents not to go to the gulch because her ghost remained. When they were old enough to disobey their parents, they were often disappointed to find that the cave, where Betty is said to have hidden, was much smaller than they imagined.

I always found the gulch to be a very peaceful place to escape to......perhaps she felt the same way......

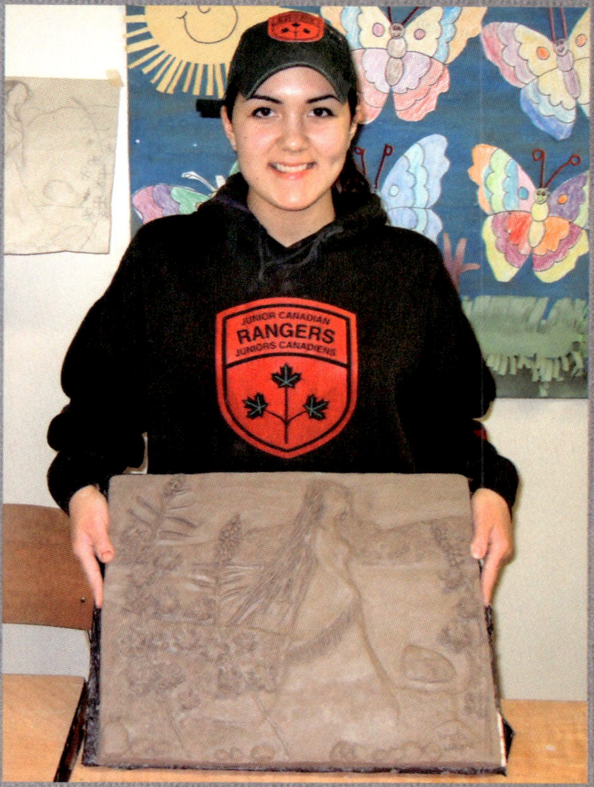

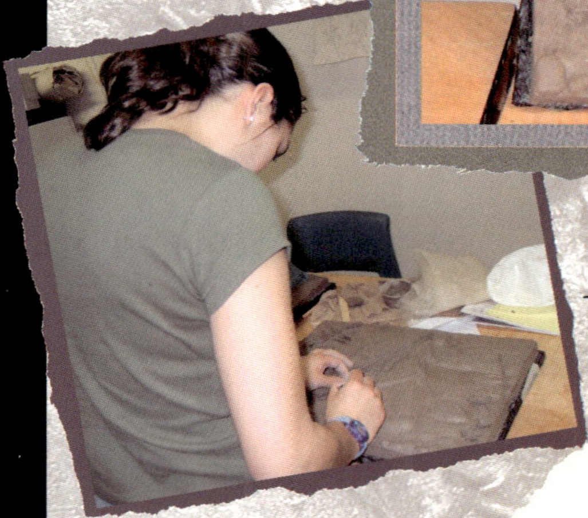

I always found the gulch to be a very peaceful place to escape to......perhaps she felt the same way......

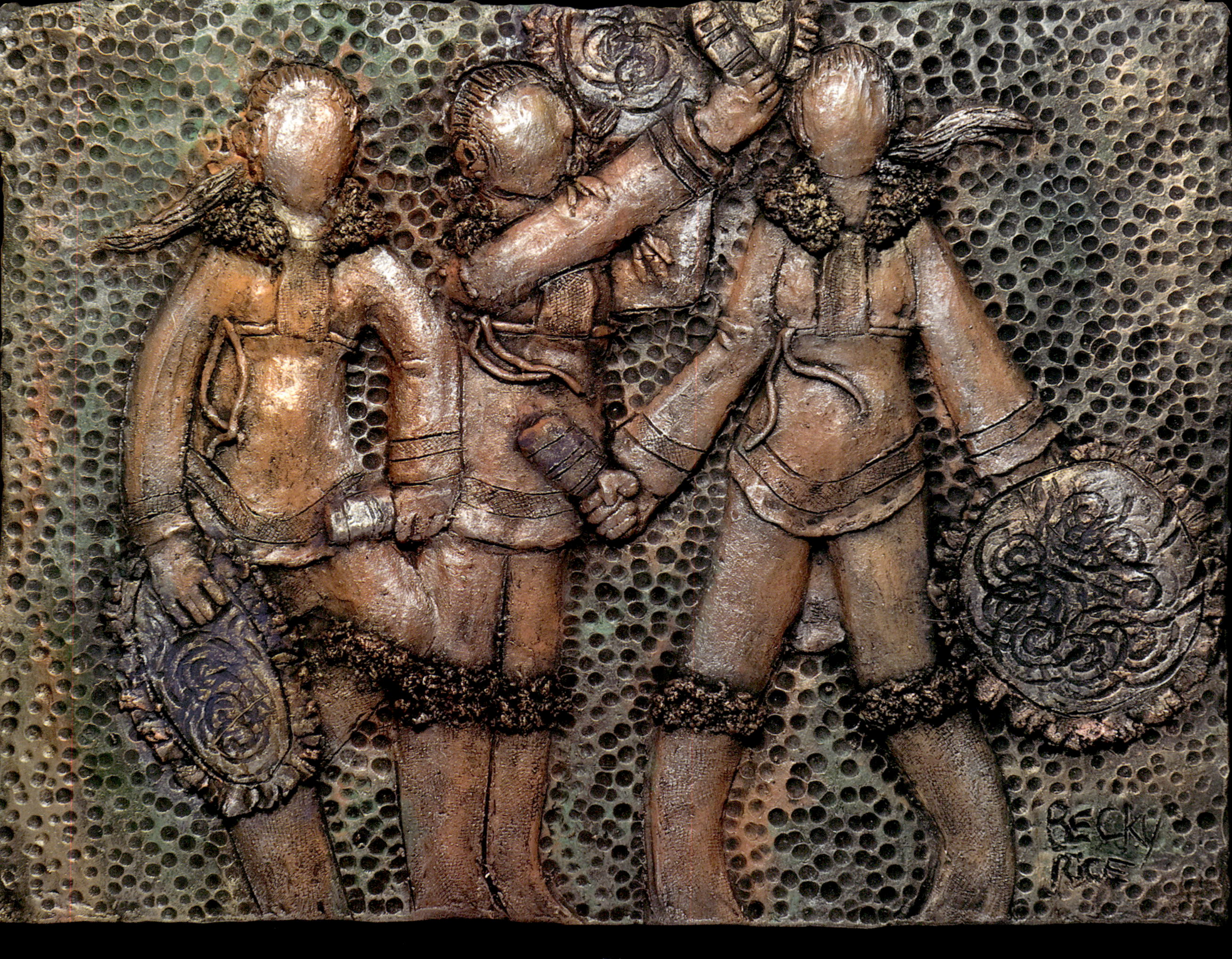
BECKY
RICE

Drumdancers & Throatsingers

Rebecca Rice, Happy Valley - Goose Bay

While others were using nature and landscape designs, I decided to develop an image based on the people of Labrador. Drumdancers just seemed to jump into my mind.

Drumdancing was discouraged and eventually disappeared after the arrival of Christian missionaries in the late 1700's, and has only recently been revived through performance groups made up of Inuit youth. Throatsinging was an early entertainment carried out by women; a friendly competition to see which partner would succumb to laughter while singing in volleys to one another. It also disappeared from Labrador but has recently reappeared, again spear-headed by youth.

The difference between then and now? Drumdancing was traditionally only done by men; throatsinging, only by women. You will notice that my drumdancers are female; I have taken some artistic liberties here, to put my own spin on the images by combining them. This also brings them up-to-date, for today's drumdance troupes include both male and female drummers. (However, throatsinging remains 'for girls only'!).

I searched the internet and some other references and sketched possible designs on paper. My proportions were off, so the teachers posed to give me real-life models to work from.

Clay presented an unfamiliar medium for me; molding the images was very hard. I was pretty happy with the result, once finished. I was surprised by the painting process – the transformation from clay to the appearance of antiqued metal. Maybe one day I can apply this technique to one of my own creations.

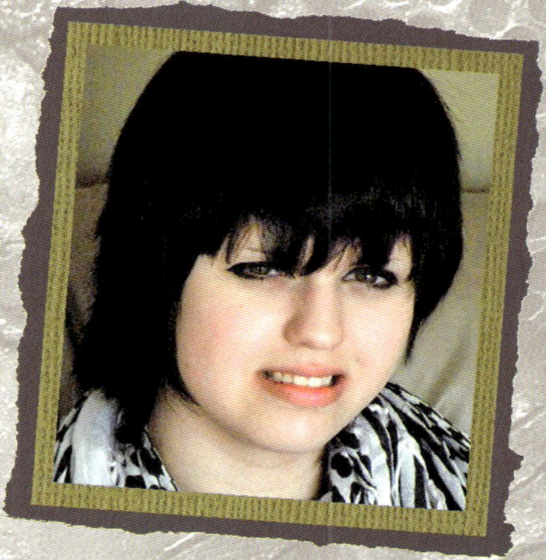

The whole experience was amazing, as were the other pieces created by fellow artists from all over Labrador. My artwork has greatly improved since I made this piece, so when I look at my tile now, I think of how much better I could have made it. Just the same, it is good to know that my piece, along with my friends' pieces, will be seen by many people in the future.

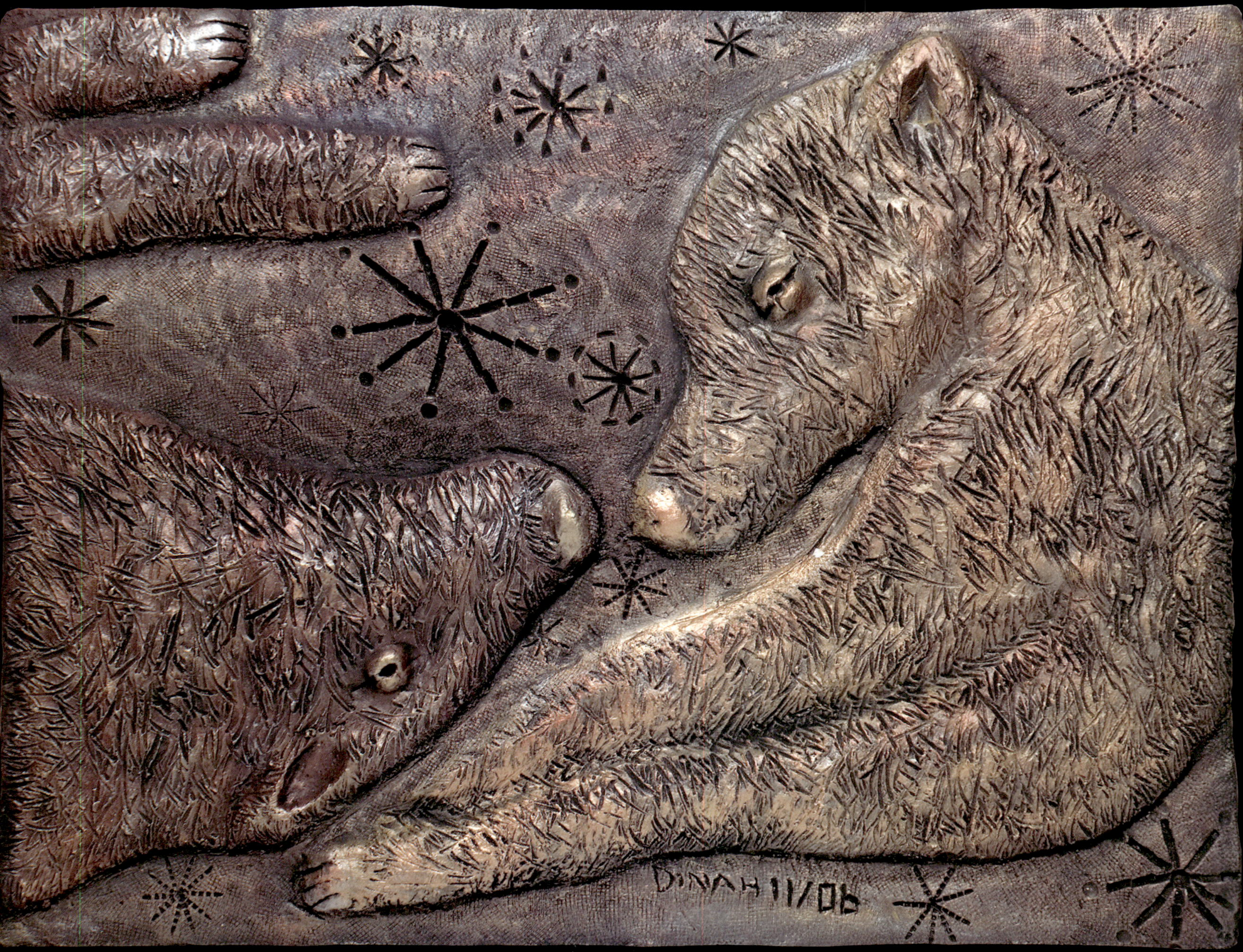
DINAH 11/06

Wolf Cubs

Dinah Wolfrey, Rigolet

I chose two playful wolf cubs for my tile image. Wolves are beautiful and wild: my favourite animal. The thick pelt could bring a nice dollar when trapping was still a way of life in Labrador. Even today, a wolf-fur *ruff* on a parka hood cuts a northern wind like nothing else can. Wolves are very important to the ecology of Labrador, for they feed on caribou; they are part of the balance of nature here.

I hope you like what I have done because I did my best, and I love what I did.

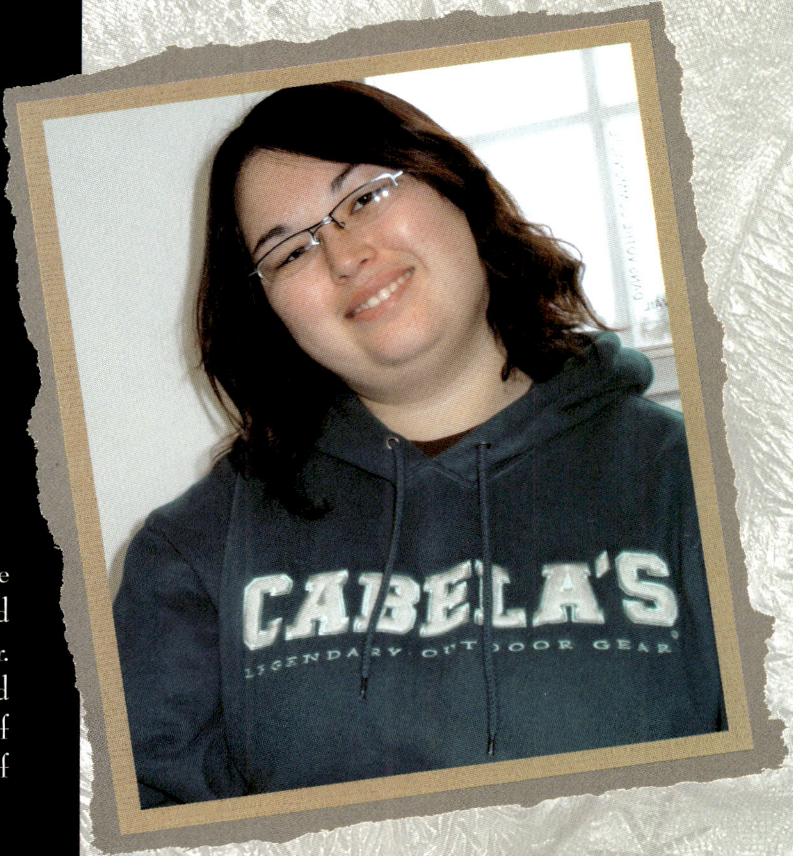

Wolves are very important to the ecology of Labrador, for they feed on caribou; they are part of the balance of nature here.

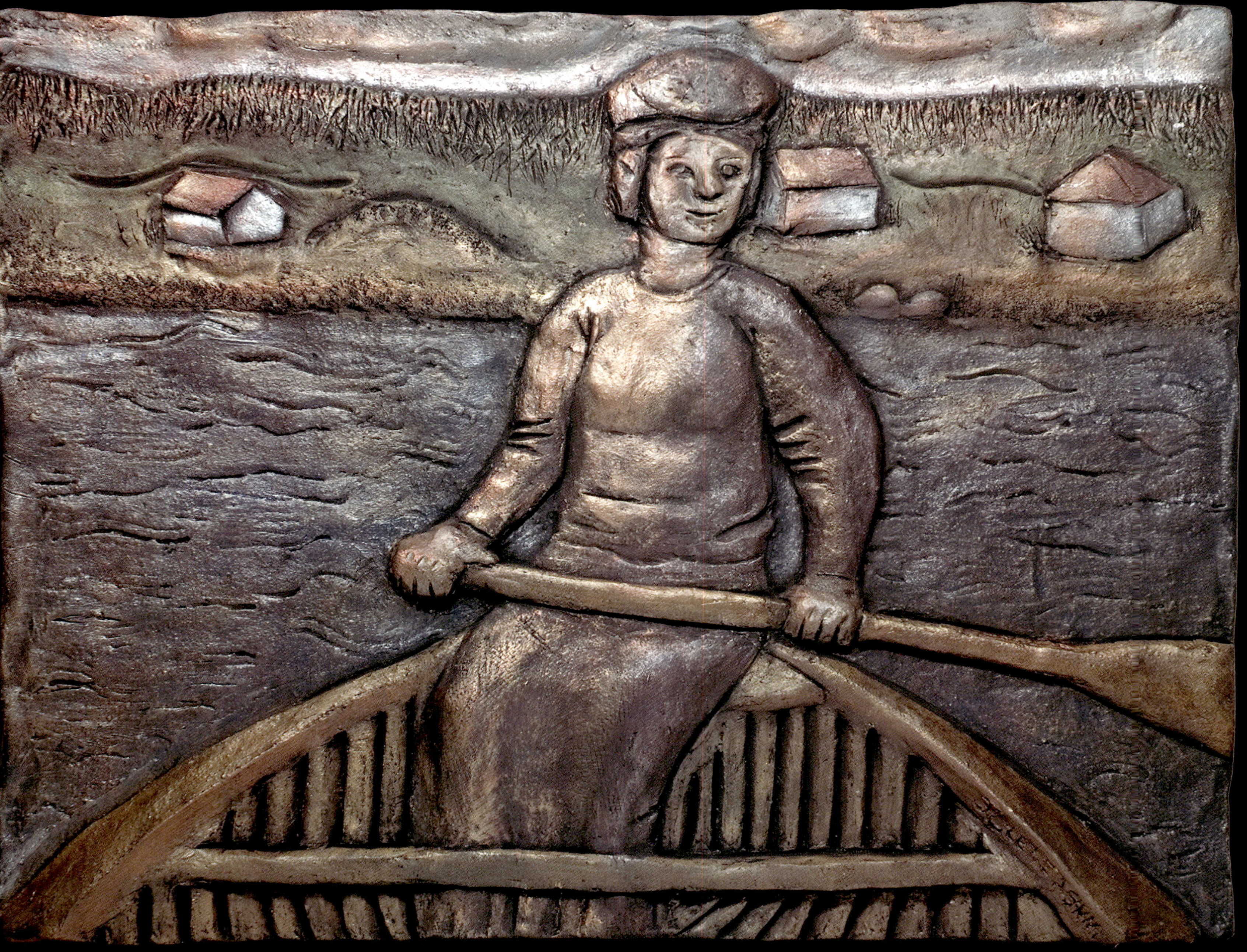

Across the River/Kamit

Jolene Ashini, Sheshatshiu

I had so many possibilities for this tile but in the end I chose to create an image which represented myself and how I thought of Labrador. The first thing that came to mind was the past, before everything, when Labrador was a nomadic home for its people. To explore this idea, I created a woman in a canoe, paddling across from Northwest River to Sheshatshiu. This represents my two heritages: my mother is from Northwest River and my father is from Sheshatshiu. I feel privileged to be part of two cultures, and honored to be the first Innu student at the United World College of the Atlantic, where I have spent two years studying with students from all over the world.

Making the tile was a learning experience, as it was my first time working with clay. It was difficult at first but it got easier as time progressed. My tile, along with the others that make up the installation, may be one way to help others understand Labrador's diversity.

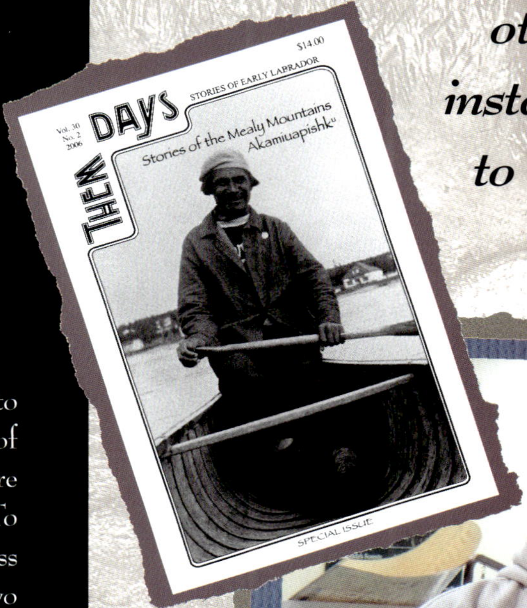

My tile, along with the others that make up the installation, may be one way to help others understand Labrador's diversity.

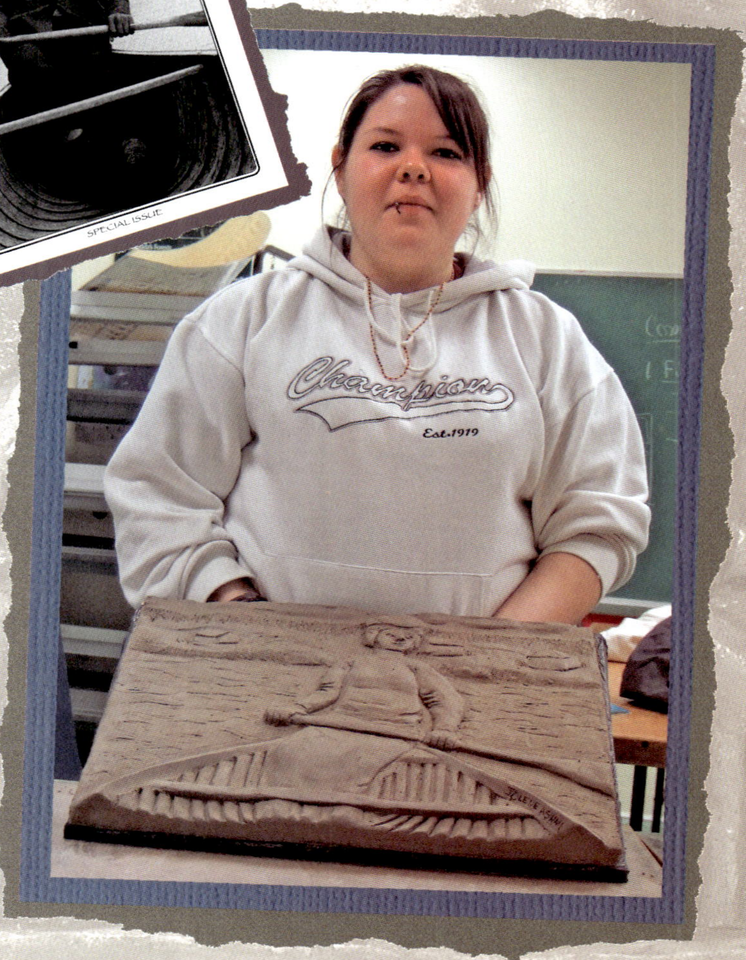

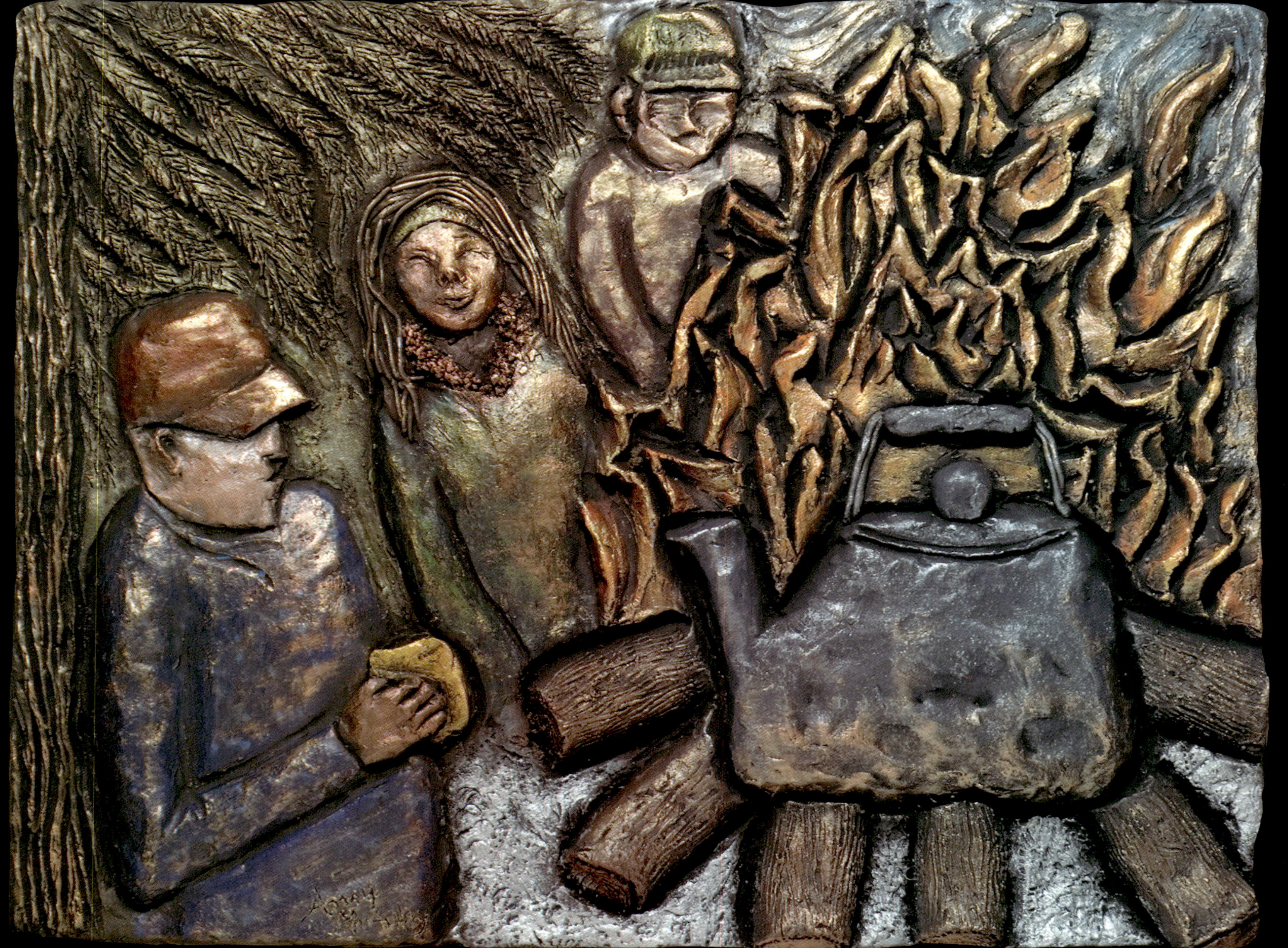

The Boil - up

Amy McAlley, Northwest River

In the "Big Land", everyone — young and old — enjoys a boil-up, including me! The boil-up is a common cultural element in Labrador: a group of people gathered around a campfire with a mug of tea.

The campfire in the foreground draws the viewer into the piece; it invites you to take your place around the fire and enjoy its warmth. The kettle, singing atop the fire, offers to fill your mug and pull you into the circle.

Hopefully, the new arts centre will fulfill a similar function in the community, inviting spectators and performers alike from all around Labrador to a warm and enjoyable shared experience.

I've never really thought of myself as an artist. At first I didn't have much confidence that I could do this, as I'd never worked with clay before. Creating the general shape of the image was not difficult, but the fine detail took much time and effort. With Dorrie's encouragement I kept going and surprised myself.

It is a real honor to have this tile displayed in the new performing arts center.

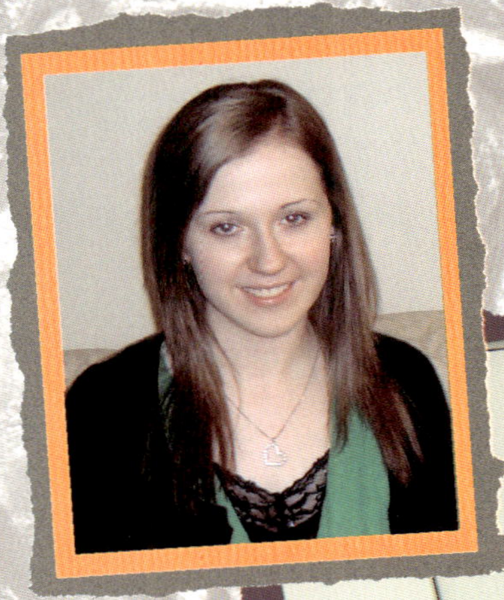

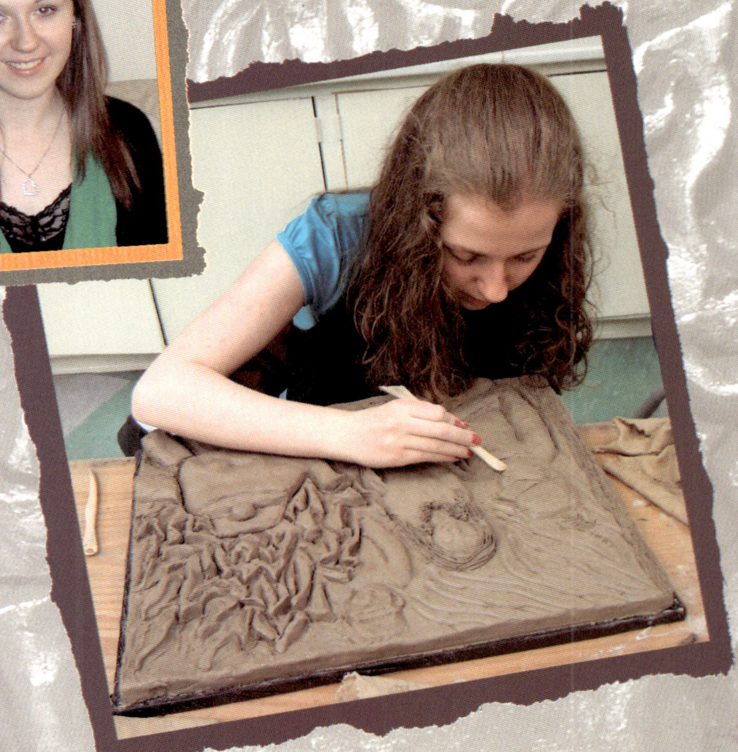

Creating the general shape of the image was not difficult, but the fine detail took much time and effort. With Dorrie's encouragement I kept going and surprised myself.

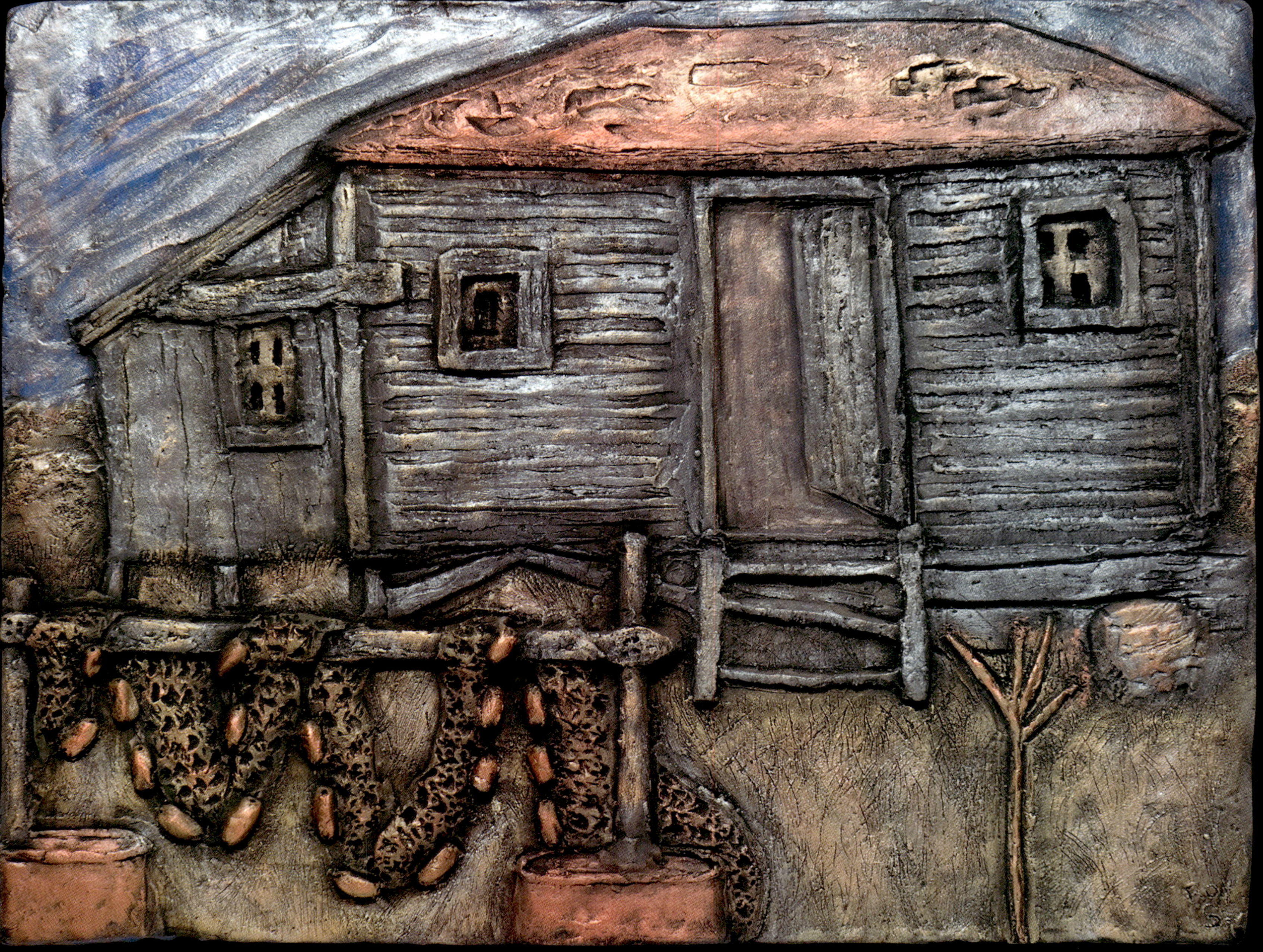

The Last Lemare, Old Man's Cove

Roy Sainsbury, Cartwright

Finlay Lemare was a bachelor fisherman; the last of his family. He had several fishing places around Sandwich Bay and everyone knew him. Everyone has a story about Finlay Lemare.

My 'story' of Finlay is a lasting one, living in my tile. I have spent a good deal of time in Old Man's Cove. My family goes there in the boat often. I had a photograph of Finlay's last fishing shack in Old Man's Cove, and had already sketched it before I started to work on the tile. It seemed a fitting image for the mural: a tumble-down building reminiscent of a family and a fishery now gone.

Working with the clay was stressful, when it wouldn't go the way I wanted it to (....and even moreso, when I got picked on by all the girls: I was the only boy in the group!)

I feel privileged to have my tile in the mural installation.

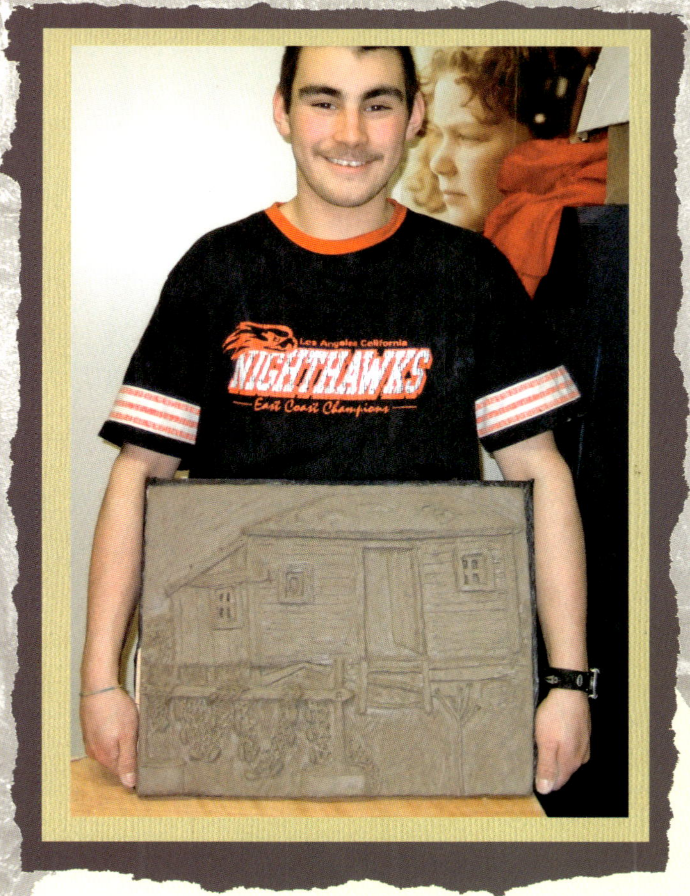

... a fitting image for the mural: a tumble-down building reminiscent of a family and a fishery now gone.

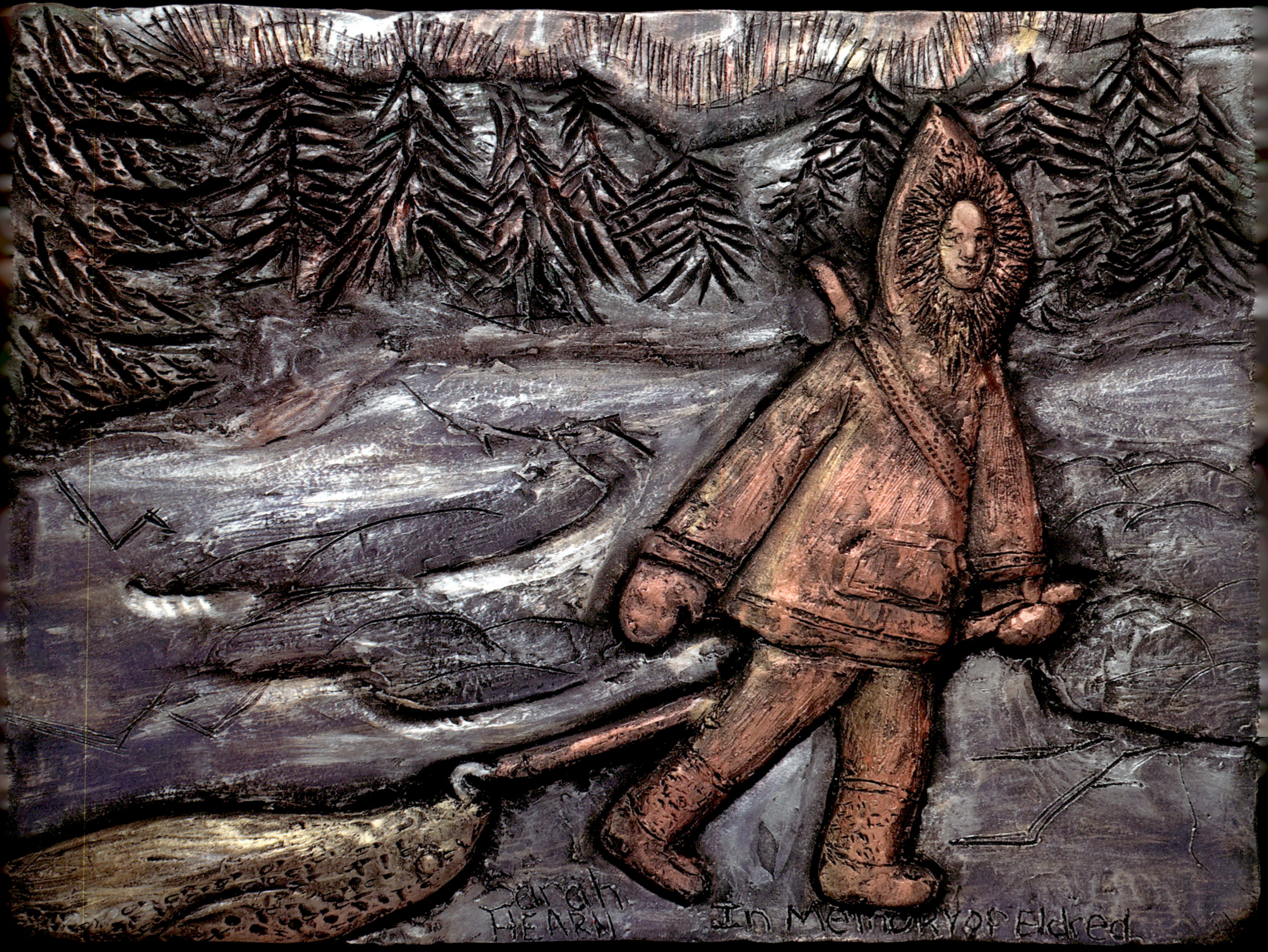
Sarah
HEARN
In Memory of Eldred

Hauling Seal

Sarah Hearn, Nain

When I'm stuck, I usually think of my stepfather, because when he came into my and my mom's lives, he inspired and encouraged me. So when I started searching for ideas for a tile image suitable for the mural, I thought of a time when he took me seal-hunting. We hid behind the *talluk*, a white sheet stretched on a five-foot-square frame, so the seal wouldn't see us. We had to park the skidoo near the shore so the seal would not hear us nor feel vibrations along the ice. My stepfather was a good hunter.

I wanted to honor his memory in my tile; I wanted him to be proud of me. He may not have been the most well-known man in Labrador, but those who knew my stepfather will remember him always with love.

This mural was a project of the Labrador Creative Arts Festival which is a sort of tradition, where students from all over Labrador come to express themselves and share arts experiences. The best part for me was getting over shyness, making friends, and learning to just be myself.

My tile lets me share a little of myself, my art, my step-father's heritage and memory – my experiences of Labrador – with anyone who wishes to take them in. It gives both ways!

My tile lets me share a little of myself, my art, my step-father's heritage and memory – my experiences of Labrador – with anyone who wishes to take them in. It gives both ways!

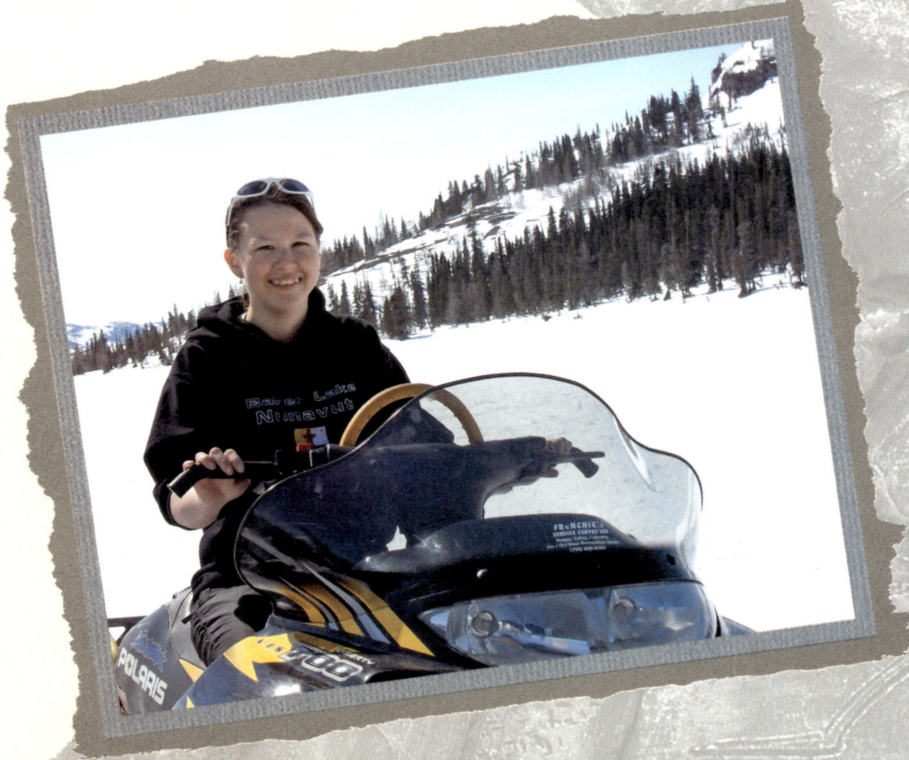

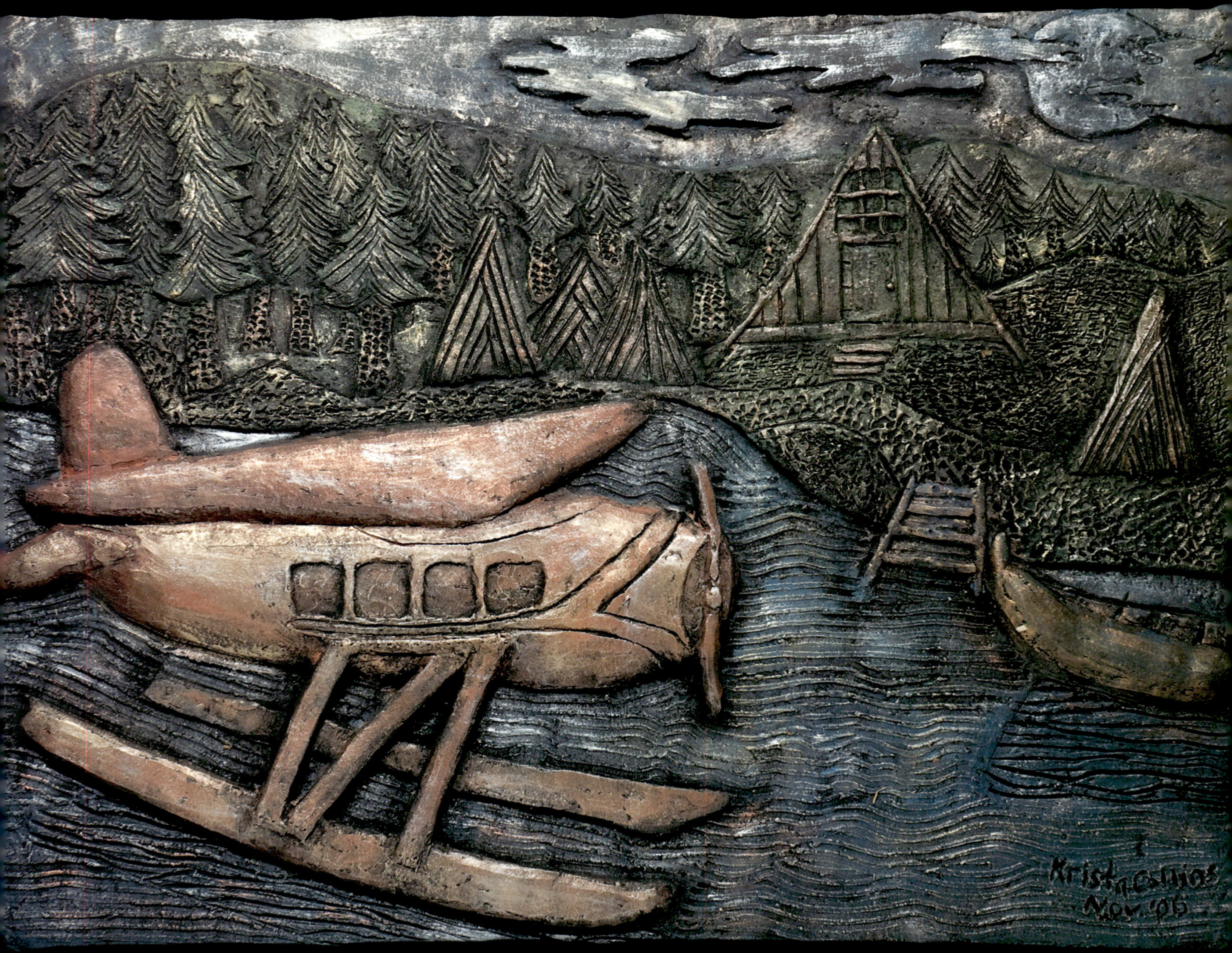
Nov. '06

Float Plane

Krista Collins, Churchill Falls

I love to travel. In Labrador, 'travel' historically involved walking, or dogteams, or boats. With the advent of the plane, mail and people and freight could move readily in all seasons. No airstrips? No problem. Float planes in the summer, and ski-planes in the winter were essential to many people in coastal communities. Float planes continue to carry fishermen into remote interior camps – just one of Labrador's tourist lures.

My inspiration for this tile came from the back cover of a **Them Days** magazine but I still thought the task impossible: how do I turn that photo into an image in clay? Working with Lynda Faulks was incredible, step-by-impossible step. I am extremely proud of my tile; to see it finished and installed with all the others that make up the mural makes it all worthwhile.

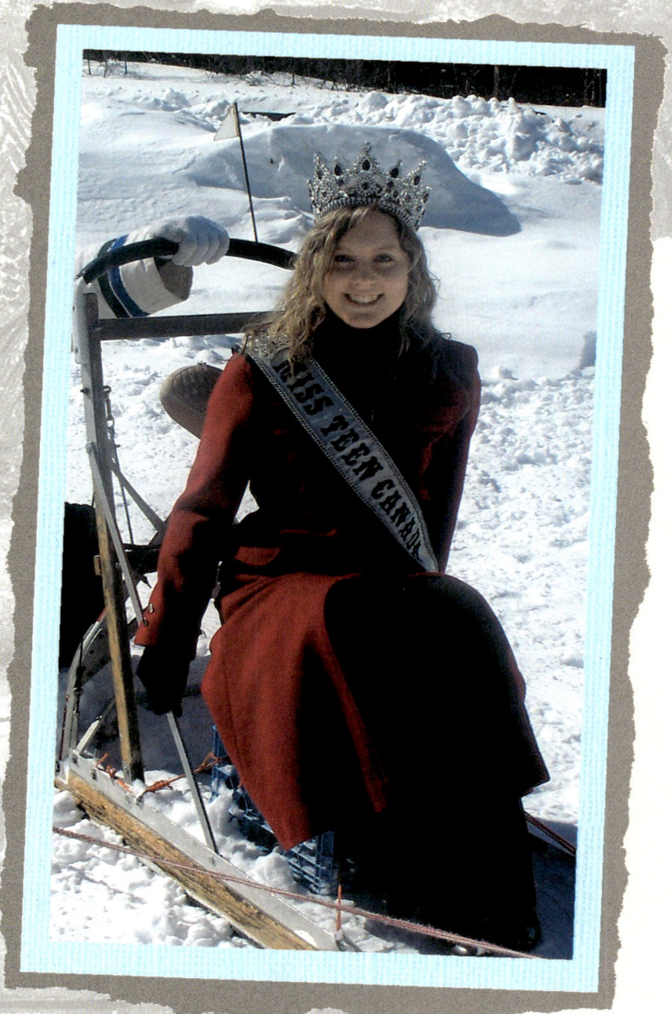

I am extremely proud of my tile; to see it finished and installed with all the others that make up the mural makes it all worthwhile.

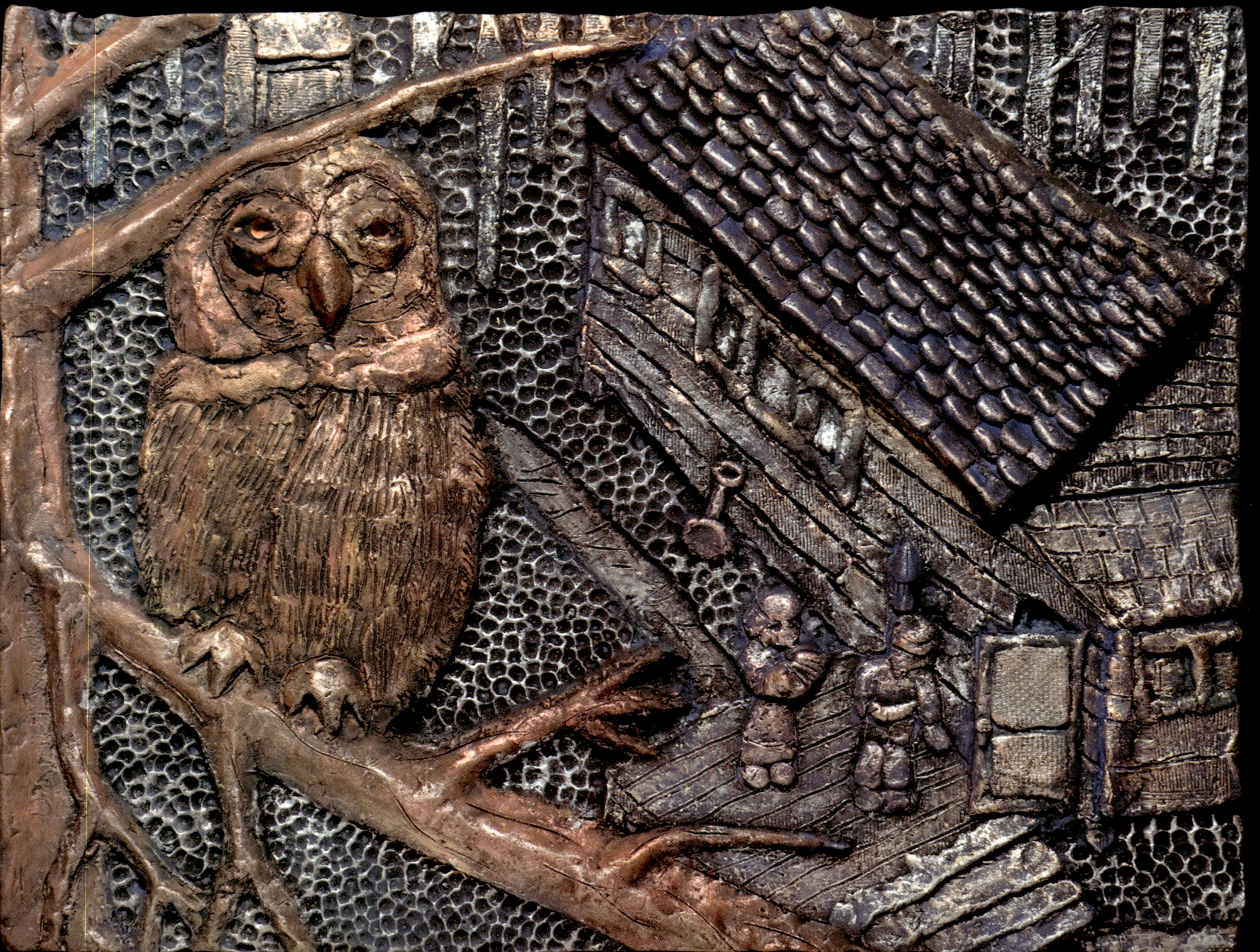

At the Cabin

Daniel Windeler,
Happy Valley - Goose Bay

For as long as I can remember, I've loved going to my family's cabin off the Churchill Falls Road. I would run through the trees, or sit on the small deck at night watching the stars. Sometimes, when I closed my eyes to savour nature's splendor, I could hear the screech of an owl – a fascinating creature. Once, mummers came to visit, clad in odd socks, hats, long underwear and rubber boots, their faces hidden under tablecloths. It was required that if they wanted a treat to eat, they must dance around the room with family members.

I have brought all these fond memories together in my tile.

And that tile exacted some skill (and patience) from me. The owl's eyes required some precision and I think I made them at least four times. Repeatedly, I placed the eyeballs in the sockets only to realize that they were lop-sided!

I feel very fortunate to have participated in the mural project. It has opened friendships that are still strong with students from other parts of Labrador. A creation of mine is memorialized in Labrador's new performance centre. As I move on to other stages in my life, I celebrate this with great pride. What a legacy!

I feel very fortunate to have participated in the mural project. It has opened friendships that are still strong with students from other parts of Labrador.

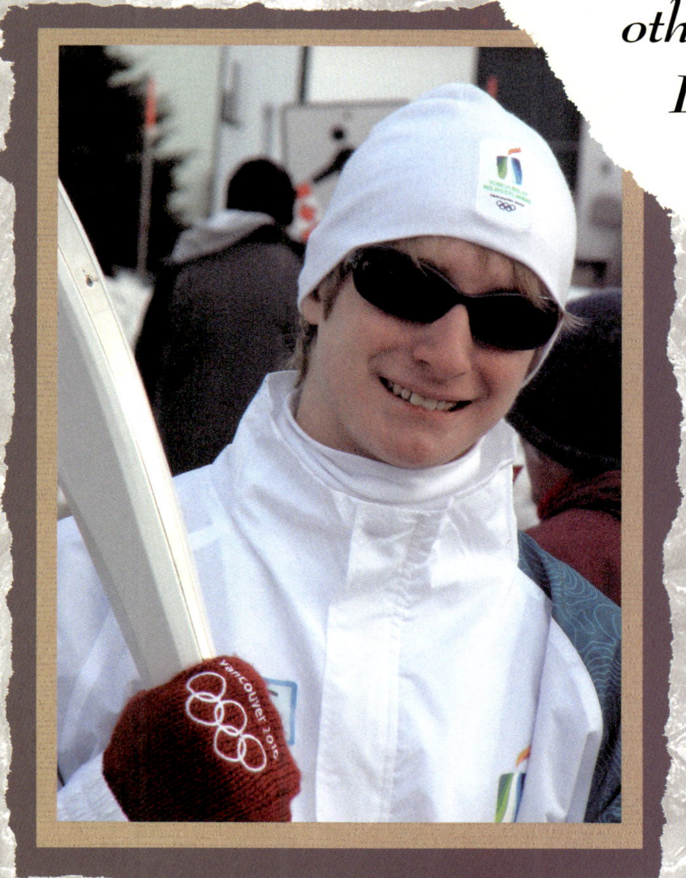

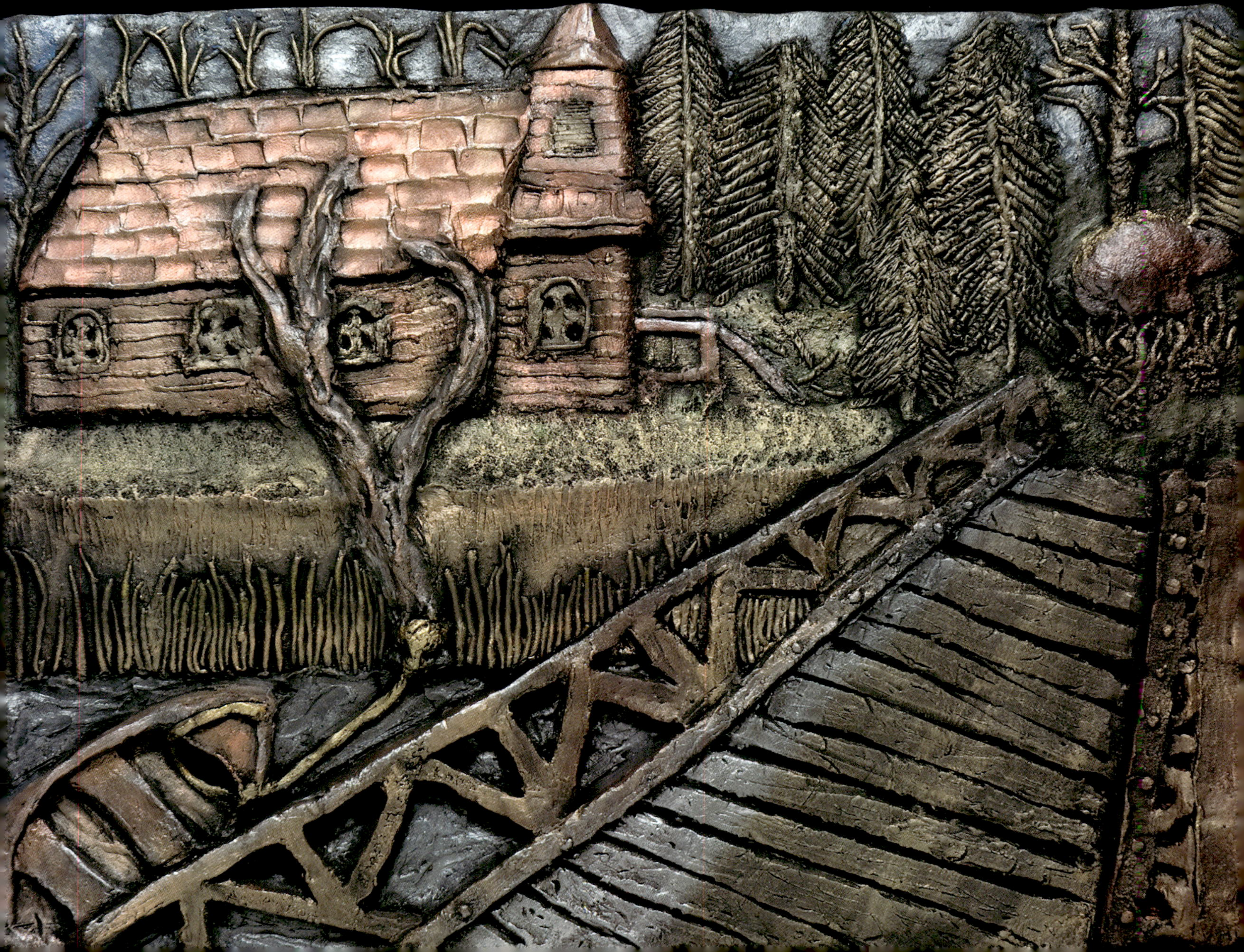

Bridge at Mud Lake

Ashley Best, Stephanie Best, Laura Chaulk

We couldn't decide what to make with our clay. All the students went outside with cameras and shot everything we saw that we thought would really 'wow' anyone who had never seen Mud Lake. We take Mud Lake for granted, so we weren't sure what to photograph: we see it all as 'regular.'

The bridge is important to the community of Mud Lake because people live on both sides of the channel and it connects us all…and, it has great textures for working in clay! It is beautiful and inspiring and it draws attention to the community.

Ashley: "At first it seemed hopeless and impossible, looking at the huge blob of clay and trying to make a picture out of it. But after long hours it came together; with each step I could see it become more and more like art, and I must say I am pleased. Others will grasp some sense of Mud Lake when they see the tile, and I will be able to say, 'I made that!' It will hang in the mural for years with my name next to it…just that fact makes me feel good."

Laura: "I thought of it as really awesome play-doh! The tile was fun to create."

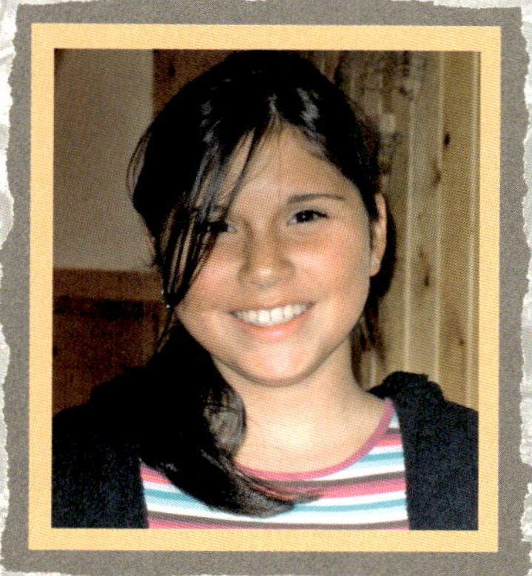

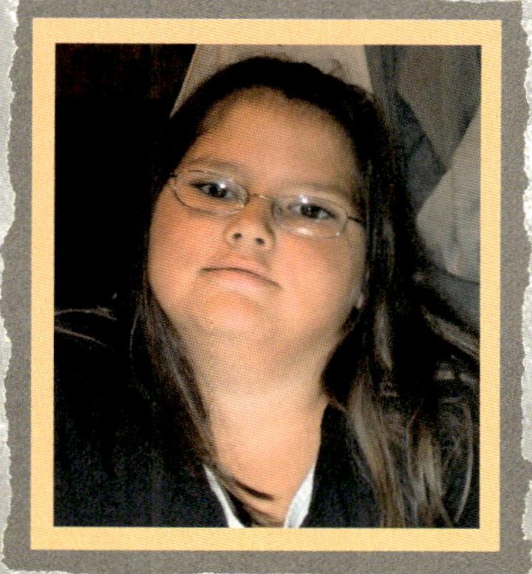

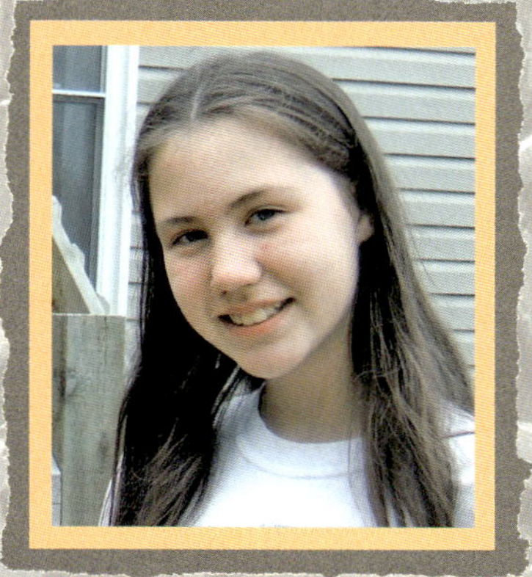

The bridge is important to the community of Mud Lake because people live on both sides of the channel and it connects us all…and, it has great textures for working in clay!

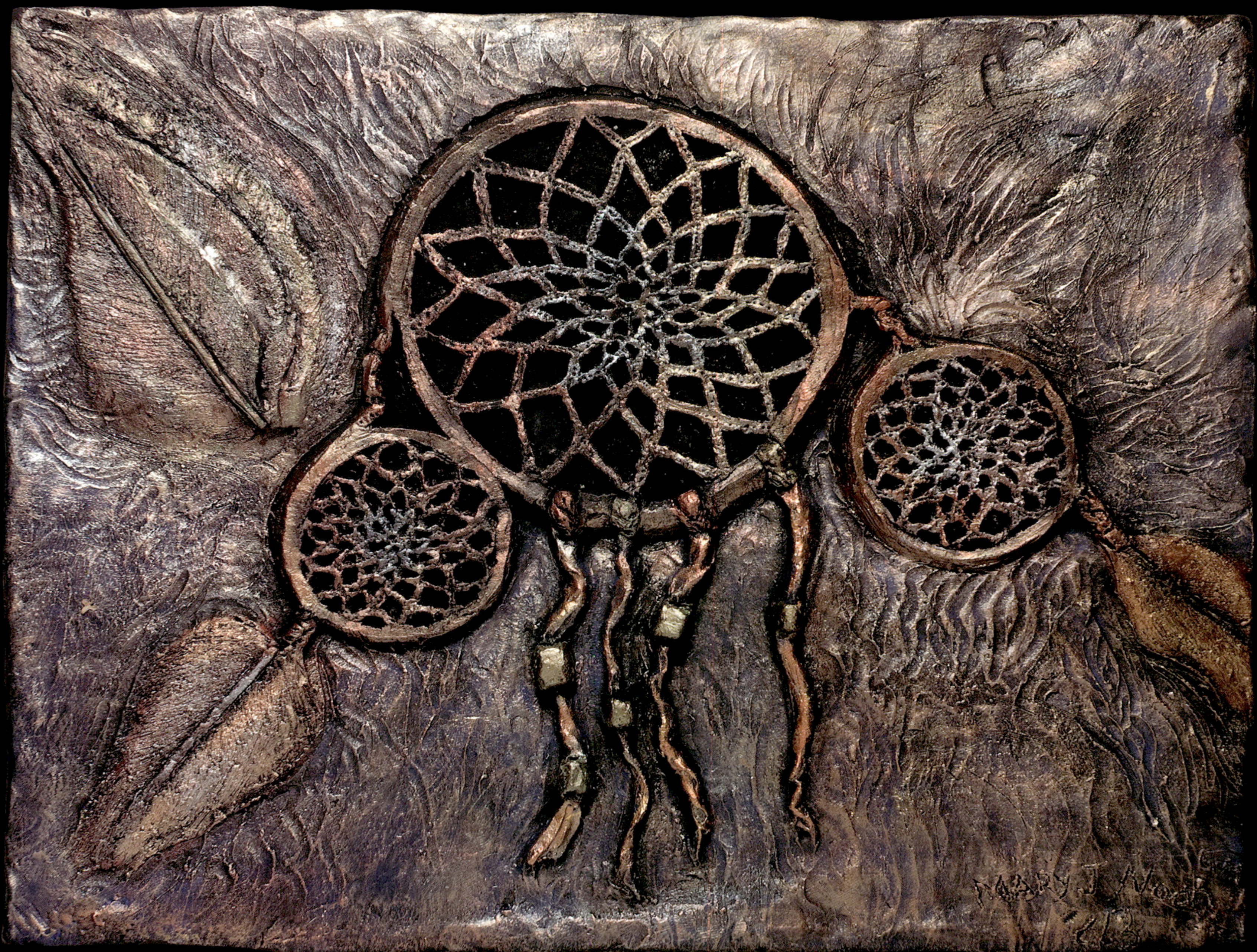
MARY J.

Dream Nui

MaryJane White, Natuashish

I chose this image because I love dream-catchers and my little cousin Dream Nui. The idea came to me when I was sitting down with my friend and I saw her dream-catcher earrings. They were beautiful, so I tried to put that beautiful image of the dream-catchers into clay.

Dream-catchers are hung where we sleep, to catch the bad dreams in their webbing. That way we will have only good dreams while we sleep peacefully.

I am very proud that my art will be up in the Arts Centre.

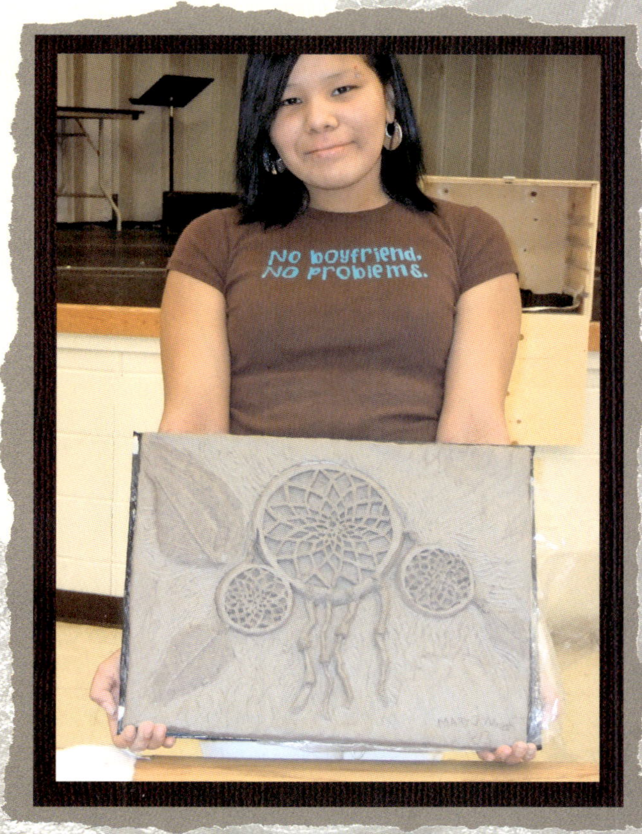

Dream-catchers are hung where we sleep, to catch the bad dreams in their webbing. That way we will have only good dreams while we sleep peacefully.

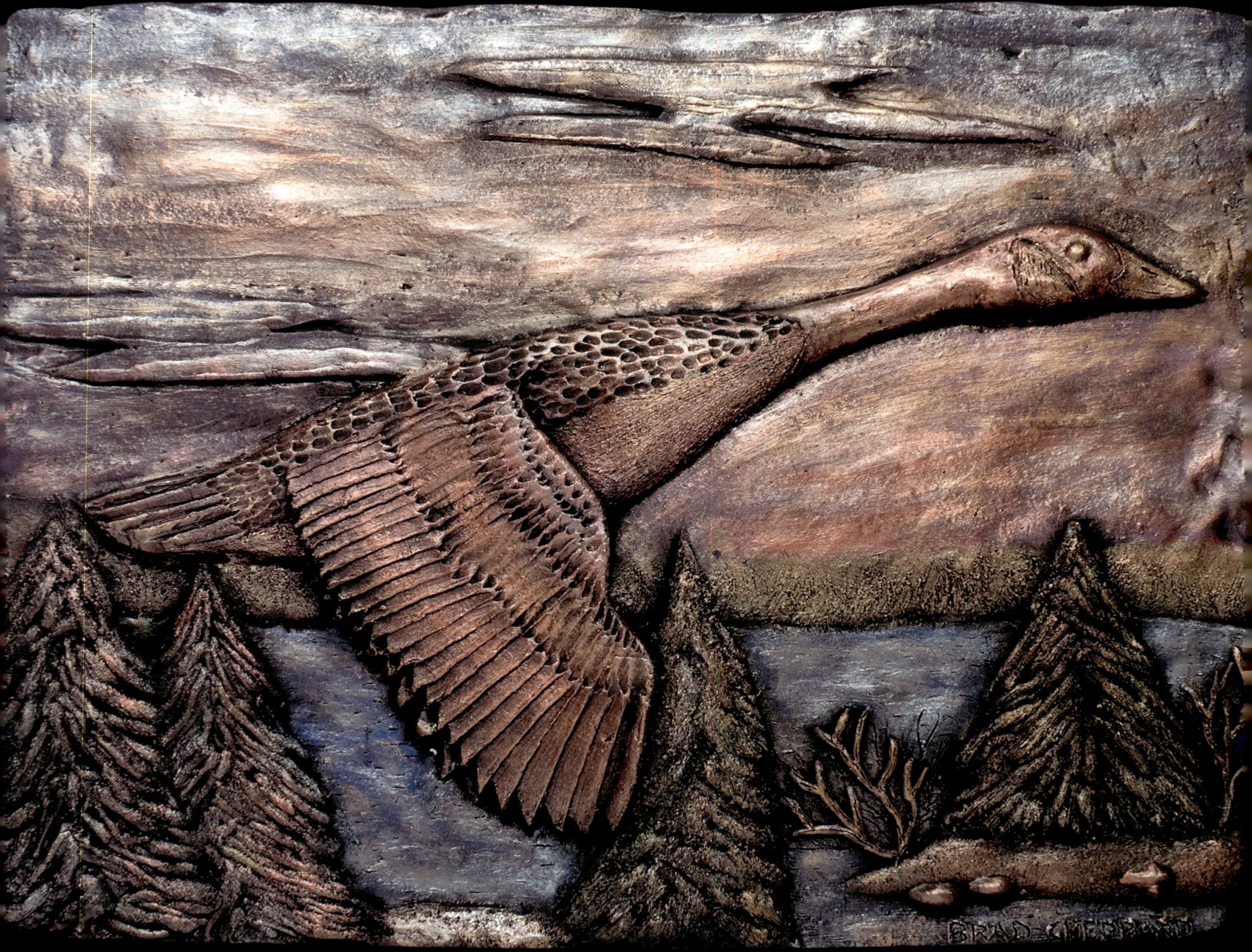
BRAD

OCTOBER HUNT

BRAD SHEPPARD, POSTVILLE

I knew from the very beginning that I wanted to make a goose. I love to go goose hunting. I drew one goose, from memory; then got a number of pictures of geese to compare my drawing to the real thing. And then, I really got to work, because now I could see differences and I needed to make some changes.

I had fun working with the clay. It gave me confidence as I got better at working with it. I even invented my own technique for making the spruce trees (I think I ruined one of Miss' tools doing it, but look at the result!). When I got as far as the tailfeathers on my goose, I just couldn't get them right. I asked Herbie, and he easily showed me what I needed to do. I hadn't been seeing them right.

I am very proud of my work. It means I will always be remembered.

I had fun working with the clay. It gave me confidence as I got better at working with it.

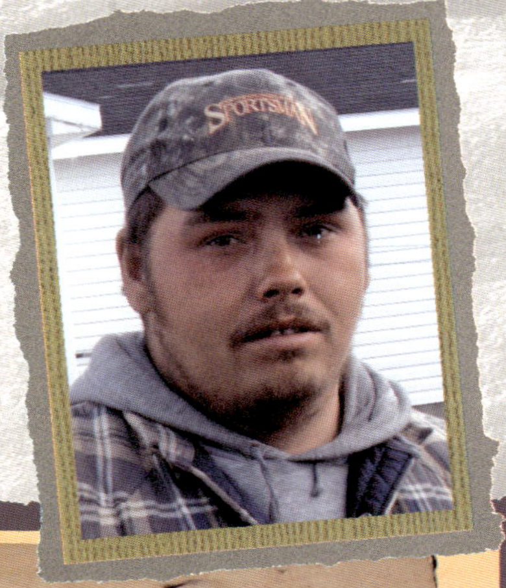

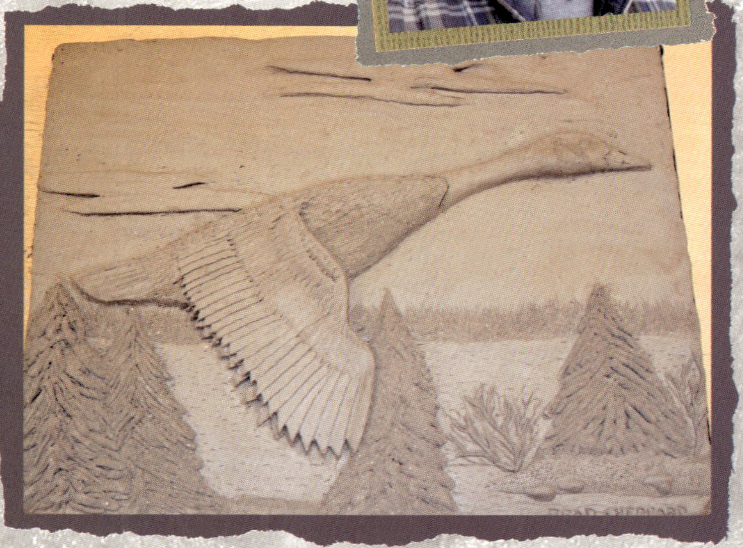

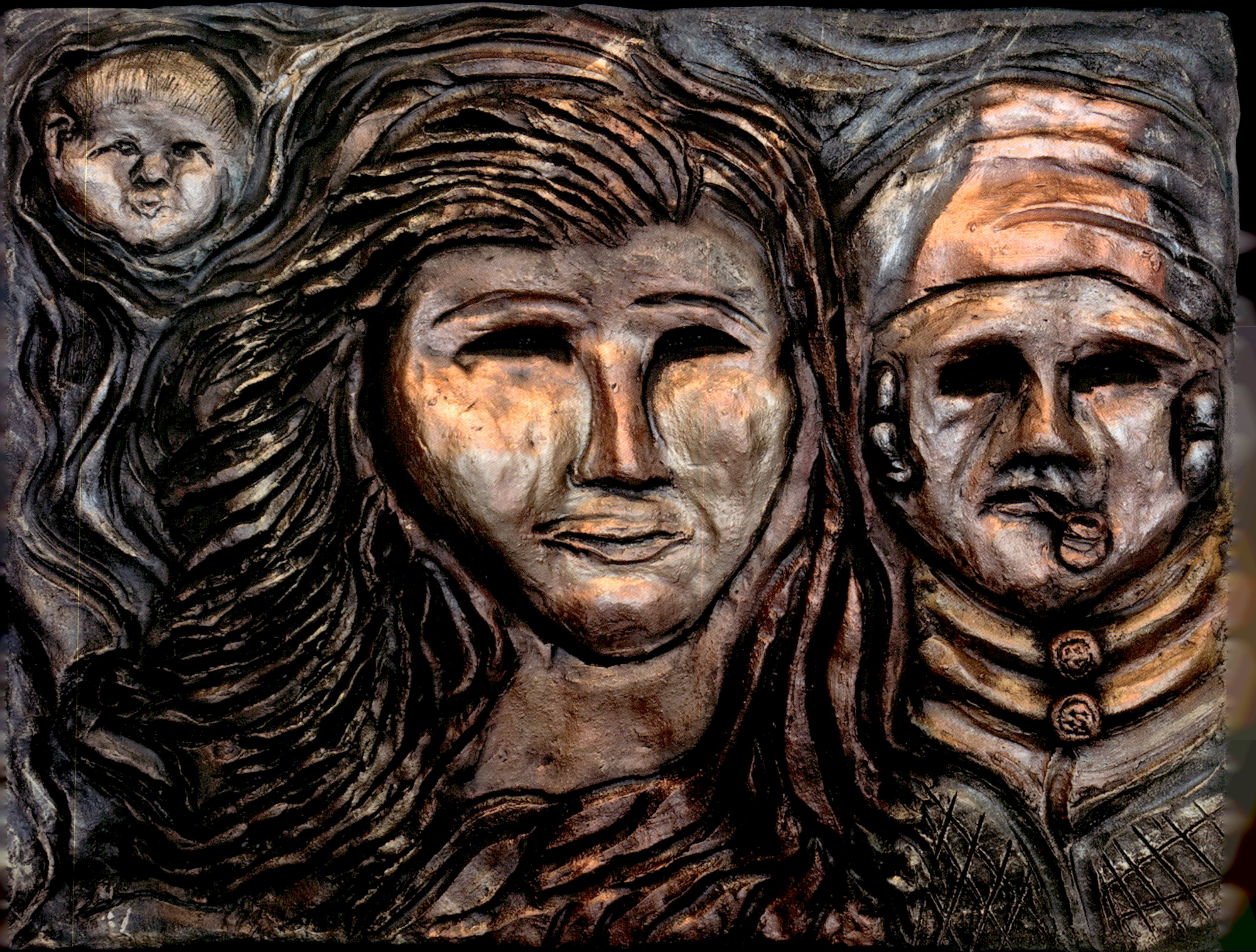

Ishkueu umeshkanam: Three Generations

Whitney Andrew, Sheshatshiu

Three Innu women, past, present, and future look at you from my tile. I am an Innu woman of the present. I am not my grandmother, but she is important to me. She helps me to know about the past, the old ways, and still she helps me to be who I am today.

The baby in my tile is not yet born. She is an Innu woman of the future. I will help her to know about her culture, and my grandmother's past. But she will not be me and she will not be my grandmother. We are different generations: all different, and still all the same.

Working with the clay was fun and I was excited to do it. I liked watching the images come out of the clay; I liked how I could make that happen. It was hard, but worth it.

I am so much proud.

Ishkueu umeshkanam

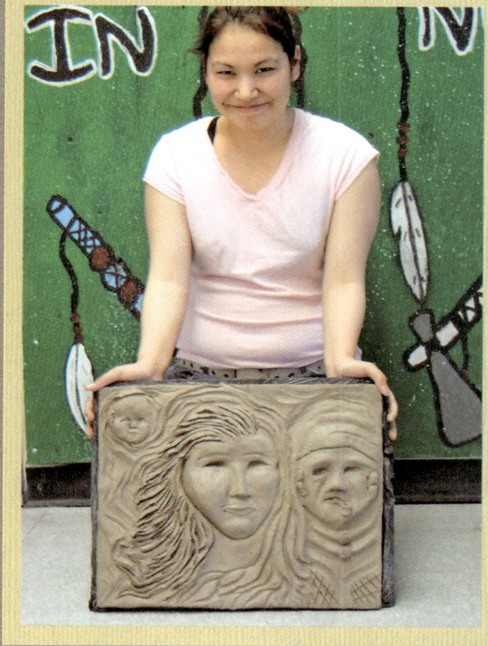

Nishtut innushkueut, ueshkat, anutshish kie ainnishkat tshe tshitapamakaut. Ninu innushkueu anutshish Mieu nin ukaumau, muk mishta ishpitenitakushu. Ni uitshik tshetshi tohissenitamuk nete ueshkat, shashish ka aitinanunit, kie eshk anutshish ni uitshik tohetshi tauk ute etaian.

Eku ne auass ka-tau-a eshk apu inniut. Eukun uin innushkueu nete aianishkat. Ni ka uitshiau tshetshi tshissenitak ka ishinniut, kie nukum-a ka ishinniuniti nete ueshkat. Muk apu tshikut nin itenitakushiht kie apu tshikut ukumitut. Tatipan ishinakunu-a ni meshkanaminan: tatipan kassinu etatishiat, kie muk ni peikushinan.

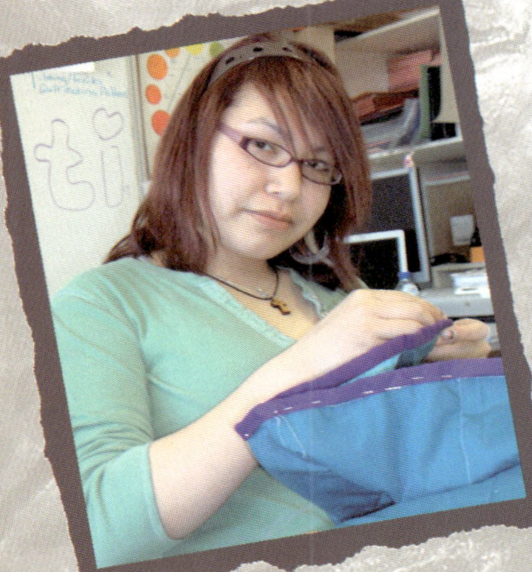

Ni mishte minuaten ka tshi atusseuatsheian ne shissu. Ni minuaten ka ishi mishkaman tshekuana tohe ishi tutakatsheian ne shissu: ni minuaten ka tohi tutaman. Animanupan, muk minuapin tshetshi tutaman tshekuan.

Ni minuenimun ka tshi tutaman.

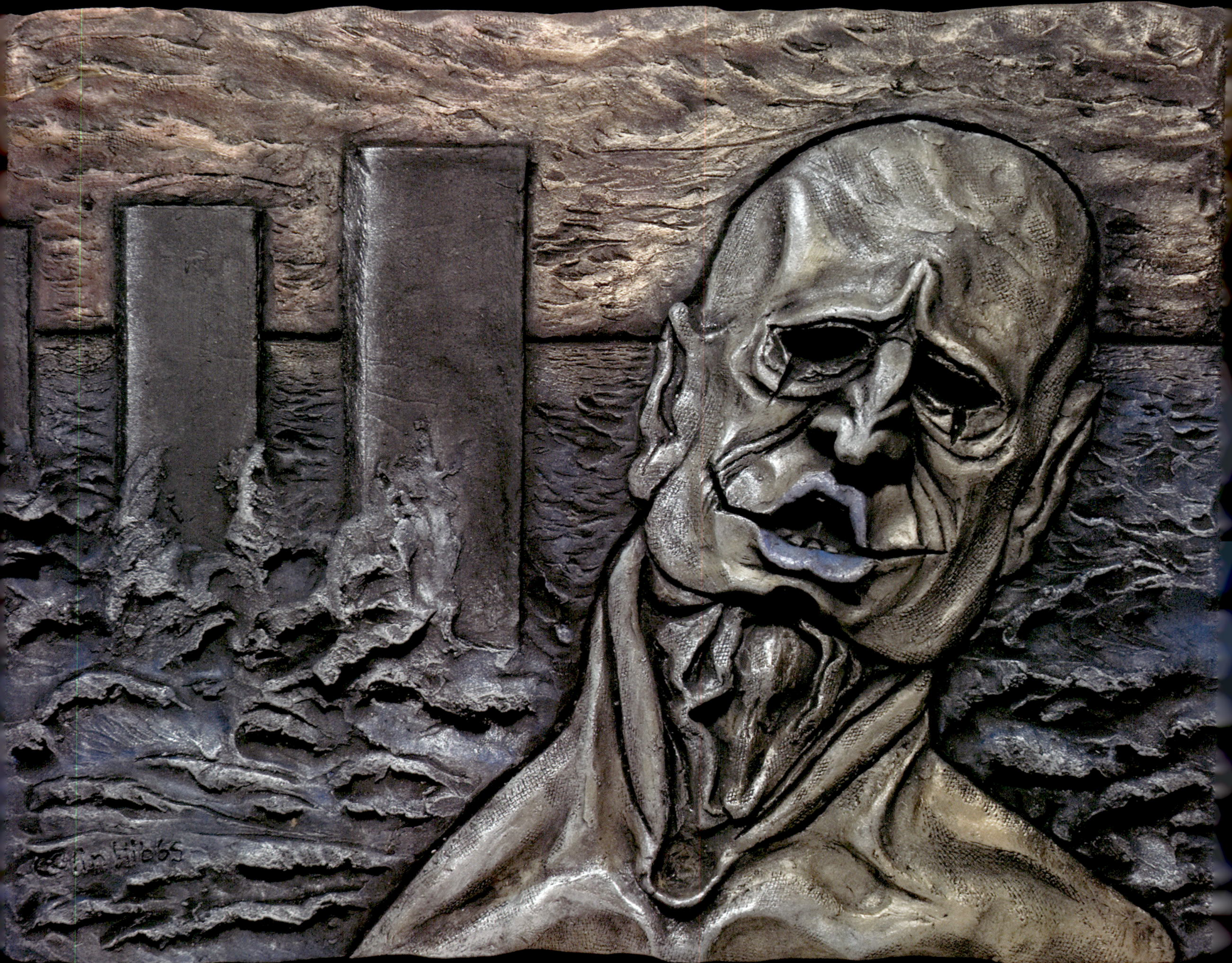

It Black Sea Shine/ A Wall of Change to Come

Colin Hibbs, Northwest River

Because I use my fingers a great deal to achieve smooth shading in my drawings, using similar technique with clay was a natural transition. Drawings must appear to be in three dimensions even though they remain in only two. With the clay I could, with little effort, achieve those three dimensions in reality. Embracing clay as a medium was pleasurable and gratifying.

Inspiration and motive for this piece of art came largely from music. Because I constantly hear unconventional, microtonal music stream through my consciousness, I try to imagine what these purely mathematical sounds might look like. Black, vibrantly cold monoliths rising from an infinitely deep body of water was one image that came to mind. A tattered being emerging from the sea, confused and purposeless, completed my vision.

I am honored to portray and represent my thoughts to the public. Though many interpretations may arise concerning the "true" meaning of the piece, I will insist, indefinitely, that it is whatever the viewer wants it to be.

I am honored to portray and represent my thoughts to the public. Though many interpretations may arise concerning the "true" meaning of the piece, I will insist, indefinitely, that it is whatever the viewer wants it to be.

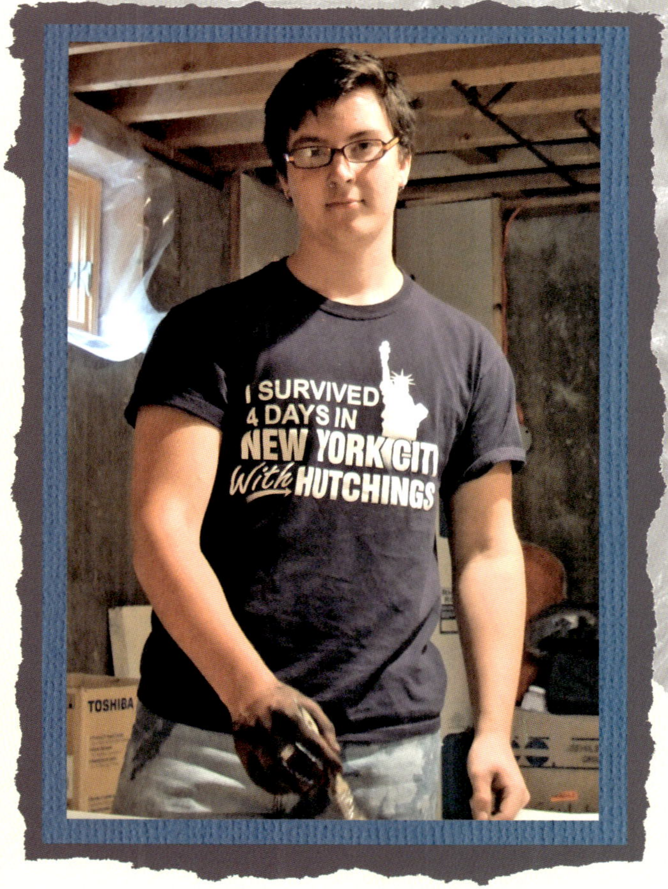

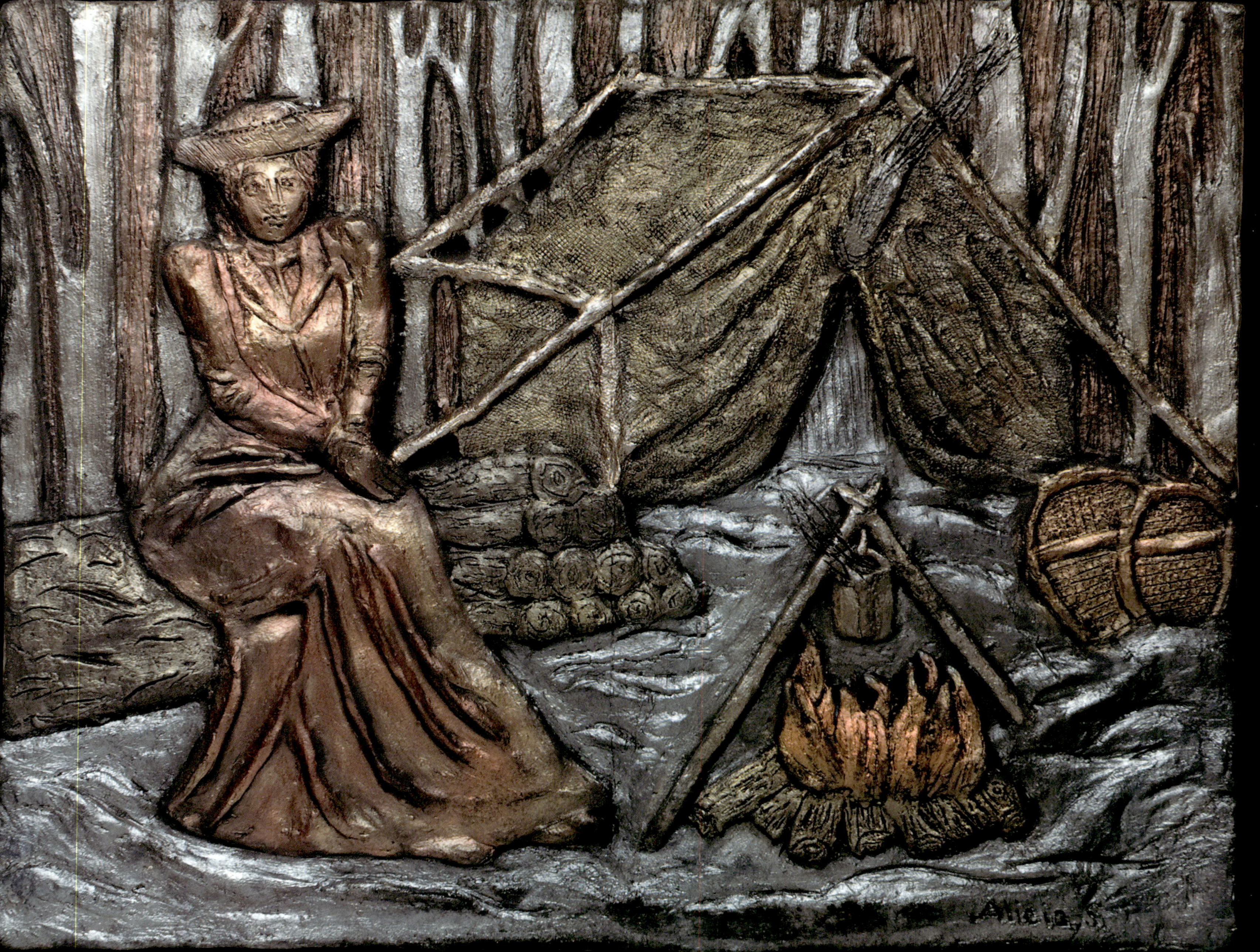

Mina Hubbard

Alicia Seaward, Happy Valley - Goose Bay

Mina Hubbard trekked across interior Labrador in 1905 from Northwest River to Ungava Bay, to complete a journey started two years earlier by her husband, Leonidas, who died of exposure and starvation before he could accomplish his goal.

I was inspired by an archival photo of Mina camping en route. Mina's story not only captures a moment in our history, but speaks to the strength of women. Her determination, organization, resilience, and optimism were qualities necessary to her survival; we could all take a lesson!

My initial confusion gave way to the joy of detail as the clay responded to my hands and the image gradually emerged. I love the way that so many different people from all over Labrador have come together in this extraordinary project; the way so many different images all connect and relate in the mural. It shows the hard work and hidden talent of our young people.

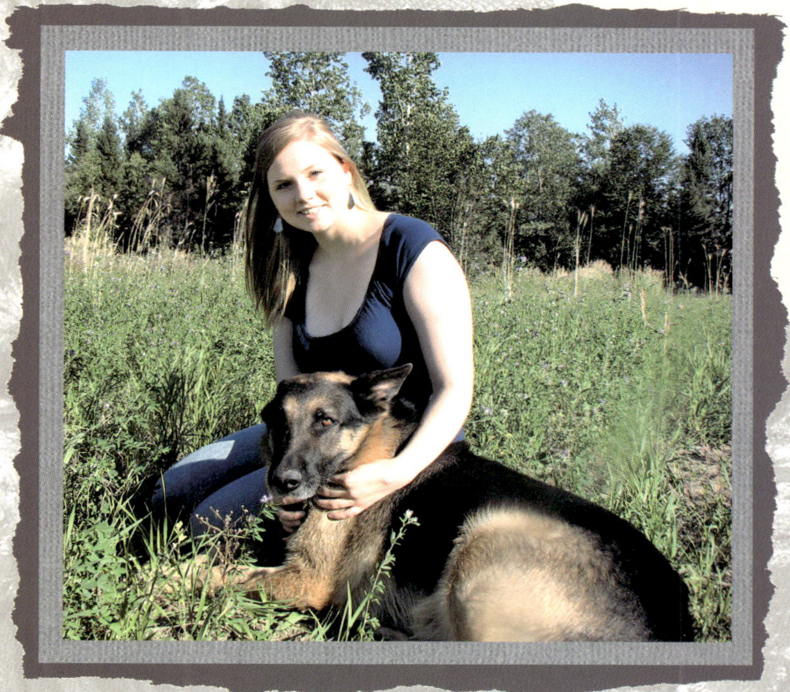

I love the way that so many different people from all over Labrador have come together in this extraordinary project; the way so many different images all connect and relate in the mural.

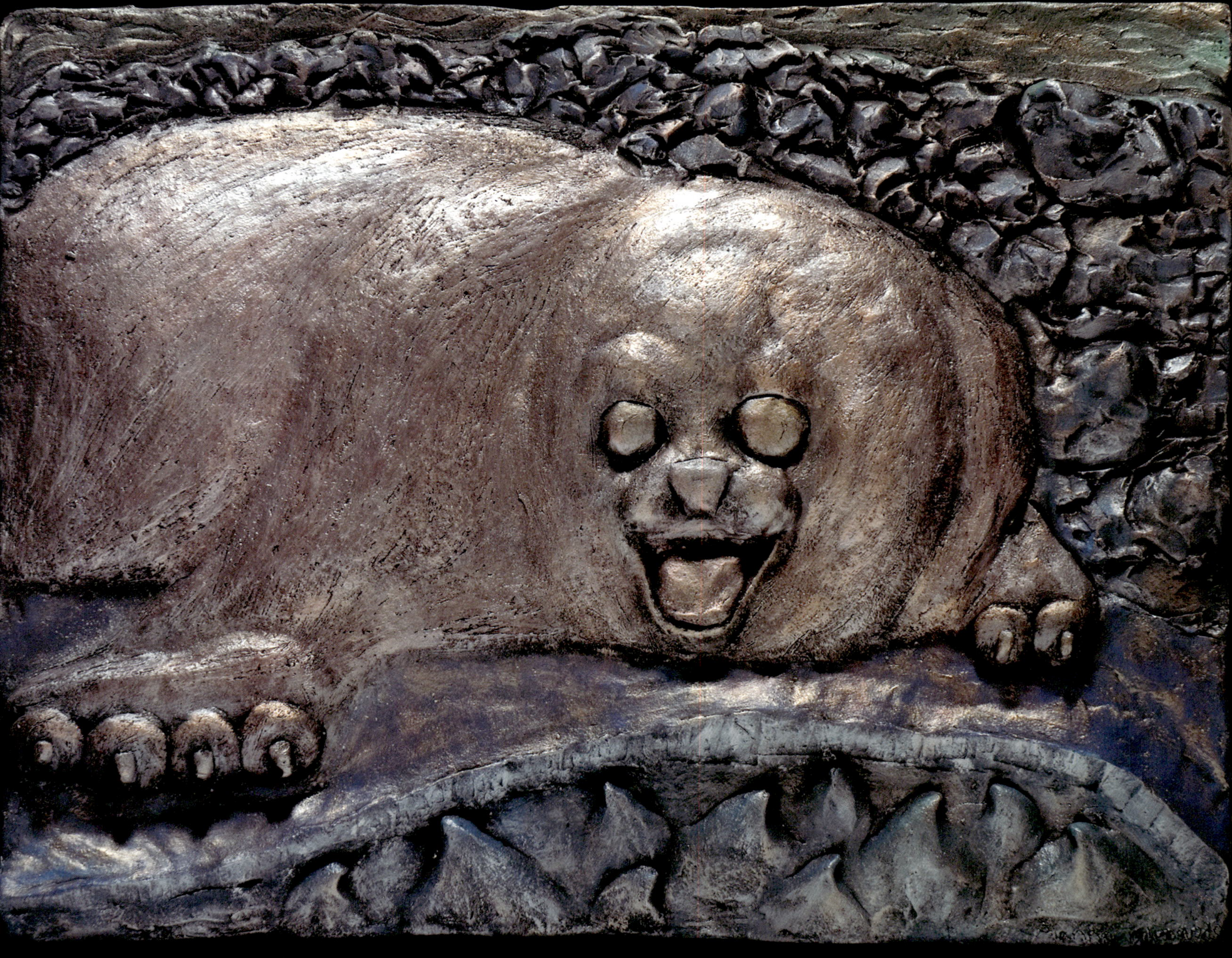

Whitecoat

Alanna Edmunds, Postville

I love the outdoors and nature, and that was my inspiration in choosing an image for my tile. I knew I wanted to show an animal, and the whitecoat certainly relates to Labrador. Whitecoats are hunted in the spring but adult seals have traditionally been hunted all year long. Seal-hunting is a specialized skill, whether using a blind and sneaking across the *sina* [ice edge] or hunting them on the water. Historically, seal meat has been an important part of the diet both for humans and for dogteams that provided transportation.

I was surprised at how realistically the whitecoat image emerged from the clay, as I worked through the steps in creating it. I am excited to think that my tile will be shown in the arts centre, and years down the road children and people of all ages will be able to see it – alongside all the others. It was a great experience.

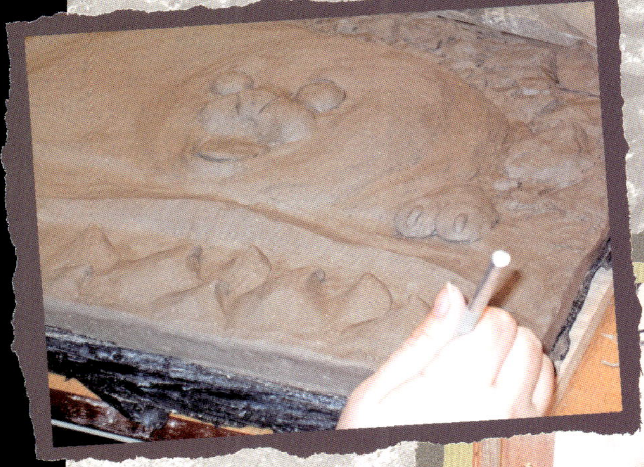

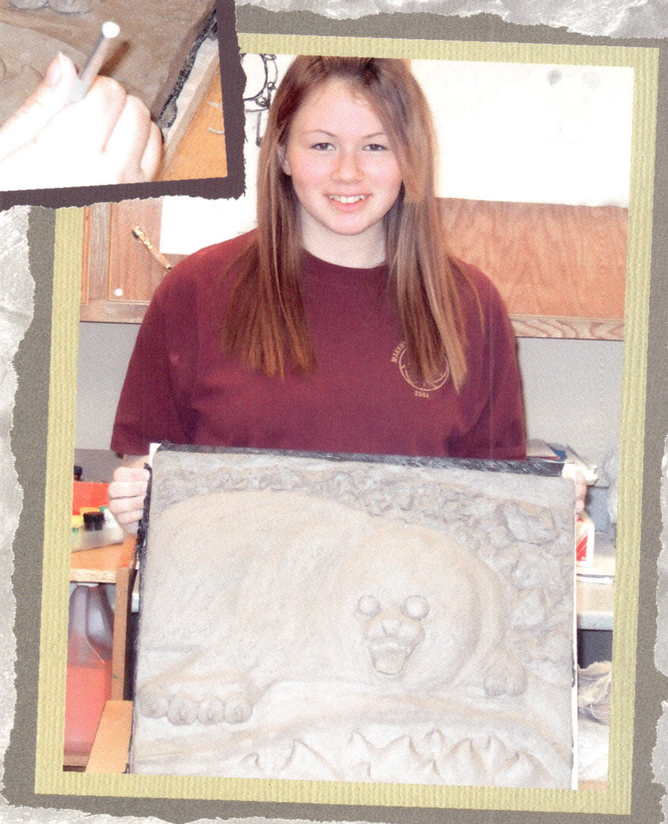

I was surprised at how realistically the whitecoat image emerged from the clay, as I worked through the steps in creating it.

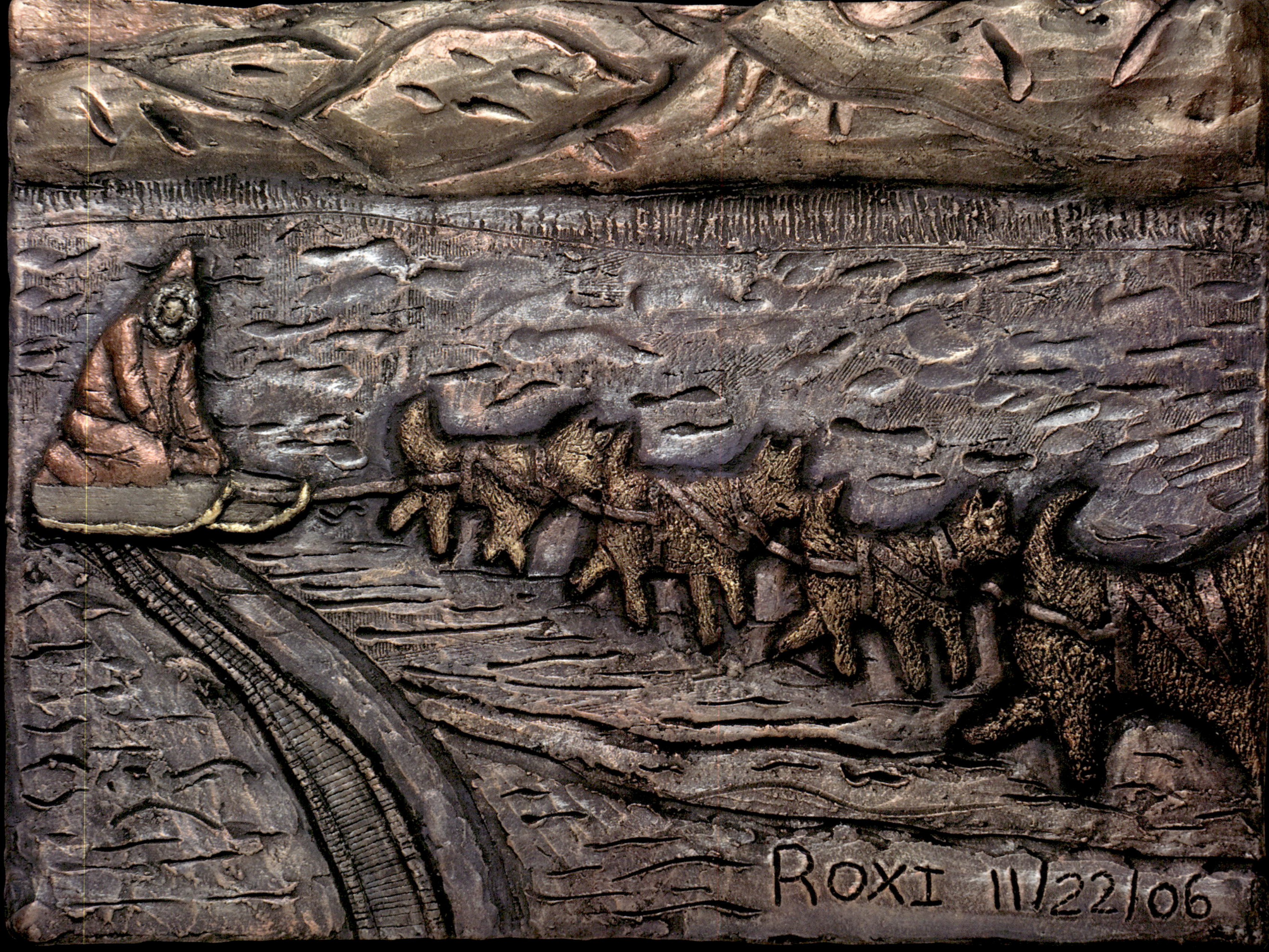
ROXI 11/22/06

RIDING WITH THE DOGS

ROXI WOLFREY, RIGOLET

Riding with a dogteam is a feeling of freedom: peaceful, serene, relaxing, and slow. Cold wind brushes against your body. Hushed sounds of dogs' feet pat in random rhythms; eager push-breaths fuel the ride; komatik runners *swoosh* confidently through parting snow-crystals, and the occasional '*Whoop!*' from driver to dog slices the silence.

Dogteams provided winter transportation in Labrador for generations. Labrador teams were tied to individual traces which fanned out in a semi-circle in front of the sled or *komatik*. Dogs were fed seal meat and cornmeal mush and were often kept on an island away from the community where they could roam freely in the summer.

But just as plastic slides have replaced bone or antler on sled runners, so has the skidoo replaced dogs for winter travel. Skidoos are faster and require less daily care; they don't have to be constantly fed, trained, and sheltered.

Then again, how many times has a skidoo found its way home through a snowstorm, or warmed its driver when waiting one out?

Riding with a dogteam is a feeling of freedom: peaceful, serene, relaxing, and slow. Cold wind brushes against your body. Hushed sounds of dogs' feet pat in random rhythms; eager push-breaths fuel the ride...

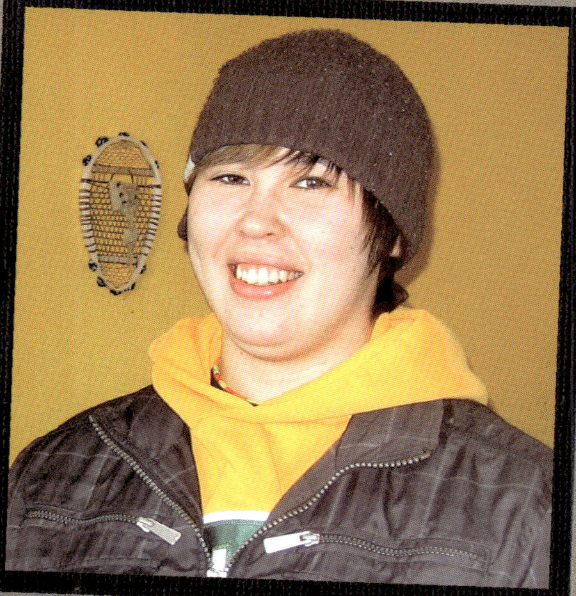

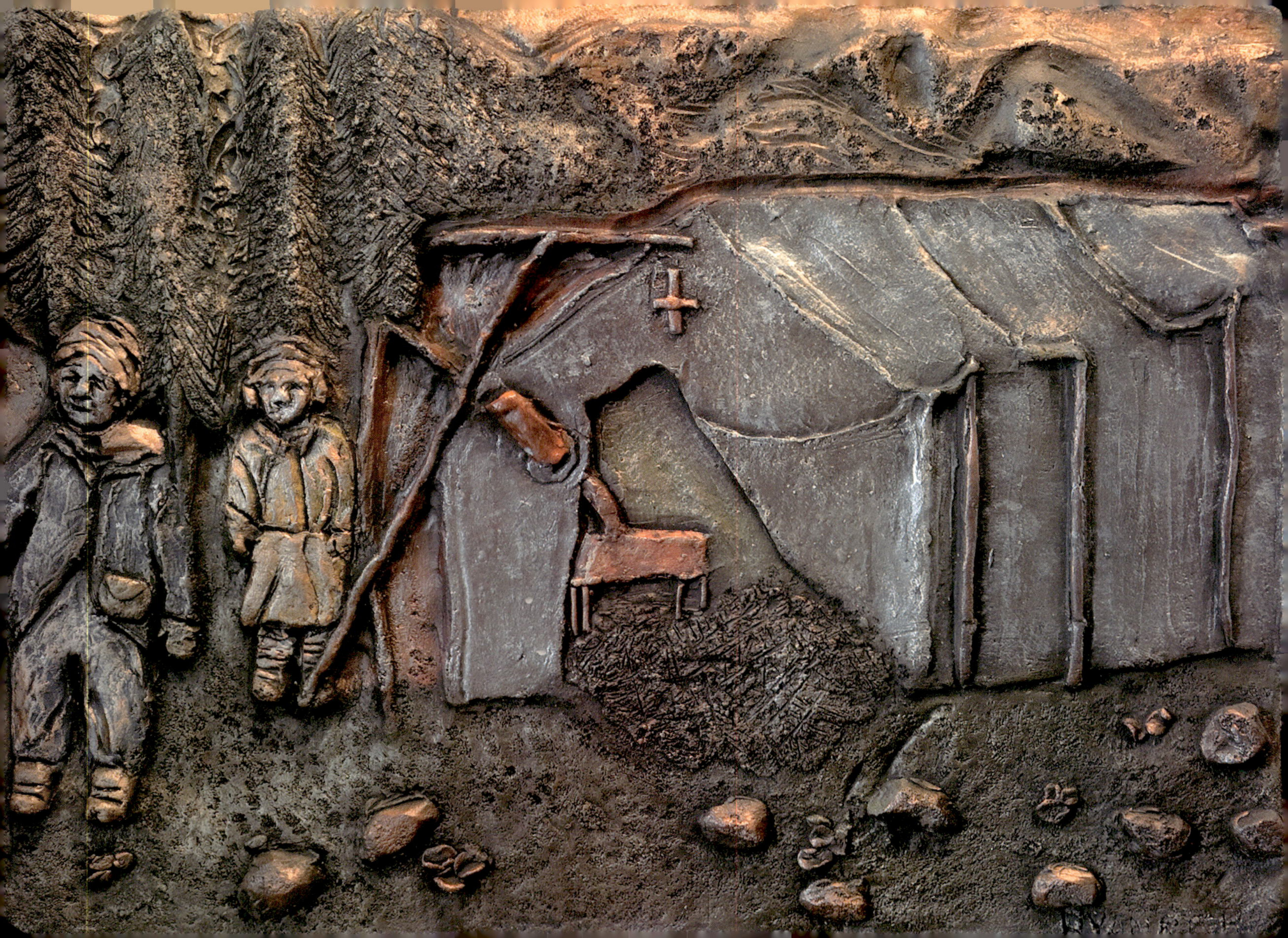

My tile image shows the traditional way of living, the way my grandfather did.

NUTSHIMIT/ IN THE COUNTRY

RYAN RICH, SHESHATSHIU

We have changed a lot since my grandfather was a boy. In his day, the Innu spent most of their time in the country, living in tents and moving with the caribou. They would come into town only to trade or maybe if the priest was here.

My tile image shows the traditional way of living, the way my grandfather did. The tent has thick layers of boughs to make a floor. They are soft, and keep a person off the damp ground. It also has a small woodstove, warming the shelter during cold Labrador winters.

You will also see a couple beside the tent. They are dressed in traditional clothing and are hunting for food. They hunt together. The **Nukum** (grandmother) might smoke some salmon or trout over a low fire, or bake some bread in the sand along the shore.

We have changed a lot since my grandfather was a boy.

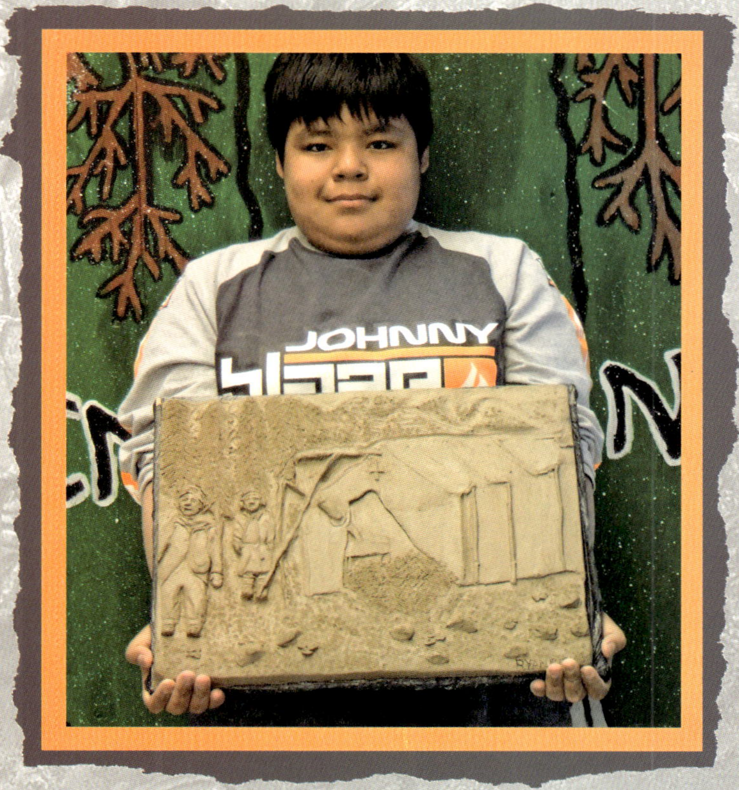

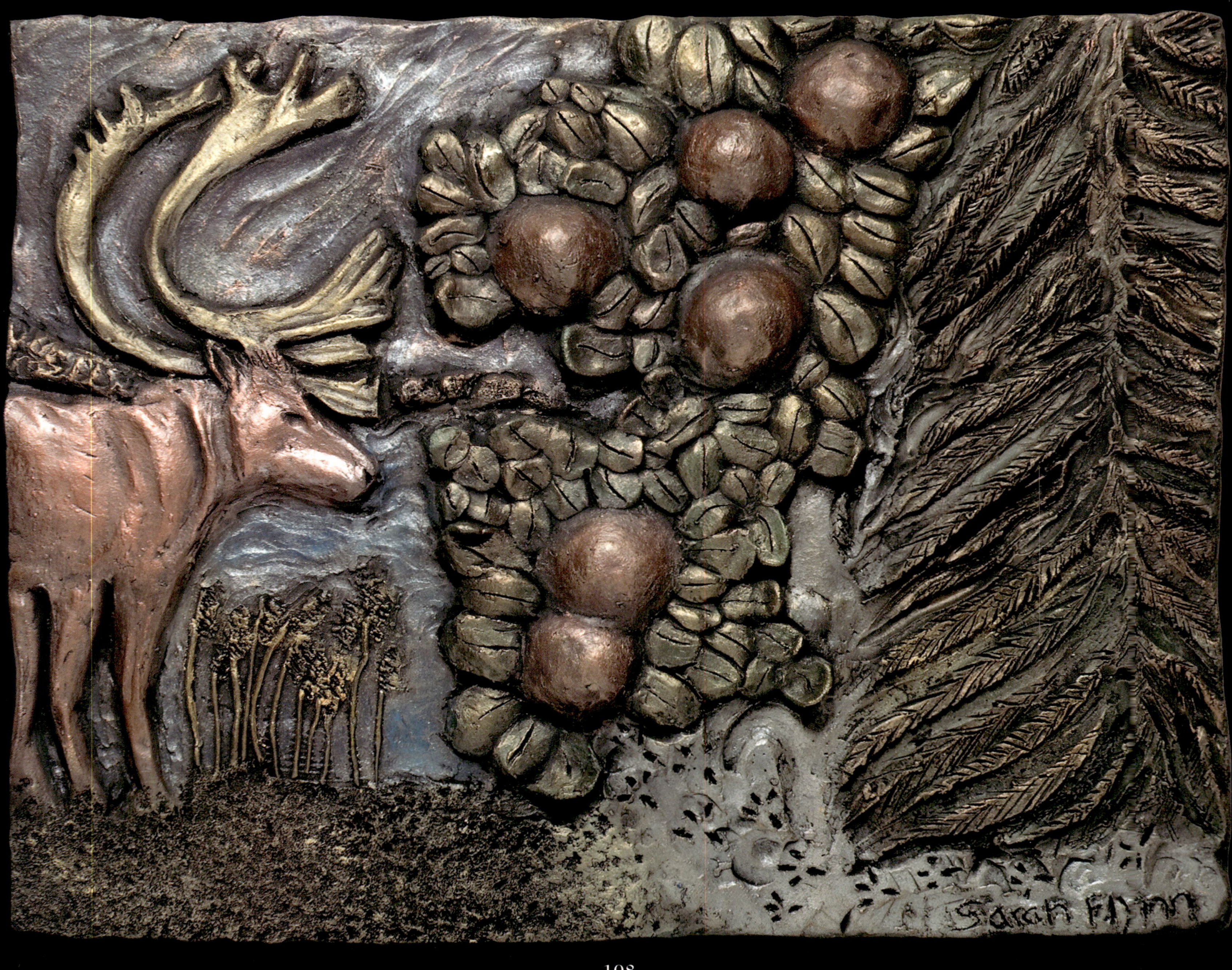
Sarah Flynn

These Are the Things I Am Made Of

Sarah Flynn, Northwest River

I had no idea where to start. We were asked to think about Labrador. Lots of possibilities there! I began to think of many different images that relate to Labrador, and all of them seemed to come from times when I had been on the land with my family.

Caribou and partridge tracks remind me of my father's hunting trips; the berries, of berry-picking expeditions; blades of beachgrass, of my mother who came from Rigolet, one of the few places where this grass is still woven into baskets; and the northern lights, of humbling northern beauty.

Instead of a realistic scene, I decided to make a collage of the images in my head that have sentimental value for me. The tile that I created has much to do with family and the places I've grown up. I welcome the chance to share these images with all who see the mural. I enjoyed being part of such a meaningful project.

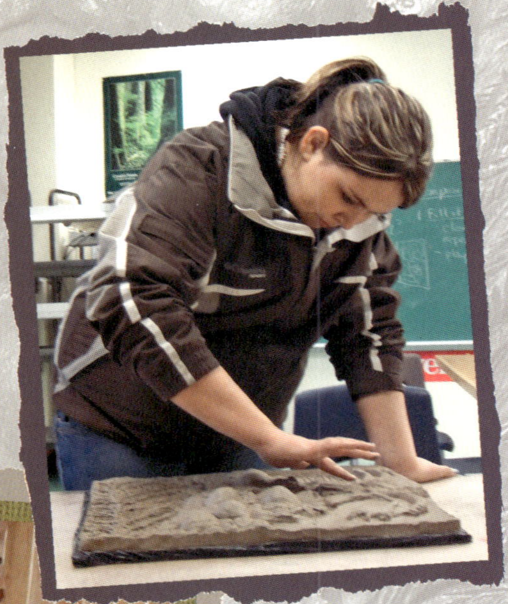

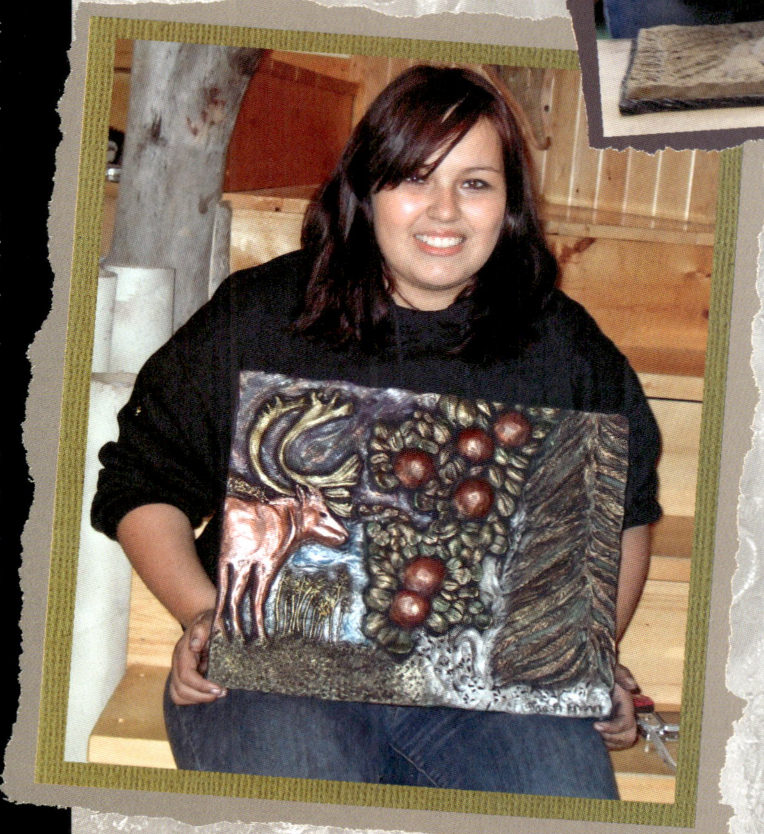

The tile that I created has much to do with family and the places I've grown up.

These images, these stories, now in common clay, are forever.

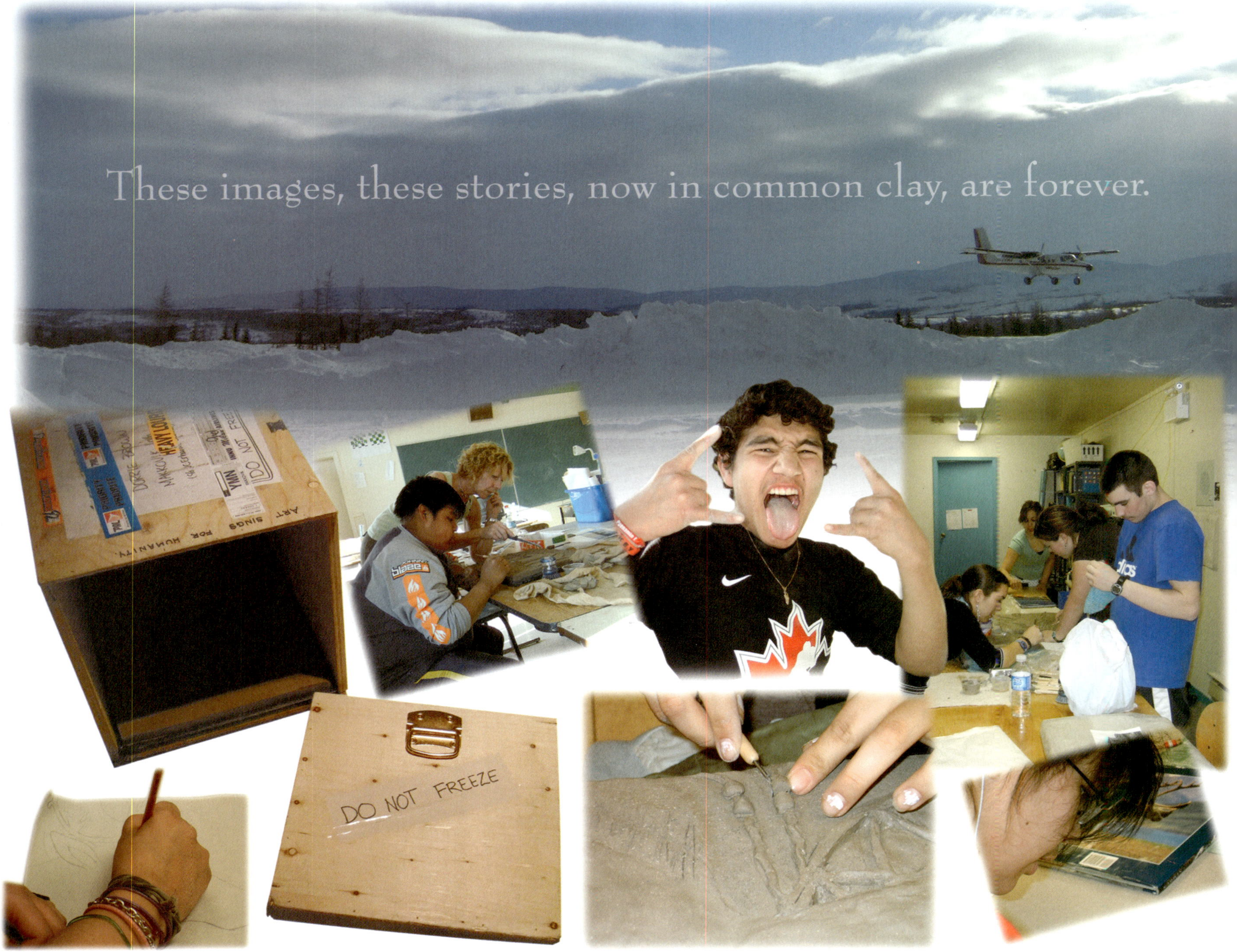

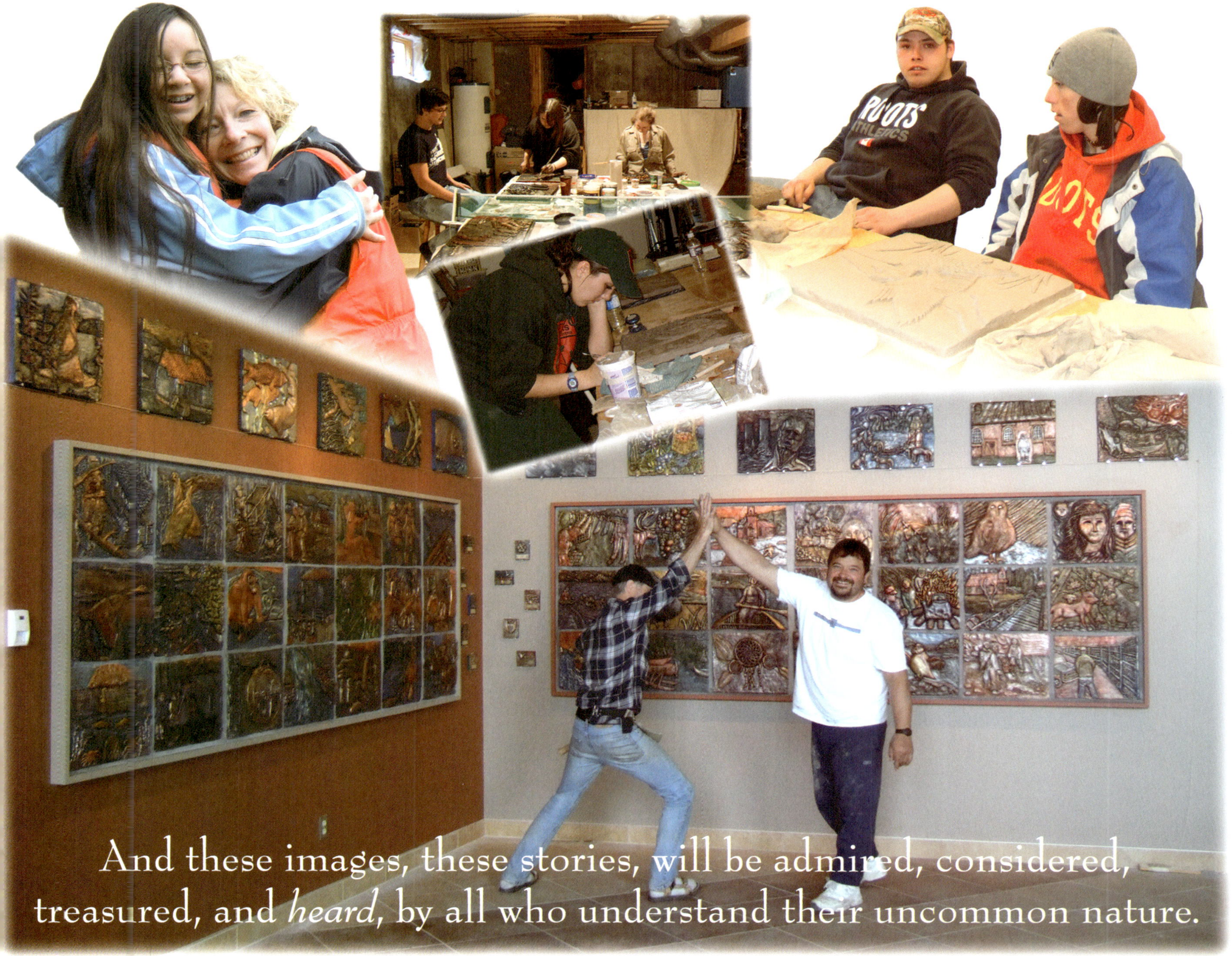

And these images, these stories, will be admired, considered, treasured, and *heard*, by all who understand their uncommon nature.

Dorrie Brown has lived and taught in Labrador for over thirty years in the communities Paradise River, Nain and Happy Valley-Goose Bay. She has been active in community arts initiatives and arts education, and won Newfoundland & Labrador Arts Council's Award for Arts Educator of the Year, 2008. The *Labradoria* Mural Project also won a Manning Award from the Newfoundland & Labrador Historic Sites Association in 2008, and the Zippie Ikkiatsiak Award in 2007.

Afterword

Etched in stone. Something both permanent and a promise fulfilled. For me, this is what the *Labradoria* Clay Mural means to the Labrador Creative Arts Festival.

In its 35 year history, the Festival has sponsored many unifying projects that have celebrated the arts, joining people and communities in collective creations of how we see ourselves as Labradorians. With the passage of time, these works disappeared or were relegated to some corner of a school, eventually to be forgotten. But for this work of art, it is different.

After years of preparation and Dorrie Brown's remarkable tenacity, this mural has a permanent home - the Lawrence O'Brien Centre. It is not to be forgotten. It hangs in a place which exemplifies an extraordinary effort by many people to find the festival a home. It is both beautiful and inspired - at the same time, one tile, yet many. It speaks to each of us who have been a part of this festival at any time. It hangs for all time. *Etched in stone.*

Tim Borlase, *Founder*
Labrador Creative Arts Festival
February 2010

Index by Artist

Photo Credits

Ashini, Jolene	*Across the River/Kamit*, *Them Days* cover, 30.2 [Monsignor Edward O'Brien collection, Them Days Archive].
Brown, Dorrie	*Amautik & Komatik: Carrying Precious Things*, based on a *Them Days* cover, 26.1 [Sydney W. Woodward photo, Labrador Institute source, Them Days Archive].
	Dorrie Brown's headshot courtesy of Michael Roop.
Kent, Heidi	*Innu Hunter*, Napeo, E83 [Kate Hettasch collection, Them Days Archive].
Lane, Ocean	*Old Makkovik Church, Burned 1949*, based on a photo from *Them Days*, 20.2, p. 30 [Moravian Mission collection, Them Days Archive].
Lidd, Maria	*The Ghosts of Hebron*, based on a photo by Bob Mesher.
Mitsuk, Marea	*Great-great-grandmother Kitora Boase*, based on a photo of Kitora Boase, Hopedale [Them Days Archive].
Tuglavina, Amos	*Moving from Place to Place*, *Them Days* cover, 17.2 [D.J. Saunders photo, Them Days archive].
White, Travis	*Hannah & Mersai Michelin*, *Them Days*, 4.3, p. 49 [Flora Baikie source, Them Days Archive].
Winters, Morgan	*Makkovik, 1929*, *Them Days*, 21.4, p. 7 [Alice Perrault collection, Them Days Archive].